ED BULLINS

Ed Bullins, 1995

ED BULLINS
A LITERARY BIOGRAPHY

Samuel A. Hay

 WAYNE STATE UNIVERSITY PRESS   DETROIT

Copyright © 1997 by Wayne State University Press, Detroit, Michigan 48201.
All rights are reserved.
No part of this book may be reproduced without formal permission.
Manufactured in the United States of America.
01 00 99 98 97   5 4 3 2 1

Library of Congress Cataloging-in-Publication Data

Hay, Samuel A.
 Ed Bullins : a literary biography / Samuel A. Hay.
  p. cm. — (African American life series)
 Includes bibliographical references and index.
 ISBN 0-8143-2616-1 (alk. paper)
 1. Bullins, Ed. 2. Afro-American dramatists—20th century—
Biography. 3. Afro-Americans—Intellectual life—20th century.
4. Afro-Americans in literature. I. Title. II. Series.
PS3552.U45Z68 1997
812'.54—dc20
[B]   96-34231

Designer: Joanne Elkin Kinney

Photo (frontispiece and p. 78) by Allen Nomura

African American Life Series
A complete listing of the books in this series can be found at the back of this volume.

To my father

Deacon Thomas Hay Jr.

CONTENTS

ACKNOWLEDGMENTS

The impetus for this study derived from my lectures on Ed Bullins at the University of Maryland, Baltimore County, in 1971. As a young teacher, I often rambled on about Bullins's plays because I liked them—basically because they reminded me so much of so many of the Geechees in my family and neighborhood. This was down in my country hometown of West Jupiter, Florida.

To my utter surprise, Bullins accepted my invitation to visit my classes. We hit it off—again to my shock because I thought he would be angry at having to hunt me down in the airport. I was playing a pinball machine. He challenged me to a game. I let him win.

After we had known each other for a year or two, I casually asked him if he planned to write his autobiography. When he said no, I quietly began planning—only to discover that he was not about to have me poking into his privacy. "Sam, you can write about my plays, but that's it," he snapped whenever I asked about his parents or children. I was never particularly bothered by his abruptness because my skin can be used for sandpaper.

But I basically stayed out of the man's private business—until I could catch him in one of his infrequent good moods. Then the questions were posed in the context of a play or character, which is the case with this book. We will look at the man through his work, with the principal focus on his many plays.

Even this was touch-and-go most of the time because we had become friends enough for him to expect me to be his intellectual bodyguard against the daily critics. Which I was. But it was a different matter when it came to writing a wanna-be scholarly literary biography some quarter century after having surreptitiously beaten him at pinball in 1971.

Bullins did not quite get this. He would read some negative comment in the manuscript and get all fired up, wondering why I was being "so hostile." I patiently explained to the brother that although I was respectful of his immense talent—and I was not being facetious this time—I had to "distance myself" in order to achieve "a believable balance between the positive and the negative."

Bullins summarily dismissed me—and I could tell from his tone over the telephone that he wanted to call off the project and come get his stuff. His son, Sun Ra, and his companion, Marva, saved the day long enough for me to prop up my quite frail trust—until, that is, he saw the next batch of "objective criticism."

Bullins eventually—and grudgingly—mustered up enough trust long enough for me to finish this exhaustive look at his life and work—without selling out, thanks to Mr. Bostic, guardian saint of Limestone Creek Road in West Jupiter. Others, too, must be thanked for helping me to weather my good friend Bullins.

We can begin with Bullins's own family, including all of his children, especially the quietly humorous Ameena and the loudly funny Sun Ra, the good-natured shield and provocateur. A juicy kiss to Ed's companion, Marva Sparks Dorsey, for her being so much unlike Ed; to his cousin, Florence Garrison of Willingboro, New Jersey, for tearing up the family album to lend me scores of photographs; and to Ed's ex-wife, Trixie, for putting up with me for hours and providing the hundreds of documents making up the Bullins Collection, most of which she carefully preserved.

I am grateful for the hard work of so many in providing information from special collections, among whom are Waltrene Canada, director of the Bluford Library at North Carolina Agricultural and Technical State University; Jim Huffman of the Schomburg Center of Research in Black Culture, the New York Public Library; Jim Hatch of the Hatch-Billops Oral History Collection in New York City; and Garry Gray of the Library of Congress for his assistance in organizing the Bullins Collection and for researching hard-to-find reviews and articles.

A special debt is owed to Dr. Errol Hill, professor emeritus at Dartmouth College, for his indispensable criticism of an early draft of the manuscript. I should have known better than to ask him to interrupt his preparations for a Christmas vacation in the Carribean and to rip apart my manuscript, which he did, calling it "a tough assignment at this busy time." I wonder if he knew how tough his many added assignments for me were. But he bandaged my wounds with his congratulations for "accomplishing such a thorough and incisive analysis of an important African-American playwright." Thanks, Errol, for sharing your vast knowledge and editorial skills.

In addition to Florence Garrison, other people were kind enough to share photographs reproduced in this book, chiefly William Lathan, M.D., of Ardsley, New York, who went through boxes and boxes of material from his days in the New Lafayette Theatre company. He spent his own money to reproduce photographs taken by him. I paid him back—I think. Thanks, too, to Roscoe Orman of Englewood, New Jersey, who interrupted his rehearsals for his one-man show, *The Confessions of STEPIN FETCHIT,* in order to help; and to Gary Fong of the *San Francisco Chronicle,* although I could not afford that ridiculously expensive photograph of Ed and me in the Pink Section on 21 August 1988.

Now, in an effort to make these acknowledgments slightly shorter than the book itself, I must briefly—but deeply— thank the following people: Robert Macbeth of Miami, Florida, for the hours he spent filling me in on details about Bullins at the New Lafayette Theatre, for identifying pictures and locating documents and plays; Woodie King Jr., for his assistance in researching the project and locating interviewees; Rev. Cecil Williams, pastor of Glide Memorial Church in San Francisco, California, for his assistance in locating interviewees; Marvin X. of Castro Valley, California, for his interviews and his research assistance; St. Clair Bourne of Guilford, Connecticut, for his research assistance; Helen Merrill of Helen Merrill Ltd. in New York City, for providing scripts, interviews, and documents; Gail Merrifield Papp, for recommending contacts; David Wheeler of the American Repertory Theatre, Harvard University, for his assistance in locating plays; Prof. Mildred Kayden of Vassar College, for her research assistance; and Rev. Michael Duke, L.L.B., D.D., minister of education and finance for the Nigritian Consulate for the Western Hemisphere, St. Petersburg, Florida, for his interviews—and for not running into that tractor trailer on the way to see the memorial to the dead Black Seminoles.

I am equally indebted to Dr. Ethel Pitts Walker of San Jose State University, Dr. Marvin Carlson of the Graduate Center at the City University of New York, Dr. Thomas Pawley of Lincoln University in Missouri, Dr. Winona Fletcher of Indiana University, and Eugene Van Horn, M.D., of Ft. Washington, Maryland, for their research assistance; Dr. S. Allen Counter, director of the Harvard Foundation, Harvard University, and Dr. Thurman W. Stanback, retired professor of speech and theatre at Bethune-Cookman College in Daytona Beach, Florida, for their friendship and assistance; Calvin L. (Muhammad) Jeffers Jr., for his research assistance; and Michael Jaffe of Jaffe-Braunstein Films, Hollywood, California, for his financial assistance in producing the play *Boy x Man.*

For sharing their experiences with and views about Ed Bullins, I will always owe the following participants in the second annual "National

Symposium on African American Theatre: Ed Bullins" at North Carolina A & T State University in Greensboro, North Carolina, 27–28 October 1995: Dr. Addell Austin Anderson of Wayne State University; Sun Ra Bullins of Oakland, California; Dr. Olen Cole of A & T; John Doyle of Florence, South Carolina; Frankie Day Greenlee of A & T; Woodie King Jr. of the Henry Street Settlement's New Federal Theatre, New York City; Susan Latham of A & T; Miller Lucky Jr. of A & T; Robert Macbeth of Miami, Florida; Sandra Mayo, St. Philip's College; Dr. Ethel Pitts Walker of San Jose State University; Richard Wesley of the Tisch School of the Arts, New York University; Glenice Troxler of A & T; and Dr. A. James Hicks, dean of the College of Arts and Sciences at A & T.

A special thank you to Chancellor Edward B. Fort and Vice Chancellor for Academic Affairs Harold L. Martin Sr. of North Carolina Agricultural and Technical State University. Chancellor Fort makes the university a nourishing environment for the arts; Vice Chancellor Martin uses theatre to help the university achieve its mission.

I am quite conscious of the debt owed to the following people at Wayne State University Press: Arthur B. Evans, director, for early seeing the need for this book and committing himself to see it completed; Kathryn Wildfong, my editor; and Ann Schwartz, marketing manager.

Finally, I thank my family for their support. If I had not already been so very long-winded, I would name all sixty-three of you, from Dad to his great-great-granddaughter, Shallante Rochelle Preston. However, I must mention Miss Lady Hay.

I thank all for their assistance, and I accept full responsibility for any shortcomings in this book.

S.A.H.

ED BULLINS'S PLAYS:
THEMATIC AND STRUCTURAL OUTLINE

I. Inner Life versus Outer Life
   A.   Race and Politics
        Malcolm: '71, or Publishing Blackness (1975)
        The Man Who Dug Fish (1973)
        The Theme is Blackness (1973)
        Safety Check (1971)
   B.   Sexual Fantasies and Desires
        A Minor Scene (1973)
        The Helper (1973)
        It Has No Choice (1973)
        Leavings (1980)
        Judge Tom Strikes Back: A Seriously Vicious Satire (1992)
        Jo Anne!!! (1993)
        The Taking of Miss Janie (1992)
II. The Black Revolution
   A.   *Umoja* (Unity)
        Black Commercial #2 (1973)
        A Street Play (1973)
        Death List (1972)
   B.   *Kujichagulia* (Self-Determination)
        Night of the Beast (1972)
        It Bees Dat Way (1972)
        A Short Play for a Small Theater (1973)

13

C. *Ujima* (Collective Work and Responsibility)
   Dialect Determinism (or The Rally) (1973)
   The Electronic Nigger (1969)
   The Gentleman Caller (1970)
D. *Nia* (Purpose)
   Education Type
      How Do You Do (1968)
   Values Type
      One-Minute Commercial (1973)
   Criminal Justice Type
      Next Time . . . (1972)
   Government Type
      State Office Bldg. Curse (1973)
      The American Flag Ritual (1973)
      We Righteous Bombers (1969)
III. Binding Relationships
   A. Rites of Passage
      In the Wine Time (1994)
      The Corner (1973)
      The Box Office (1969)
      Dirty Pool (1985)
   B. Lies
      Michael (1978)
      A Sunday Afternoon (1987), with Marshall Borden
      A Teacup Full of Roses (1985)
      The Home (1974)
      C'mon Back to Heavenly House (1977)
      City Preacher (1993)
   C. Gay and Lesbian Relations
      Snickers (1985)
      Hunk (1980)
      Clara's Ole Man (1969)
IV. The Flow
   A. Musicals
      1. Historical
         I Am Lucy Terry: An Historical Fantasy for Young Americans (1993)
         The Mystery of Phillis Wheatley: An Historical Play for Young Americans (1993)
         High John Da Conqueror: The Musical (1993)
         Storyville (1977), with Mildred Kayden
         Sepia Star (1977), with Mildred Kayden

14

      2. Social

         American Griot (1991), with Idris Ackamoor

         Raining Down Stars (1992), with Idris Ackamoor and
            Rhodessa Jones

         Emergency Report (1993), with Rhodessa Jones and Danny
            Duncan

         Sinning in Sun City (1987), with Salaelo Maredi

         Home Boy (1976)

      3. Romantic

         House Party (1973), also known as

         Women I Have Known (1976)

      4. Personality

         Satchmo (1981)

         I Think It's Gonna Work Out Fine: A Rock and Roll Fable
            (1989), with Idris Ackamoor, Rhodessa Jones, and Brian
            Freeman

      5. Sacred

         The Work Gets Done (1980)

   B. Forms

      1. Happening

         The Play of the Play (1973)

      2. Prose Poetry

         Street Sounds (1973)

         Salaam, Huey Newton, Salaam (1993)

      3. Film for the Stage

         *Dr. Geechee and the Blood Junkies: A Modern Hoodoo Horror
            Yarn* (1986)

         Go Go: A Story of Dancing Girls (1969), with Bill Lathan

      4. Musical Structures

         The Fabulous Miss Marie (1974)

         Steve and Velma (1978)

         The Duplex (1971)

V. Inner Life versus Inner Life

   A. Truth

      Goin' a Buffalo (1974)

   B. Order

      In New England Winter (1969)

   C. Logic

      The Pig Pen (1972)

      Daddy (1977)

   D. New Spirituality

      *A Ritual to Bind Together and Strengthen Black People So That
      They Can Survive the Long Struggle to Come* (1969)

A Black Time for Black Folk (1970)
A Ritual To Raise the Dead and Foretell the Future (1970)
The Devil Catchers (1970)
The Psychic Pretenders (1971)

E. Certainty

A Son, Come Home (1969)
Boy x Man (1995)
Blacklist (1982)

When it came to that mean and short Ed Bullins, I would have gladly gone to Miss Julia in West Jupiter, Florida, to have her work some roots on him. As much as I hate graveyards, I would have gotten some dirt off of a fresh grave out at Mt. Carmel Missionary Baptist Church. I would have folded it up in one of his handkerchiefs, and, as we were talking, I would have pretended that I was wiping my mouth with it. Miss Julia would have shut him up for good. He deserved it. There we were, cast and crew, working our skulls thin in 1987 to change an Oakland, California, storefront on San Pablo Avenue into a presentable place for a production of his *Street Sounds* (1973). There he was, saying nastier and nastier things—all because I had paid absolutely no mind to what he said about how I should direct his play. It looked to me as if he had only brought me over from Baltimore so that he could direct my directing. It ran across my mind to quit, but that would have been spiting my real reason for putting up with him in the first place—for my critical study of his plays, I wanted a fresh look at his contrary ways.

I already had most of his papers. He had asked me to go to the Bronx in 1985 to get them from his estranged wife, Trixie, a pretty brown woman from Montserrat. She had laughed honest laughs as we boxed up the many manuscripts, diaries, memorabilia, and letters. She had started to give me a bunch of his love letters, but blushed before stuffing them under a cushion. Her devilish smile was the same as when I first met her, in 1972. Bullins had invited me up to see a play, because he liked what I had said about him in a *Black World* article. His whole happy family was so proud

17

of him, as were all the fine women who rubbed up against him as he took me to his spots. (Trixie was busy with their two youngest, Ameena and Sun Ra.) I had felt important.

I suppose this caused me, in 1971, to invite him to speak at the University of Maryland, Baltimore County, where I was then assistant professor of African American studies and English. Walking around with him and introducing him boosted my lowly stature on campus, which probably led me to design a course on him and invite him back. The students enjoyed his irreverence, and they told me to bring him back for the opening of *Street Sounds,* which I directed in 1973. It was this visit that caused my later troubles. Bullins came spouting suggestions—all of which I took because I was too eager to please. Like a fool, I even changed my 1975 production of his *In New England Winter* (1971) at Purdue University because of his "I'm not trying to tell you what to do, but. . . ." To be honest, the man really knew more about directing than I—back then. Things were different now, almost twenty years later. I planned to be stubborn—and even rude—about this production of *Street Sounds*—even though he was putting me up in his writing space in Berkeley.

Bullins wrote in the tiny kitchen of a four-room frame duplex that belonged to the Right Reverend Michael Duke, Esquire. That fast-talking greybeard, who drove a homemade purple van, saw himself as Bullins's patron. He could tie you up with stories of how he had taken Bullins in when he came to Berkeley in 1982, with his then thirteen-year-old daughter, Ameena, and his twelve-year-old son, Sun Ra. Duke never stopped fussing at Bullins about rent, but he, too, liked the notion of being around Ed Bullins. Bullins knew this. So he was still there in 1988, at that formica-top expandable table, which took up half of the kitchen. In front of the one window he typed, mumbling to himself and looking up at people over his half-rims. The window would not stay up, so he put a Brasso can under it—so as not to let in too much air. A breeze might mess up his filing system on the floor, which held a whole new slew of notes, first drafts, diaries, letters, appointment books, bills, and legal documents.

I had no business messing with that man's stuff. I ought not ever forgive myself for rummaging through every piece I could find within minutes after he dropped me off. (He was off to San Francisco, where he stayed with his girlfriend, Marva Dorsey Sparks, a sweet mango-colored property tax administrator.) The looks that Sun Ra gave me—Ameena had the good sense to be back East, away from Duke's roaches—did not say stop, probably because he and I had just made up after a big to-do we had had the summer of 1986 in Maryland, when I sent his butt back to the Bronx for staying out overnight because "it just happened." Sun Ra would become now not only the medium and mediator between Bullins and me but also a co-conspirator on both sides. More importantly, he was a mighty

fine actor and the backbone of *Street Sounds*: He did six of the monologues. The audiences and the critics loved him. He will hit it big one day.

Full-scale war broke out when Bullins caught me reading some of his
papers. He got his revenge at the rehearsals for *Street Sounds*. One night
he invited a shapely actress to sit with him. After a particularly good run-
through of the play, she said loud enough for all to hear: "Well, what we
have here is every cliché in the book." Bullins looked at me and laughed.
I asked the stylish woman to join the company, which she did. The poor
dear paid dearly as I made the sweat pour through her mascara. We became friends, though, thanks to her pitchers of virgin bloody Marys. I
stayed away from Bullins's papers.[1]

Things did not get all that much better, though. After only thirteen
days of rehearsals, the producer Bullins announced that we would start
previews. I fumed, although I later grudgingly admitted—to myself, of
course—that the audiences probably would help me to decide which of
the twenty-six monologues were not working. Two weeks before opening,
the executive producer Bullins announced that everybody in the company
needed to help him support the organization. This meant that everybody—especially I—had to take turns selling oils and incenses in front of
the theatre. I did not mind this so much, but I argued about having to go
out to the Berkeley Flea Market. Bullins supported his theatre by selling
everything from used party dresses to automobile radiators. He just loved
being out there in the hot broiling sun with thousands of weekend bargain
hunters. He religiously emptied the theatre of his "goods," which he
loaded into his 1976 slime-green Plymouth Volare. He squeezed in and
off he went, spewing oil down San Pablo Avenue. No one would have
taken this Sanford-without-son (Sun Ra found every excuse to avoid the
flea market) for one of America's finest playwrights, as evidenced by his
101 plays, which have garnered more than fourteen prestigious awards.
Nobody would have a hint that he had literally changed American theatre—not if anybody saw him haggling back and forth with some drunk
woman over the price of some hat, which looked like it had been worn by
Sojourner Truth.

Bullins barged into theatre in 1965, the year Malcolm Shabazz was
assassinated in New York and Martin Luther King led about two hundred
marchers from Selma to Montgomery. Bullins was thirty, having been born
two days shy of Independence Day to Edward (Dawson) and Bertha Marie
Queen Bullins in Philadelphia, Pennsylvania, right in the middle of the
Great Depression. By 1965 he had already filled the pages of some upstart
West Coast magazines with a few of his mediocre short stories and worse
poems.[2] African American theatre at the time was stably in the hands of
respectable educators and professionals. The Florida A. & M. theatre educator S. Randolph "Prof" Edmonds (1900–83), joined by the likes of the

director Richard (Dick) Campbell (1903–95), had seen to that. They were the fountainheads for organizing theatre companies and for training theatre people. It was to these middle-class people that both the sociologist W. E. B. Du Bois (1868–1963) and the philosopher Alain Locke (1886–1954) had turned when they wanted theatre to take a more active role in the political and the cultural lives of African Americans. While starting two antipodal schools of theatre—Protest and Art—both men worked hard to keep from white people's eyes what the critic Darwin T. Turner called the cracker-box animals of African American life: shoeshiners, moonshiners, beauticians, numbers runners, homosexuals, West Indians, Father Divine followers, and gangsters, all of whom cut, shoot, drink, make love, gossip, play numbers, flirt, and mouth-off without saying a single significant thing.[3] Du Bois's and Locke's plans worked beautifully.

Du Bois started the Protest School of Theatre, which became the Black Arts School in 1965. The school underwent four smoothly intelligent periods: Early Protest Drama (1913–32), Era of Warnings (1932–51), Attack Era (1951–65), Black Revolutionary Drama (1965–72), and Black Arts School (since 1972).[4] The school showed to whites that African Americans (a) would contribute if permitted, (b) would threaten if ignored, (c) would verbally assault if pushed, and (d) would kill if attacked. Alain Locke founded the Art-Theatre School, which specialized in showing people as they were, regardless of political concerns. This school, whose name Bullins changed to Black Experience in 1965, went through five periods: Early Musicals Period of Art-Theatre (1898–1923), Early Straight Drama (1923–38), Experimentation and Diversification (1938–68), Black Experience Theatre (1968–75), and Bridge Black Experience Theatre (since 1975).[5] This school showed (a) that it could turn huge profits from singing and dancing and (b) that it could adapt to African American causes already established playwriting formulas and standards, whether they be realistic, expressionistic, absurdist, or any other ismistic.

It did not help the Protest Theatre people's cause to have the former Greenwich Village Beat poet Amiri Baraka (LeRoi Jones) (b. 1934) interrupt their musings in 1964—the year Sidney Poitier won the Oscar for best actor and President Lyndon B. Johnson signed the Civil Rights Bill—by raising questions about public accommodations and fair employment. To many middle-income African Americans, this was such a promising time that there was no particular need for a James Baldwin to stir up trouble with his *Blues for Mr. Charlie*, or for a Baraka to make white people uncomfortable with his *Dutchman* (1964). Baraka had founded his Black Arts Repertory Theatre/School in Harlem, a short-lived project that revolutionized black theatre and ushered in the Black Arts Movement. In 1966 he was out at San Francisco State College, encouraging the Black Student Union president Jimmy Garrett to write more plays like *We Own the Night*, in which a revolutionary son shoots down his own mother (wearing a blond wig), on her way to report him to the police.

The trouble started for the Art-Theatre School when Bullins bumped into Baraka at San Francisco State in 1966, the year that Robert Weaver became the first African American member of a presidential cabinet and Milton Olive Jr. was awarded the Congressional Medal of Honor for gallantry in the Vietnam War. Baraka was on the West Coast starting his Black Communications Project, a system for delivering consciousness-raising information to the African American community.[6] Bullins was just up from Los Angeles City College, where the white Texan professor James Parker had told Bullins to forget about writing. Bullins did not listen—not even after being told that he did not belong in college, this after having his writing flung back into his face.[7] When Parker finished with Bullins, the English teacher Otis D. Richardson took him on. Bullins complained

> [Richardson] was a fascist. He hated me. He always ran me out of his classes when I tried to take them. He taught the History of English Literature, which I found fascinating, but he wouldn't let me through. I was the only black in the Contemporary Literature Club, which I founded and headed. And when he saw me sitting on the campus green with the other club members, Richardson would come over and talk to them, turning his back on me until I left.[8]

Bullins toughed it out, thanks to two other teachers (James Simmons, instructor in composition, and Isabelle Ziegler, teacher of creative writing). It was with Ziegler that Bullins founded the campus literary magazine, *Citadel*, which was later edited by the respected poet Quincy Troupe.[9] Bullins was probably determined to ignore the tough times at Los Angeles City College because he had decided while he was in the navy in 1953 that nothing would stop him from getting a formal education and becoming a writer. In fact, he had joined the navy on his seventeenth birthday, in 1952, a year after Gen. Matthew Ridgway received permission to integrate African Americans throughout his command in the Far East. Bullins saw this as a good time to take advantage of the military's educational benefits. He knew about the GI Bill: "My stepfather had not used his bill, much to the sorrow of my mother, who was a get-ahead type of person"—the subject of *Boy x Man* (1995).[10] In the navy, Bullins saw for the first time that he was not as well-equipped for the world as he had previously thought: "I read a lot while I was there. . . . And, being brighter than most of the people around me, I had to do something to change my life."[11]

Within days after he had been discharged in December 1955, the year that Emmett Till was lynched in Money, Mississippi, and the Georgia Board of Education adopted a resolution revoking the license of any teacher of integrated classes, Bullins enrolled in the William Penn Business Institute in Philadelphia. He chose this school partly because he had followed into a building a "beautiful light-skinned sister . . . who looked like a model straight out of New York City."[12] She led him to the president of the school, a Mr. Maxwell, who tried to persuade Bullins to forget about being a journalist and become a businessman. Maxwell was not successful—until Bullins noticed the string of light-skinned young women periodically entering Maxwell's office to get memos signed. Bullins could not take his eyes off their big stockinged legs and firm titties.[13] He enrolled in business school. A Mr. Jason at that school can be blamed for pushing Bullins in the direction of theatre:

> He was an old blackman who was probably educated at a black college in proper English or classics, no doubt, because his pleading to us veterans, boobs, buffoons and misplaced southern girls was sprinkled with the Oxbridge Canon. He invoked Socrates, in prophet-like wrath, along with all the other white guys. But he taught me how to conjugate, something which worked magic on my thinking and later on my writing. And I became a favorite of his, since I was the single student who could hold my ground with him in debate—having read more than any of the other students, [even] the graduates from four-year southern black schools. But I didn't get to write anything more than letters and memos the year and a half I was with Mr. Jason. But he taught me something about the life of the mind, the beauty of writing, the greatness of the language, for a blackman, in still segregated America.[14]

After this epiphany, Bullins furthered his non-street education by following another woman into the Temple University High School—Temple Prep it was called—which had been set up for veterans and underprepared students who wished to get into the university. This woman, Gloria, taught Bullins the art of manipulating people through their sexual desires. After he had bought her clothes and books, she stood him up.[15] When Gloria finished with him, Bullins caught a Greyhound to Los Angeles during the Christmas holidays of 1958, the year that Ernest Green graduated from Little Rock's Central High School. In early 1959, Bullins enrolled in the Los Angeles Manual Arts Adult High School, where he got his General Education Diploma. That summer, while Prince Edward County, Virginia, was abandoning its public school system in an attempt to prevent school integration, Bullins studied at Los Angeles City College (LACC), where his first course was remedial English, "not because I failed the placement test, but because I scored too low for my satisfaction."[16] It was at LACC that he got to know many of the fledgling black activists of the very early sixties, such people as Leon Smith, who exerted a strong intellectual in-

22

fluence on Bullins by taking him to several black cultural activities. He later roomed with Smith and—for a short while—with the president of the student government, Ron Everett, who later became Ron Karenga, father of Cultural Nationalism, founder of the US organization, and creator of Kwanza. After "almost smothering" in Los Angeles for six years, Bullins moved permanently to San Francisco in 1964. It was there that Bullins the playwright was born.

The importance of San Francisco in the 1960s must take a back seat to the man in this time-space. Who he was became insignificant because of what he was—simply contrary. Whatever already existed was there only to be opposed. It is predictable, then, that his plays were unlike anything ever seen in African American theatre. Bullins's plays *had* to directly oppose such "proper" and "right" Art-Theatre classics as Willis Richardson's *The Chip Woman's Fortune* (1923), Marita Bonner's expressionist *Purple Flower* (1928), and Randolph Edmonds's realistic *The Bad Man* (1934). Bullins's plays had to be different even from Baraka's *Dutchman*, which Bullins took as the New "right-proper."

A better understanding of this self-willed need for contrariness might be gained through a discussion of Bullins's first short play, *How Do You Do* (1968). It tells the anti-story of an encounter among three people/mind-states: Paul (the Image Maker), Dora (Stereotype), and Roger (Stereotype):

PAUL

I must make music today, poet music. I've sat here too long making nothing, and I know I've been born to make song.

(*A figure appears from the wings. It dances in the shadows to a small plaintive melody, mingled with the blues, and DORA bumps and grinds into the light to the incongruous music. She stops behind the man, and when the music changes to barrel-house blues, she dances like a child around the bench.*)

How shall I begin? Should I find the words first, or the melody? Should I suggest a theme?

DORA

(*Strutting in front of PAUL like a streetwalker*)
What are you doing? Are you talking to yourself, man? Why are you here alone?

PAUL

Who the hell are you?

DORA

I asked you first! If you're talking to yourself that means you're crazy. I think I'd better report you.

23

(She starts off, twisting her hips to the quickly blinking light.)[17]

This birthmark piece was a rare sight in African American theatre in that it made words into musical instruments, accompanied by blues guitar and multi-hued sight. Bullins tried to get several African American theatre companies in the San Francisco Bay Area to perform this play. All of them refused. Bullins eventually persuaded the director Robert Hartman of the San Francisco Drama Circle to produce this play, along with *Clara's Ole Man* (1969) and *Dialect Determinism* (1973), at the Firehouse Repertory Theater in San Francisco on 5 August 1965. The black revolutionary poet and playwright Marvin X. Jackmon heard about these plays, and invited Bullins, along with Ethna Wyatt, Duncan Barber, Hillery Broadous, and Carl Bossiere to found Black Arts/West,[18] which opened in 1966 in an abandoned theatre on Fillmore Street in San Francisco.[19]

Black Arts/West put on *How Do You Do* with Marie Bell as the first Dora Stereotype (the now-noted actress Vonetta McGee later played Dora). The theatre began with performances in the Fillmore, at Merritt College, in bars, in community places, and wherever Black people might be reached. Before closing in 1969,[20] the theatre became the training ground for such actors as Danny Glover, such activist/actors as Bobby Seale, and the playwright Jimmy Garrett.[21] Marvin X presented some readings at Soledad Prison, where he gave the budding revolutionary Eldridge Cleaver a letter of encouragement from Bullins. Cleaver was released in 1966, the year that Kwame Ture (Stokely Carmichael) was elected chairman of the Student Nonviolent Coordinating Commitee, whose communications director, Julian Bond, had been denied his seat in the Georgia House of Representatives, purportedly because of his opposition to the Vietnam War. Marvin X and Ethna Wyatt then persuaded Cleaver to use the advance for his book, *Soul on Ice,* to convert a large, two-story Victorian house at 1711 Broderick Street in San Francisco into something called Black House, the birthing place of black revolutionary thought and activity in Northern California.[22] Thanks to the money from Cleaver's *Ramparts* magazine articles, as well as substantial contributions from the black middle class, Black House prospered, fueled by the weekly poetry readings and theatre performances of the theatre group called the Black Troupe. After Marvin X introduced Cleaver to the newly organized Black Panther Party co-founder Bobby Seale, Black House became the San Francisco headquarters of the party.

Although Bullins and Marvin X put on plays about the Panther philosophy, Panther founder Huey Newton—influenced by Cleaver—had almost no tolerance for the black artists, who opposed the policy of allowing white leftists to become comrades in the Black Liberation Movement. This caused Newton to complain that the artists were simply reactionary cultural nationalists. He put pressure on Cleaver to evict them. Bullins tried to intercede, but Black House closed in late 1966 because of this rift, which Bullins called an "idiotological" falling out.[23] Supreme Commander Huey Newton ordered all the young people who gathered daily in the basement of Black House to stop coming there because of reported gang rapes.[24] Newton did not want the police to use this as an excuse to raid the place and to confiscate the stockpile of weapons. Marvin X, who felt that he and Huey were equals, refused the order. The Panthers "were packing," according to Marvin, and they wanted to kill him that moment. But "they waited. All night, Ethna and I could hear the Panthers pacing in front of my door. We could hear them cocking their forty-five automatics. Nothing happened that night, but Eldridge told me to get out the next day."[25]

Bullins, reportedly, was run out of Black House in the middle of the night:

> A kneegrow writer, whose name I've presently forgotten, published in *Black Players* some years ago that I had been put out of the Black House in my drawers. On the contrary, I was not living at The Black House at the time. I was staying with a young woman, but I was working sixteen hours or so daily at the House. Therefore, it may have seemed that I, too, lived there with Eldridge, Marvin, Etna (one of the names she used then), and others. After the explosive meeting in which Eldridge and Marvin drew their lines in the sand, nothing seemed to happen for a day. Then the next, word came that the "Artists and cultural people" were being purged from the house. Next came a small security force from the Panthers to move in. They began patrolling. Finally, within a short time, threats began being made by the Panthers to everyone on Marvin's side of the argument concerning White radicals being a part of and sharing in the decisions of the house. I tried to act as mediator between the groups. I could talk to Eldridge. And I could talk to Marvin. But the die had been cast. Eldridge cooked some pork chops. Etna and he got in an argument about it. Little Bobby Hutton pulled his .45 and jacked a shell into the chamber. "Power Comes Out of the Barrel of a Gun," I thought. Okay, you got it. When the actual purge went down, I was out of the situation. I wasn't sleeping there in my drawers.[26]

The closing left Bullins with no place to perform his plays. He was planning to emigrate to Paris when the artistic director of the New Lafayette Theatre, Robert Macbeth, asked Bullins to relocate to New York City. By 1968, almost before Bullins finished unpacking, he had many of "the proper" folks of Sugar Hill Harlem out of sorts. To advertise his New York debut, he had posted on an off-Broadway marquee the title *The Electronic*

Nigger and Others—"others" being *Clara's Ole Man* (1969) and *A Son, Come Home* (1969). When "refined" Afro-American theatregoers saw that sign, they simply refused to go to the theatre. They dismissed Bullins as a low-class heathen. That, as strange as it might sound, was exactly what Bullins wanted them to believe. His contrariness was not capricious. It was always directed, for diametrically opposed reasons, at the well-off, the dispossessed, and the uninitiated. Wynn Handman, director of the American Place Theater, selected these plays, which had been written three years earlier in San Francisco, for Bullins's first New York City outing for their shock value. The Harlem elite was outraged. In a compromise designed to lure them into the theatre, he changed the marquee to the more acceptable title "Ed Bullins Plays." Once Bullins got the people inside, however, he slapped them with *Electronic Nigger,* a satire on "Negroes" who fully accept white values, and who become gross distortions of what African Americans should be.[27] Before the people could catch their breath, he put *Clara's Ole Man* on them. In this twelve-page short, the sociopathic characters mouthe no fewer than thirty-eight vulgar words, twelve of which are that unspeakable insult to mothers. The people dismissed Bullins as godless.

They did not know that this "infidel" had what he later admitted was a "strong Christian foundation for life."[28] Although his mother had rebelled against the church when he was born, and was "an intermittent agnostic for the next twenty years," she "gradually became a fundamentalist religious Pentecostal to such an extent that she alienated and shunned the whole of the family"—the subject of *A Son, Come Home.*[29] His aunt, Beatrice Garrison Williams, saw to it, however, that the young Bullins attended Sunday school and service at the Williams Institutional Baptist Church in Philadelphia every week. She caused him in 1991 to thank "God for the influence of the church that had shepherded me to successful manhood."[30] Because of this upbringing, he seldom invited either his mother or his Aunt Bea to see any of his plays, because they would "not want a whole lot of cussing, undressing, wayout-of-sight and off-the-wall stuff. They want to have a good time that they can take back with them to relate to their church choir members."[31] Although he spared his mother and aunt, Bullins served up choice paganism for the pharisees:

> I found that the black . . . churches were hypocritical and crooked. To me, they became the seat of degeneracy and decadence. At least the hustlers, gangsters, and street people were honest about what they were about, I believed. . . . I would not become the preacher that my mother prayed I would. I would not become a hypocrite. I would rather martyr myself on the streets of the ghetto, in the den of thieves, in the diseased wombs of whores than become that.[32]

26

This stubborn abstinence from organized religion, which, ironically, was spiritually motivated, shaped this man, who was often called the "most prolific writer in American theatre"—before "prolific" became vaguely insulting to a writer.[33] By aiming his contrariness not only at the church and the well-off but also at the dispossessed and the uninitiated, Bullins eventually made three singularly important contributions to American theatre.

The most significant of these benefactions was the creation of a whole new method of playwriting, which he called "films for the stage." Although most playwrights during the sixties were still influenced by the structure of either the well-made or the agit-prop play, Bullins devised a structure geared toward the deprived urban dwellers. It was difficult to get the people away from television and cinema and into theatres in order to see non-comical, non-protesting, and non-revolutionary plays. The reason was that the people preferred the fast-paced episodes of television and film over the slower-paced non-guerilla theatre. Bullins solved this problem not with the presentational methods popularized by such groups as the Open Theatre; he, instead, shortened the beginning and end of the play, enlivened and elaborated the middle, and urbanized the characters, themes, and slight plots. His atypical structure has been severely and continually castigated. But Bullins has dismissed the criticism because he had some other models in mind:

> [My] structure is almost improvisational. This approach to form I learned best from the black avant-garde musicians that I grew up listening to: Miles Davis, John Coltrane, Dizzy Gillespie, Max Roach, Charlie Parker, Clifford Brown, Thelonious Monk and many others. I learned early in my explorations of my craft that these supreme creators of abstract musical structures had an answer for me, a writer, that would enable me to continually create fresh forms for my work that took place in time, space and confinement of staged reality.[34]

The result is highly crafted plays containing motion-filled snapshots of urban American life and culture. This innovation influenced his second major gift to American theatre: Bullins popularized certain themes and characters. His early plays all but ignore the theme found in most of his contemporaries' plays, that all whites are enemies of African Americans. Bullins's themes concern people's needs for sexual satisfaction, safety, economic security, family, esteem, and self-improvement. The people and the themes are "things" that he "had experienced or seen. These subjects came out of a world that a young urban Blackman inhabited, a world that white Americans ruled so ruthlessly and totally."[35] Bullins felt that many in the theatre establishment disliked his themes and characters because "the establishment has no desire to recognize the contemporary black urban experience as subject for great literature. But it is not surprising in America: How could it be possible for children of slaves to aspire to attempt greatness?"[36] The plays proved quite popular, as indicated by their being performed in such reputable theatres as the Lincoln Center, the New Lafayette Theatre, the American Place Theatre, La Mama, the New Federal Theatre, and the Public Theater. Bullins probably overstated his case against the theatre establishment, which thought so highly of him that it awarded him the New York Drama Critics Award and the Drama Desk-Vernon Rice Award—along with three Obie awards, two Guggenheim fellowships, four Rockefeller Foundation playwriting grants, and two National Endowment for the Arts playwriting grants.

More important than these awards, however, is Bullins's third contribution to American theatre, which was directed at the uninitiated. He raised a whole generation of young playwrights. Through his Black Theatre Workshop at the New Lafayette Theatre and the New York Shakespeare Festival Writers' Unit, Bullins shaped such authors as Amhir Bahati, Martie Charles, Doug Fallon, Fatisha, J. e. Franklin, Kermit Frazier, Abbie Gehman, Neil Harris, Herb Liebman, Winston Lovett, OyamO, Sonia Sanchez, Barbara Schneider, and Richard Wesley.[37] These people looked to him for guidance in dramatic style, content, and technique.[38] Though it was kept quiet, Bullins in 1971 helped to change the "kill-whitey" rhetoric in Black Revolutionary drama and the cussing and fussing in Black Experience drama. He influenced Richard Wesley to quiet the revolutionaries with *The Black Terror* (1971), which told them to stop waging war without first engaging in "painstaking and self-deflating political analysis of the situation."[39] Bullins even stopped the representation of the lurid street life, a subject that he himself had popularized. Wesley's *The Last Street Play* (1977)—renamed *The Mighty Gents*—is really the last of such plays.

Bullins assisted the young writers not only by conducting workshops but also by publishing and producing their plays. He published the plays in *The Drama Review* (1968), *Black Theatre Magazine* (1968–1972), *New Plays from the Black Theatre* (1969), and *The New Lafayette Theatre Presents* (1974). He produced his students' plays not only in New York City theatres but also at the New Lafayette Theatre Workshop (1968) and the Bullins Memorial Theater (BMT) in Oakland, California (1987). All the while, he continued his formal education, getting a bachelor's degree from Antioch University/San Francisco in 1989 in liberal studies (English and playwriting), and an M.F.A. in playwriting from San Francisco State University in 1994. He accepted the appointment of professor of theatre at Northeastern University in 1995.

Although understanding Bullins can be extremely difficult, it might be helpful to know that he cares deeply about anything or anybody down-

and-out. In some ways, his short story "The Hungered One" is autobiographical. It tells of a young man's efforts to help an ugly duckling, a ghoulish, big blue bird with no feathers, just scaly skin. It has four legs, which sprout from its squat and muscular body. Black talons shield its toes. Splintered dewclaws dangle from the backs of its legs. Its stubby neck holds a small head with round, yellow snake eyes set deep above a hooked and vicious beak. It eats whole any careless bird that gets too close. Bullins places this "hungered one" opposite a gentle and kind man who enjoys "touring" among the pigeons in the park. The man feels sorry for the creature, which he offers a handful of nuts. It tears off the outer joint of his index finger. This is not enough for the young fool, who picks up the bird to take it home in a taxi in order to nourish the thing. On the way, the hungered one bites a hole in the man's chin and breastbone. During a frantic fight, the man splits the monster's head. No blood oozes from its brain. The mutant knocks the man unconscious. It tears a strip from his thigh before jumping out of the car. The beast scrambles down the street. It looks like some huge rodent or diseased hen with a large worm dangling in its beak.[40]

Bullins might be both ghoul and fool, connected by a diamond-hard head and a gelatin heart. His hidden soft-heartedness had better not be taken for granted, however, because it takes almost nothing to turn the missionary into the monster. There is no better example of this than in Bullins's battle with an Oakland, California, land baron to save the BMT Theater. The landlord told Bullins in 1987 to get out of the storefront because he was putting the building up for sale. This was right in the middle of the well-attended previews of *Street Sounds*. Bullins tried to humor the landlord, who would have none of it. Bullins ran to the press. The landlord gave the put-out date. Bullins told me to come with him to "have it out" with this "cracker." With about five dollars between us, we went to this meeting. It was there that I gained an odd respect for the man Bullins.

He put on a masterly performance, thanking the man for seeing us, and for working out a plan to pay back rent. During the pleasantries, he had the man laughing. This soon changed, however, when Bullins asked for a postponement of the quit-property date. "Absolutely not," the man said, which he repeated to Bullins's request for another spot in one of the landlord's many other properties. Bullins accused the man of not even trying to understand "what we are doing." When this did not work, he threatened to file a series of lawsuits that would have the building tied up in court for years. What amazed me was that Bullins never once raised his menacingly quiet voice. We left—wondering if we would have to start street theatre. Bullins's empty threat worked, however. The man rented us a building in Emeryville, a 99 percent white town squeezed between

Berkeley and Oakland. The mayor, along with other top officials, came to the re-opening of the (better polished) *Street Sounds*.

A poignant example of Bullins's change from monster to nurse occurred after that opening. Although the African American and suburban papers loved the show, the highly influential (among arts people) *East Bay Express* gave a mixed review. The critic loved some of the actors, especially Bullins's son Sun Ra. The review gave thumbs down, however, to my failure to sufficiently individualize the twenty-six characters. It was a downer, probably because the critic was right. Seeing me depressed, Bullins, who had publicly second-guessed and ridiculed much of what I had done, told me that he loved the show. I did not believe him. He expertly—and without misquoting—pulled out just enough of the *Express* review to turn it from lukewarm to rave. He poured money into advertising. As a result, the show ran on weekends for 256 performances. Although producer Bullins was trying to make money, there was something about his demand for professionalism, as well as his new-found genuine caring, that made me even more wary of this profoundly unusual man: When I got ready to leave town to go home to West Jupiter, Florida, he told me: "Take all of my stuff that you've been peeping at in the kitchen." Although I was happy, I still started to stop by to see Miss Julia.

1

INNER LIFE VERSUS OUTER LIFE CLASS OF THE BLACK EXPERIENCE SCHOOL OF DRAMA

E d Bullins was asked recently if the theatre critics had run him out of New York City in 1982. "Not really," he answered. "I left because I felt as if somebody was setting me up to be shot."[1] The question was inspired by what appeared to have been an orchestrated onslaught of negative reviews of his plays. This barrage began in 1976 with the critic Erika Munk's attack on Bullins in *The Village Voice* for what she believed was his use of rape as a political act in his *Jo Anne!!!* (1993), the story of the Joan Little murder trial in North Carolina. Women were in no mood for such. Three years earlier, in 1973, the African American educator Barbara A. Sizemore had already advised black women to "exact more accountability from black men in response to problems by demanding parity at the decision-making table of organizations and associations designed to promote survival and achieve liberation, for black men must work toward liberation through means that do not oppress and exploit women."[2]

Some women's angry reaction to *Jo Anne!!!*, then, was not at all surprising—especially from Erika Munk, the highly respected feminist pioneer who had edited *The Drama Review, Performance,* and *Scripts,* before becoming critic and later theatre editor of the *Village Voice,* from 1978 to 1990. In 1992 she became editor of *Theater Magazine,* published by the Yale School of Drama. Munk and Bullins had become acquainted when she, as managing editor of *The Drama Review (TDR),* helped him do—"coedit," she said—the landmark Black Theatre issue in 1968. Bullins said that she did not co-edit because "outside of Larry Neal's Black Arts essay, she understood little."[3] Nonetheless, Bullins and Munk became and remained friendly until *Jo Anne!!!,* which prompted her to publish that Bullins was a "lying hypocrite who manipulated history to create half-truths."[4]

The review is so personal that it makes one wonder what went wrong. Why did she—and later almost every other critic at *The Voice*—dislike Bullins so? Could it be that they misunderstood his love of pulling people's legs, of always looking for a chance "to stir up something," as he put it?[5] This urge is particularly evident in Bullins's plays about race relations, a type of play that the philosopher Alain Locke called in 1925 the "Inner Life versus Outer Life" class of drama. Locke argued that protests against racism might be mounted in plays that are not too moralistic or sickeningly sentimental:

> Not all the new art is in the field of pure art values. There is poetry of sturdy social protest, and fiction of calm dispassionate social analysis. But reason and realism have cured us of sentimentality; instead of wail and appeal, there is challange and indictment. Satire is just beneath the surface of our latest prose, and tonic irony has come into our poetic wells. . . . It is no longer true that the Negro mind is too engulfed in its own social dilemmas for control of the necessary perspective art, or too depressed to attain the full horizons of self and social criticism.[6]

Bullins's efforts to write this ironic and satiric play that protested racism created for him all kinds of professional and private dilemmas. He realized that the most enlightening and entertaining protest plays were written in the tradition of the W. E. B. Du Bois Protest School of Drama, led in 1965 by Amiri Baraka. These plays were not satisfying to Bullins. Like Locke, Bullins believes that protest plays fail to analyze and indict racial discrimination. Artists become so engulfed in and depressed by their own social predicaments that they lose control of the necessary artistic distance. As Locke had warned, such losses often led playwrights to create false plots and characters that in no way represented people's daily lives as they were (i.e., "Inner Life"). This encouraged the selecting, polishing, and idealizing of characters so as to present good faces and arguments to white people (i.e., "Outer Life").

Although Bullins did not want any of this, neither did he relish carrying on the Lockean tradition of simply indicting racism through well-made plays. This practice had been established from the middle 1920s to the middle 1960s through the likes of Willis Richardson's (1889–1977) *Compromise* (1925), in which real characters express honest emotions without being maudlin or preachy. Other plays that exemplify this method

32

are Langston Hughes's (1902–1967) expressionistic *Don't You Want to Be Free?* (1938), which mixes protest and culture; Alice Childress's (1920–1994) realistic *Florence* (1950), which protests—and radically altered—the African American "Mama" stereotype; and Ossie Davis's (b. 1917) *Purlie Victorious* (1961) and Douglas Turner Ward's (b. 1930) *Day of Absence* and *Happy Ending* (1965), which exemplify Locke's wish to weld laughter and indictment.

Bullins's need to be different caused him to reject these models, all of which simultaneously analyze and indict racism while calmly promoting racial harmony. The best way of bringing about harmony, Bullins believes, is to get people upset by making them look at racism in totally new ways. He set out to do just that in the plays that make up the two subclasses of the Inner Life versus Outer Life plays. The four plays making up the Race and Politics subclass ask, What are some new and different ways that the African American might correct race discrimination in publishing houses, financial institutions, entertainment industries, and legal systems? The print media, he suggests in *Malcolm: '71, or Publishing Blackness* (1975), should be handled quietly—but firmly.[7] He wrote the play in 1971 because of a personal encounter with a white editor of African American material. The play suggests how black authors can stop being manipulated by such people: A white girl in a "mini-mini dress" speaks hundreds of words on the phone to a revolutionary poet. Her dog, Malcolm, barks. She drops names and makes claims as she tells the poet that although she cannot use any of his poems in her upcoming collection of poetry by "anarchists, wobblies, nihilists, etc.," she would very much appreciate his collecting some black revolutionary poems for her. When he discovers that she has named her dog after Malcolm X, "the BLACKMAN gently hangs the phone up. LIGHTS DOWN. Blackness." Such restraint stands out because other black dramatists of the time were scoring racism with shoutings and shootings. Although less dramatic, the hang-up shows just how much control BLACKMAN exercises over his life and image.

This revolutionary quiet matches the second way of dealing with bigotry—this time in banks, which, according to Thomas Angotti, redline minorities out of the home-owning market while landlords and real estate agents steer blacks away from decent rental housing.[8] In *The Man Who Dug Fish* (1973), Bullins recommended handling bankers' redlining with devastating charm. In the play, a tall, impeccably dressed African American man in his mid forties rents a safety deposit box after he gets the bank to agree that the box "cannot be touched by another human hand besides" his. He pays the rent for ten years. Into the box he puts a fish and a shovel. He leaves.[9] Atypically, this protest piece tickled the audience's imagination about a fish odor that almost matched that of a banker's redlining. Sparked as well was a delayed recognition of how Bullins had tapped minds: The differences between the denotation of shoveling and the connotation of enjoyment found in the slang verb "to dig" in the title *The Man Who Dug Fish* allowed the audience to smile at how Bullins had pulled their legs and slammed heads.

Bullins's recommendation for dealing with the entertainment industry, however, is as subtle as a sunset. In *The Theme Is Blackness* (1973), which was to be performed before a predominantly white audience, he shows how black people could better announce their presence:

SPEAKER

The theme of our drama tonight will be Blackness. Within Blackness, one may discover all the self-illuminating universes in creation.

And now BLACKNESS—
  (Lights go out for twenty minutes.
  Lights up)

SPEAKER

Will blackness please step out and take a curtain call?
  (Lights out)

BLACKNESS[10]

It might be argued that in 1966 such fun-making begged to be misunderstood, given the fact that almost every black political organization had elected more revolutionary leaders. Theatre critics like Erika Munk had no reference for Bullins's black theatre language of double sense, for his playing up the contradiction between what "was" and what "seemed" for all of its entertainment value. Baraka and company had all but ruled out this protocol in the Black Arts Movement. However, Bullins uses it continually. For example, in the unpublished and unproduced scenario *Safety Check* (1971), which is about trusting police, two white police officers stop an African American couple because the right front headlight in the man's car is out. The police ask the man if he knows about the light:

BLACKMAN

Yes, I did, officer. I've been having trouble with it. I got a ticket for it earlier and I'm on my way now to have it repaired.

1ST COP

Do you have any proof of this?

BLACKMAN

Sure . . . the ticket and written instructions are on my ticket here in the dashboard.
  (to Blackwoman)

34

Honey . . . reach into the glove compartment and hand me that ticket, please.[11]

As she does, the second officer "blows her brains out. The startled BLACK-MAN jerks about in time to catch the WOMAN's body falling across his chest. And the 1ST COP reaches in and shoots him in the back of the head." The police plant a pistol. They call to have an ambulance remove "two bodies" of "Black and dangerous" people. The fun of this title, *Safety Check,* makes the piece even more terrifying.

How can one ever know when to take Bullins at face value? The seven plays that make up the Sexual Fantasies and Desires subclass of the Inner Life versus Outer life class of the Black Experience Dramas by Bullins certainly clear up little. Almost impishly, Bullins asks, When, after all, does talking, staring, or thinking become rape? Is it when the character Peter Black converses in *A Minor Scene* (1973) with a white woman at a bus stop?

PETER

Hey, you white scummy-lookin' bourgeois bitch, take me to dinner?

ANN

Wha . . .

PETER

I said suck mah dick! In fact, suck outta mah ass!

ANN

Oh, dear . . .

PETER

You heard what I said, bitch . . . take me to dinner and suck mah dick and et cetera fa dessert.

ANN

Are you mad? I don't even know you![12]

She refuses him until he introduces white paternalism, police brutality, white liberal hypocrisy, and reparation:

PETER

Don't look at me out of your fuckin' ignorant, white face and ask stupid questions! You seen my pretty black face a hundred years snif-fin' round your door for crusts of bread, pats on my wooly ass and for sniffs out of ya asshole and armpits.

Bullins makes Peter such a bad boy in order to show how saintly he might seem in the context of the historically quiescent rape of African Americans—seen in the fleeting glances and painful words in *The Helper*

(1973). In this play, a day laborer helps to move a white family (the wife, called Sister; her husband, Buddy; her mother; and her father). Something sparks between Sister and The Helper. The only evidence, however, is a brief meeting of eyes in the mirror. She is scared wet by her feelings, made even more alarming when her loose-lipped mother voices them:

MOTHER

(After THE HELPER passes)
Sister, doesn't he have the most marvelous skin?

SISTER

(Disinterested, starting up the stairs)
Yeah, Mother . . .

MOTHER
So dark and rich . . . so . . . so African . . .[13]

Sister runs to the bathroom, only to be followed by Mother, going on and on about wanting a grandchild. The Helper finally gets a moment alone with Sister:

(HE finds SISTER in the bedroom changing her pants. HE stands in the doorway watching her for a while, her back to him.)

THE HELPER
Is there anything else, Miss?

SISTER

(Furious)
WILL YOU PLEASE PARDON ME!
(HE walks downstairs and finds BUDDY and the two older people in the hallway. BUDDY opens his wallet and pulls out several bills and hands them to THE HELPER)

THE HELPER
Thanks.
(BUDDY nods, SISTER comes downstairs. Before THE HELPER turns to leave, HE catches DADDY's stare for the first time)

DADDY

(Saluting)
See you again, boy.
(THE HELPER smiles, nods, pocketing his money, and exits.)

The importance of these polar examples of rape might be that the definition itself is insignificant only because the poles are intended only to raise questions. This is atypical of Black Protest theatre, which offers answers. In both The Helper and A Minor Scene, people with no answers act as if the non-answers themselves are workable. This is not the case with Steve, in the third Sexual Fantasies and Desires play, *It Has No Choice* (1973), however. Instead of walking away or hyperventilating, he forces a white woman to pay for having played with his feelings. Grace tries to break off a short relationship with Steve because "I just can't have the things I want if I keep loving you!"[14] He reminds her of his earlier warning that she should not make love to him if she was not in it for the long haul. When she later yells that the affair is over, Steve chokes her almost to death. After dressing, he tells the barely recovered Grace: "I think I'll enjoy making love to you tomorrow, darling." The play, significantly, shows Bullins's uses of race and sexual politics as what Locke called "idioms of expression": Grace and Steve bring up race only to win important personal battles. Whenever the brawl is in danger of being lost, each character plays the race card, as might be seen when Grace points out Steve's inconsistent racial identity: "Oh, I forget! I forget you don't want me to say *colored* . . . that you want to be called at least *Negro* by stupid whites like me, or better, just plain *black*, for the more enlightened . . . did you catch the pun, dear? . . . *Afro-American*."

That Grace's real argument is not about race but about her right to quit a relationship whenever she wishes makes the race issue secondary to character and plot but primary to theme. The importance of the divide is that situations, characters, and themes are better dramatized and developed. The fuller dramatizations surgically implant—and make entertaining—tired issues and arguments:

GRACE

Do you hate me so much?

STEVE

Hating is a foolish waste of emotional energies. Psychologically, it's defeating.

GRACE

See . . . you even forget to talk like a Negro sometimes when you're alone with me!

STEVE

How should Negroes talk, Grace?

GRACE

(Sorry)
Oh, you know what I meant, darling.

STEVE

How should we niggers speak to white folks, Miss Grace?

GRACE

I'm sorry, let's forget about it.

STEVE

How should we happy-go-lucky coons talk to you, Miss Ann?

GRACE

See, you do hate me!

STEVE

(Relieved)
Yeah . . . I guess I do, baby.

Bullins's extension of this use of the political to speak for the personal signals a principal difference between his and other Inner Life versus Outer Life plays. He uses this device, as well, to compare—and weigh—historical and current abuses, as was seen in *A Minor Scene.* The result is surprisingly penetrating insights. He argues that whereas the contemporary assault always paints the character into beastly corners, the character's actions must be judged within the context of history. History has a way, after all, of unearthing full views. To drive home this point in *It Has No Choice,* he relies on an unusually straightforward title taken from the Franz Kafka tenet that one need not do anything but wait for the world to reveal itself because the world has no choice but to show its hand. The title plays this notion against the natural urges, shaped by history, between two simple mortals. The title simultaneously reduces the scope to respective race histories, governed by personal idiosyncracies. The unsaid, then, balloons, making substantive what might have otherwise been deemed pedestrian.

These troubling plays really did not cause Bullins any problems because they were not widely seen or reviewed. They were first produced either in workshops (*The Helper* at New Dramatists, directed by Richard Graziano) or in California (*A Minor Scene* and *It Has No Choice* at Black Arts/West, directed by Hillery L. Broadous). However, this was not the case with *Leavings* (1980), the fourth play in this subclass, which Omar Shapli directed at Syncopation in Greenwich Village. All hell smiled at what was to come. In the play, which has only two white characters, Bullins says that much of the feminist movement is nothing but gameswomanship—or worse, studied hypocrisy. He wrote the play for two reasons. The first is his lifelong hatred of hypocrisy. Bullins tries to live by the code that public image should match private behavior. Whenever he finds vast gaps between the two, he pokes fun at the situations, as well as at the people in them and the people writing about them. He goes about this so casually and humorously that some people—black revolutionaries, for example—assumed from the very start of Bullins's literary life that he was an apolitical lightweight who was not to be taken very seriously. These folks discovered otherwise, as much of his early writing about race, sex, and politics aims deadly blows at black revolutionaries he considered hypocritical for simultaneously damning white people but sleeping with white women. These "cowboys" ranked almost as low down as ministers, who were the first to pique Bullins's obsession with the distance between public stance and private behavior:

> Each preacher that I met soon became exposed as corrupt and two-faced. . . . One preacher stole the church funds and started another church. . . . Another committed crimes and was given thirty-five years in prison, but I was told not to condemn him; it was the Lord's providence. The others seemed only jacklegged shysters, stereotypical slobbering pretenders and wimps, mealymouthed petticoat chasers, and worse. Once, when it was almost time for my baptism, when I had to join and commit myself to their God and ways of worship, I was almost overcome by religious ecstasy, or the Holy Ghost, or whatever that ecclesiastical feeling could be called. The church was jumping, the singing, the preaching, the beat, the music. And I felt I was losing control, being taken over by a celestial power, but I rebelled. I escaped. I ran from there. I would not become the preacher that my mother prayed I would. I would not become a hypocrite.[15]

Bullins came to accept this childhood encounter with sinful preachers as a given for ministers, a situation which congregants offhandedly pass off as "the Lord's providence." As a child he was told, nevertheless, to live up to the publicly preached precepts, which proved for him—along with many others—to be unrealizable, thereby severely damaging the child and the group psychology, as Locke put it. Among the most important of these religious canons was abstinence from premarital sex, which was confusing to the narrator (Bullins's surrogate) in the short story "He Couldn't Say Sex":

> He couldn't say sex and he wondered why. Ten years he wondered, fearing to tell himself he didn't fear to say it—not even to the God he knew that wasn't.
>
> "If I ever hear you say that nasty filth, boy, under this roof again, I'll give you a lesson you'll never forget," his mother said.
>
> But the word oozed off syrupy July pavements filling his muggy playstreets in asphalt-thick waves. . . . The word drifted down midnight hallways of tenements, finding him awake in frigid beds envying the couples clawing in the stairwell. It surmounted the whimpered snores of his pregnant husbandless sister on the first night he cried from fear of his drenched belly. The word mingled with the strained grunts of coughs of his mother and his latest "uncle" in their closed door revelry.[16]

When the narrator escapes his mother and her church, he blames them for the fact that he has fathered bastards throughout the world. More importantly, he cleanses himself. This holy communion of the private and public selves caused white feminists to resent the narrators' redemption at the expense of such hapless figures as Sister in *The Helper,* Ann of *A Minor Scene,* and Grace in *It Has No Choice.* The bitterness flared again when Bullins published his novel, *The Reluctant Rapist* (1973), the story of Steve Benson's youth on a state adoption farm: his sexual and political awakening, and his growing awareness of a quixotic world of casual loves and sudden deaths. As he grows from street fighter to admired boxer and businessman, he treats women like "dogs": he rapes both black and white women only for the excitement. Bullins views the novel as only a "parody on that Eldridge Cleaver 'thing' about rape as a political act": "It was a satire that contained some autobiographical story elements—a comic existential black novel. The feminists got on to the book and went crazy."[17] Not only did they kill the novel, but they also spread the word that Bullins himself enjoyed raping. This attack did not let up.

Bullins struck back with the one-act play, *Leavings* (1980), which is his only play without any black characters. *Leavings* features only Joyce and Freddie, ex-hippies who finally come down from their sixties high by rediscovering their true racial feelings.[18] Joyce, a feminist, says continually that she plans to leave her live-in boyfriend because, among other reasons, he refuses to "stop playing nigger"—although "black people are passé now." Freddie's nigger games include an original blues song:

Mah momma's done left me
She gone out de door
Mah momma's fixin' to split
And I don't know what for

Dese is hard times fo' white men
De world ain't de same no how
Dese is bad lovin' days fo' me
'Cause mah baby's mad as she can be
It must be de times, lawd
Can't be mah fault
It must gonna change soon
Or we's white folks sho is caught

In ah trick bag
Yes, lawd
In ah trick bag
Yes, indeed
In ah trick bag, a brick bag, trick bag, etc.[19]

The song is a microcosm of the play's action: A man is put in "ah trick bag" by a "mad" woman who threatens to leave only because such caveats are fashionable. Furthermore, her leaving is but an empty game designed to wrest and keep control in the relationship. Man's only recourse according to Bullins, is to play along. When Joyce first leaves, therefore, Freddie fashions a noose in order to fool Joyce into thinking—upon her inevitable return—that without her he will commit suicide. Joyce relishes the compliment:

JOYCE

(*Enters.*)
Oh, Freddie . . . you shouldn't have.

FREDDIE

Shouldn't have what?

JOYCE

Shouldn't have done what you almost did . . . or tried to do.

FREDDIE

Shouldn't I have? . . .

JOYCE

Come on . . . don't be so bloody modest. Your love for me is so great that you were about to take yourself out-of-the-picture, as the saying goes, permanently, rather than endure another moment without me. Right?

FREDDIE

Well, almost.

JOYCE

Hey, that's really tough man. It's not like I have no heart or anything like that, but I'm leaving.

She does not leave, however. Freddie punishes her with harrowing tales of how the boxer Jack Johnson not only won the heavyweight championship during a race riot but also violated every feminist principle by marrying and abusing three white women. This causes the expected reaction:

JOYCE

STOP! STOP! STOP IT! If I'm going to stay in this place with you, you must alter your conversation. I don't care what happened then. I don't want to think about it. These are new times. Colored people can be treated as good or as bad as anybody else. They have their equality now. Didn't we fire Andrew Young? And nobody felt guilty about it. Nobody! Those days are gone . . . forever! And another thing: I think that Reggie Jackson is impudent.

The feminists assaulted Bullins upon the first production of *Leavings* in 1980. The *Village Voice* critic Thulani Davis wrote that Bullins created two characters who had nothing in common but their "dubious and tangential relationships to Black people." Davis said that Joyce seemed to have been leaving Freddie more because she was sick of his "playing nigger" than because she wanted her "freedom." Freddie seemed to be holding on to her to keep an audience for his Lenny Bruce antics. Davis felt that Bullins's familiarity with whites was limited to a list of sixties rock groups and Bauhaus references and some worn out notions about white women's sexuality. "What informs the characters of Joyce and Freddie," she concluded, "is the playwright's impassioned dislike of them."[20]

Bullins's 650-word reply, which he negotiated with the *Voice* to publish, says that for years he had been burdened by critics' (false) contentions that he created characters whom he disliked because they stood for the kinds of people that merited his disdain. Bullins had in the main simply ignored such misunderstanding on the grounds that it was the critics' projections and hang-ups. Instead of hating his characters, the opposite was true. It was, in fact, impossible for him to create something or someone that he personally hated because there was too much of himself invested in the invention. To this patent lie, he added that he actually liked Joyce and Freddie "fairly well":

> I have learned from them, and I have taught them things. I grew with them. . . . I evolved with them through the activist-integration-civil rights cum Black Revolutionary separatism sixties. I hung out with them in North Beach and Haight Ashbury, in Tangiers, Earl's Court, Sausalito, and the Village. So, I know Joyce and Freddie, at a distance, and I enjoy them at times. But hate them? Not at all. They represent certain things American to me, so I fashion their presentation for an audience. As I write them at the end of the seventies and the beginning of the eighties, perhaps I am trying to say to Joyce and Freddie that if they don't get themselves together, then we are all closer to being totally doomed. (Like, who's taking care of the store?)[21]

Davis shot back: "It helps those of us concerned with Mr. Bullins's work to have a clear statement of the aims of his play; however, it is a loss for us that the closeness and the feelings for the characters described here did not lend more credibility to the work itself. I did not so much 'project' my insecurities as my expectations."[22] For some strange reason, which might become evident later, Davis did not rest her case against the play solely on the poor character development. She added elaborate theoretical grounds: The play was poor satire because it neglected to "reveal some true absurdity, extravagance, or limitation inherent in observed life." There was no substance to these whites because they did not seem to be true. Therefore, they were not satirized because they did not embody qualities that were "larger than their own particulars."[23]

Although Bullins needed no defending—especially by someone who might smile to see him publicly flogged—Thulani Davis barked up the right tree but in the wrong forest. Bullins called his play a "comic drama."[24] He did not label it a satire, as he did his first draft of *Judge Tom Strikes Back* (1992), the story of the manipulation and emasculation of an African American who looks "amazingly like Clarence Thomas."[25] Freddie and Joyce are intended to be laughable stereotypes, void of any motivation, individuality, or complexity. They are but Bullins's double-edged tools for proving how wrong Eldridge Cleaver had been in 1966 for having kicked Bullins's Cultural Nationalists out of Black House in San Francisco in order to make room for Cleaver's white Maoist friends. More importantly, Bullins connected Cleaver's historic mistake to the notion that the feminist movement itself was but a fickle—and dishonest—game.

Davis's dramaturgical and racial arguments against *Leavings* simply continued the battle begun four years earlier by her editor, Erika Munk, who had made some very serious charges against Bullins. Munk despised the way that Bullins used rape as a political act in his *Jo Anne!!!* (1993), the sixth play in the Sexual Fantasies and Desires subclass.

Jo Anne!!! tells the story of the Joan Little murder trial:

> Sometime between three and four o'clock on the morning of August 11, 1975, a deputy sheriff, bringing a drunken woman into the Beaufort County Jail in the eastern part of North Carolina, found the jailer, Clarence T. Alligood, white, dead on a bunk in a cell in the women's section. There was an ice pick held loosely in his hand; his pants were off; he had sperm on his thigh, and he had seven puncture wounds in his chest and others on other parts of his body. The occupant of cell No. 2, Joan Little, a young black woman, was gone.[26]

Munk claimed that Bullins uses this case "to get credit for a pro-woman, militant play while maintaining anti-woman and anti-political ideas. Underneath, I smell a profound cynicism." She called him a lying hypocrite who manipulated history to create half-truths.[27] Bullins gulped. This very damaging charge must be closely scrutinized through the details of the last two plays in the Sexual Fantasies and Desires subclass: *Jo Anne!!!*—first produced at the Theatre of the Riverside Church in New York City and directed by Carl Weber, a veteran of the Berliner Ensemble and a specialist in the German drama of Bertolt Brecht; and *The Taking of Miss Janie* (1992), first performed at the Henry Street Settlement's New Federal Theatre, and directed by Gilbert Moses. The question might be asked, What textual or other proof is there that these plays are anti-woman, anti-political, and anti-white?

The plot of *Jo Anne!!!*, which could have easily been made into an anti-white theatre essay, consists of four versions of the murder, preceded by the murder itself:

Two oversized silhouettes appear on a scrim—a large male and a smallish female. The MALE gets the best of the FEMALE. HE has a weapon in his hand. HE raises his arm to plunge the weapon in her, but he slips on something upon the the deck and falls. The Two SIL-HOUETTES freeze. . . . The FEMALE FIGURE grabs the weapon away from the fallen man and backs off. The MALE FIGURE lunges at her. As HE closes on her, the FEMALE strikes out at the male in fear, desperation and hate. . . . The MALE fights to kill her with bestial energy. HE knocks her down and kicks and stomps her. SHE strikes again and again with the weapon, and slows him down by hitting his legs. SHE fights her way to her feet and plunges the weapon into the MAN again, as he rushes her. . . . Like a wounded animal, the man beats and pummels the woman. HE is about to kill her with his brute strength, except that she strikes once more. . . . ALL GOODE pulls an ice pick from his bleeding chest and tries to get to JO ANNE. HE freezes before he touches her. . . . JO ANNE rushes off.

ALL GOODE
(Half-drunk, wild-eyed)
She killed me! . . . That nigger bitch killed me. Do ya hear that! A nigger bitch killed me!!! Ya hear that, brothers? Killed. Me. Guard All Goode—a whiteman . . . a southern whiteman, in a southern town. Now ain't that the limit?[28]

Significantly, this *prologos* action articulates the plot—along with the device of the periodic appearance of an elderly black Townsman (really Father Time) helping a matronly white woman (Justice) to find the claims office (Judgment). Each of the four versions of the murder visually or verbally embellishes the act, implying, as critic Erika Munk said, that each has validity.[29] In the first version, Jo Anne tells how that "huge, drunken, depraved monster" comes to where she sleeps and makes her "suck his . . . his *penis*, that's right, give him up some 'head.' " Later this action is narrated by Jo Anne and All Goode in a voice-over as the actors enact Jo Anne's version behind the scrim. In the second account, which is All Goode's, Jo Anne seduces him. While dreaming, she whispers how she wants to suck his "brains out through [his] toes":

ALL GOODE
Oooeeee, hot dawg! I knew I was into something then. I pulled my pants off, then mah drawers and my sport shirt that they got for evidence now. I was clean bareassed buck naked, except for mah tee

shirt. Then you was undressin', throwin' your bra over the cell door and kickin' your panties under the bunk, and your hands . . . gawd . . . your hands was doin' things to mah pecker that I can't ever describe, much less imagine. . . .

Jo Anne and All Goode play out the action of the narrative.

ALL GOODE

I had forgotten that I still held the ice pick in mah left hand. All I could do was place mah right one on the top of your head as you went down on me . . . aahhh . . . and close my eyes and hold on. Oooosss, Jo Anne . . . gal, you love me so much that night.

The third story, which is speculation by a black activist, is that All Goode commits suicide, a conclusion reached based on the fact that the body has been moved, the blood is wiped up, the pants are missing, and the shirt has been washed. The final tale is the prosecutor's. It supports All Goode's seduction theory—with a twist:

ALL GOODE opens the door and enters the cell. The Lights dim so that [Jo ANNE's and ALL GOODE's] bodies can be hardly seen. As soon as the lights dim, the COUPLE embraces, pulls their clothes off, hastily, and ALL GOODE takes her in his arms again and eases her down upon the bunk after THEY kiss passionately. THEY begin to make love.

PROSECUTOR

And this temptress, this Jezebel, this Delilah, this Pandora, this siren seduced this weak, good man, and in his weakest moment of desire and passion, she committed upon him the act of MURDER!
Sound of love-making.

JO ANNE

Oh, Goody. Oh, daddy. You gonna let me get out? You gonna let your little Jo Jo get away?

ALL GOODE

Oh, baby. Oh, Jo Anne . . . this is so good.

JO ANNE

You gonna open the door to freedom for me, daddy?

ALL GOODE

Freedom? Oh, this is so good! What you know about freedom, gal?
Jo ANNE pushes him off.

JO ANNE

What you think I know about freedom, punk! You're my one-way ticket, what you mean by that shit?

ALL GOODE

I'm keepin' you hare, gal, as long as I can. You the best jail cunt I could ever imagine. Open your legs up now!

Jo Anne reaches under her pillow and brings out an ice pick.

ALL GOODE

What the hell? Where's that one come from?

JO ANNE

Don't you recognize it, sucker? I took it out of your desk drawer and kept it for you.

ALL GOODE

Black bitch!

These different stories provide desperately needed suspense for the well-known facts in the case, along with old-hat arguments and analyses. The stories are reinforced by Bullins's signature absurdist structure, which makes appear fresh the possibilities represented. The choice of absurdism for a linearly unfolding trial made Bullins more vulnerable than usual to Munk's charges because he, more so than usual, could play with not only incidents, issues, and spectacles but also their order, size, and time. The importance of using arbitrary time connected by associations instead of real time for real events in a documented situation is that the very time-choice itself becomes a tool for shaping and shading theme—or prejudices. When that time, as in the first episode, is mostly past or past perfect, with quick dashes into the future and present, time can confuse more than clarify. Added to the mix is the ingenious use of the spectator-preferred present time, which Bullins uses for exposition (which the audience disliked), and for brief comic relief (for which the spectator thirsted). Present time in skillful hands, then, made the author even more masterly at satisfying his dramatic needs by manipulating audience preferences. To be fair to Bullins, however, he warned the audience right from the start to watch out for his sleight of hand: The already dead All Goode seats the spectators and sets the ground rules:

SPECTATOR

(Dignified)
Pardon me? Pardon me, sir? What's going on here? Who's on trial.

ALL GOODE

(Indignant)
Who's on trial?

ALL GOODE

(Indignant)
Who's on trial? Why that black nigrah gal—Jo Anne!

> SPECTATOR

But . . . but . . . but who got killed?

> ALL GOODE

> *(Amazed)*

Who got killed? Need ya ask? Why yours truly . . .

> *(He takes a deep bow.)*

> *(proud)*

Me! One of the good ole boys . . . *Guard All Goode.*

> SPECTATOR

Excuse me . . . I thought this was Radio City Music Hall.

The audience, strapped and trapped, is whirligigged through time zones, which are bridged by light, silence, darkness, freeze, and music. Anything missed simply adds to the magic, and makes spinning the sub-plots of a cut-and-dried trial into well-stitched episodes, cut and manipulated for point of view possible. That point of view, gained from Bullins's brief two-day visit to the trial, is that it was a metaphor for American justice, a perfect example of money buying an acquittal—just as Little's attorney Jerry Paul had boasted.[30] Jo Anne was still a victim, however, because the trial, which turned her into a star, was as much make-believe as any Hollywood hype. Paul had found the dream case, said Bullins, and Paul played it as far as he could go. He even went to Hollywood and negotiated the rights to the movie.[31] Bullins felt so badly about this that he sent a letter excoriating Paul to the New York City media saying that Paul had pulled off a "sting" on Little.[32] Bullins said that "when she was acquitted and returned to serve a sentence for a crime committed when she was a minor, no one seemed to care about her any more."[33] Paul was not the only person ripping off Little, however: The black activists got their share of the Little media/money pie, and the feminist movement took the Little case and ran with it for the movement's own ends.[34] Bullins's feelings about these particular feminists did not prevent him, however, from making Jo Anne into a feminist.

Predictably, Jo Anne is more sympathetically drawn than All Goode, notwithstanding Bullins's efforts to make both complex and contradictory. She is tough, independent, hardheaded, mean, and vindictive: "If you [All Goode] mess with me any more, I'll kill your memory by never mentioning you again and destroy your image by creating curse poems about your deeds."[35] Yet, she is fragile, vulnerable, sensitive, and afraid, not only of all white men but also of her own abilities: "It's so hard . . . to believe in anyone, even myself. My body and brain are paralyzed by numb fear and hopeless panic." Whereas this undereducated woman is in many ways naive, she is also bright and thoughtful. She fights not only for a better life but also for respect: "Now, there's two things I really want out of this life I love so much: That's to be somebody, somebody important. And I want my people to be proud of me." Significantly, this complex, sensitive, and intelligent characterization shows Bullins to be quite pro-woman. This was not necessarily at the risk of being racist because Bullins makes an equally sympathetic and difficult character out of All Goode— notwithstanding Erika Munk's contention that he is basically a comic figure.[36] All Goode, as guard, is typically bossy and grotesque: "I'm bossman here. . . . When I tell ya to spread open ya legs, gal, you better open up like a goddamn bloomin' rose just kissed by the sun." Although he is racist and sexist, All Goode is also sympathetic, as seen in his concern that Jo Anne not be angry with him. He even cries at her feet. He is in many ways as self-doubting as she:

> I didn't know what to do. I couldn't see what was makin' the noise over the closed circuit TV from where I was sittin'. And I was scared to come back to the cells. And if I called up to the main building and got the chief night guard back there, and if he heard and found nothin', well, he'd probably laugh at me or get mad and write me up and say I was drinkin' too much on the job.

More importantly, All Goode is God-fearing and truthful. He admits to the prosecutor that his story about Jo Anne's dream about him is a lie, that he does not remember what has happened. He confesses to his plan to rape and kill Jo Anne. He refuses to lie any more in order to make Jo Anne conform to the prosecutor's projected public image. He wants to redeem his place in history. Munk's real concern, then, was not so much with the protagonist and antagonist as drawn as with the use of a woman as All Goode's dog Dixie, which is a "coal black doberman" used to search for the escaped Jo Anne:

> *DIXIE, the dog, is an ACTRESS who wears a menacing looking black leather and metal costume. Spikes jut out of HER huge collar, and a chain is used as a leash by ALL GOODE to hold back the terrible beast.*

> *Arching HER spine at the waist, DIXIE walks on HER hands and the balls of HER feet like a squat monster. While on stage, SHE does not crawl on her knees, nor stop HER hungry, predatory movements and ferocious sounds.*

> *DIXIE is muzzled, for SHE barks fiercely at the SPECTATORS, while dripping saliva and showing HER fangs, as SHE lunges for victims.*

Compounding this representation is that of female nudity, which the critic Barbara Lewis joined Munk in decrying as pornographic simplicity and transparent commercialism. Lewis claimed that Bullins was trying to have it both ways by claiming to uphold the dignity and honor of the black woman while capitalizing on the titillation of rape and nudity. Not once does the jello-belly All Goode bare his flesh, complained Lewis, but the character Jo Anne and another actress who substitutes for her in one scene strip to the quick. Lewis was upset as well by a white women's libber parading through the aisle with a placard boldy stating Pussy Power, brazenly yelling, "Power to the Bitches." The coup de grace, however, was this libber's "shamelessly displaying to the audience her hind section, hair and all."[37] Munk, then, appears justified in her angry claim that this play benefits from the very sexism and exploitation that it purportedly deplores.

The Taking of Miss Janie (1992) also appears to have profited from exploiting while deploring sexism. Written in just sixty days, *Miss Janie* concerns the loss of control and idealism.[38] The absurdist and didactic plot opens with the end of Monty's rape of Janie, and ends with the start of the rape. Sandwiched between are the events leading up to the sexual assault: Janie befriends Monty in a creative writing class. She makes him not only her confidant but also her spiritual custodian, a role that includes taking her for an abortion of some other man's baby. She knows that Monty wants her. In fact, she fantasizes about him—and even about his raping her. She enforces a no-sex rule, however, in order not to lose him, or, more importantly, not to lose control over him. When he rapes her, he steals not only her body but also her lie that she does not know of the act's inevitability.[39]

The principal difference between this and *Jo Anne*'s plot is that *Miss Janie* plays upon contradictions: Bullins sets up assumptions, which are often painted in broad melodramatic strokes. Then he counters the proposition with cold and contrary cunning. He uses Bertolt Brecht's alienation effect in order to keep his spectators thinking and re-evaluating. The audience empathizes with Janie's lesbian friend Peggy, for example, for withstanding a savage attack by Monty's revolutionary friend Rick:

RICK

(Self-righteous and pompous.)

Sister you must admit . . . you live a very unnatural way of life. . . . I know it developed over a time of suffering . . . your disillusionment with your unfulfilled life . . . your loss through resignation of your baby . . . your exploitation by your black man . . . your search for love and emotional and physical security . . . your penis envy . . . and, ah, other masculine-feminine conflicts and encounters. . . . Now, take this scene. This is where your relationship with Brother Monty was nurtured. That's heavy. At wine and pot parties to impress white girls!

49

Just as the audience's heart bleeds for Peggy, she and Rick turn on the spectators by stepping outside of their characters and commenting on the real cause of their failure to make lasting social change:

> We all failed. Failed ourselves in that serious time known as the six-ties. And by failing ourselves, we failed in the test of the times. We had so much going for us . . . so much potential. Do you realize it . . . ? We were the youth of our times . . . and we blew it. Blew it completely. Look where it all ended. Look what happened. (*They are looking out front at the audience.*) We just turned out lookin' like a bunch of punks and freaks and fuck-offs.

The play abounds in such audience-alienation devices, framed by the overriding question raised by the critic Martin Gottfried: Does Monty take (or rape) Janie, or does she take him?[40] Bullins centers the answer in the obvious: Monty not only sacrifices Janie on the altar/bed, but he also hu-miliates her. The later act, well-designed by Bullins to be taken at face value, grated already raw nerves. The *Village Voice* critic Julius Novick joined Erika Munk in the belief that Bullins pretended to address specific social realities, but really distorted those realities in order to gratify his fantasy-desires.[41] Novick hit even harder than Munk: "Virtually everything in the play is rigged to offer Monty/Bullins a maximum of sexual and egotistical gratification, and that is a characteristic of pornography, not of life—or art":

> Is it possible that this moral indignation of mine conceals a psycho-logical hangup? Was I made angry by *Miss Janie* because I suspect that humiliating women really is a satisfying and rewarding thing to do, and that I may be missing something by not trying it? Perhaps, a little; I think most men have a rape fantasy down in there somewhere. (The question is what we do, or don't do about it.) Or could I really be angry because Mr. Bullins celebrates a *black* man humiliating a *white* woman? Am I really reacting as a racist? Again, perhaps; but frankly I doubt it. And if I am a racist, it seems clear that Mr. Bullins is even more of one, and a particularly vicious sexist to boot.[42]

This *ad hominem* attack so angered Bullins that he refused to attend the ceremony to pick up his *Voice*-sponsored Obie Award for this play, which he received for best play. Bullins noted in his journal: "I might win an Obie. Got an invitation to the awards. Tore it up. Ain't going. *Village Voice* slandered me. Called me morally corrupt. So I'll take Trixie to see *Chorus Line*. Didn't want to go anyway."[43] Novick's charge resulted from not knowing—or not accepting—that Bullins likes to pull legs: Monty was seduced. As indicated in his notes, Bullins viewed Monty from the outset as a victim of "the theatrical menace of Janie, the fate-worse-than-death syndrome. She was simultaneously fascinated and disturbed by being raped. She's the kind that will refuse to see [Monty] again, since she has lost control of part of the situation. She should play innocent. He should be calculating, truthful and deliberate."[44] Because she knows what, when, and how she wants what she wants, she "rapes" him from the moment they first meet:

JANIE

Hello. You're in my Creative Writing class, aren't you?

MONTY

Yeah . . . I think so.

JANIE

I love the poetry you read today.

MONTY

Thanks.

JANIE

But it was so bitter.

MONTY

Oh.

JANIE

Do you call that Black Poetry?

MONTY

Hey . . . my name's Monty.

JANIE

Mine's Janie.

MONTY

Pleased to meet 'cha, Miss Janie.

JANIE

(*Surprised.*)
What did you say?

MONTY

What did ya think I said?

JANIE

(*Curious.*)
Why did you say that?

MONTY

Oh, just a little joke of mine, I guess.

51

She never lets up, playing upon—and being—his palsied perception, his broken confidence, his forbidden fruit, and his blurred imagination. Her power flows from things as simple as not only altering his perceived place in her pecking order but also loading his historic self- and race-view. As Monty inches away from the merely "colorful" and farther up her chain, she continually teases, alternately reeling him in and letting him go.

That Bullins created this contradiction of who raped whom left him too open to Munk's charge that he was anti-woman and racist: Janie and All Goode are, after all, compatriots. Bullins countered by making victim Monty anything but a sacred lamb: he is the source of revolutionary Rick's nonsensical verbiage. Furthermore, Monty is selfish and cruel, caring about nothing much beyond his poetry and his penis. It is his sexual cravings, in fact, that cause him to lose the war with Janie. He believes that no matter how many battles she wins, the rape will assure him of ultimate victory. Even the rape, however, is a loss, as indicated by Bullins in an important interview with the writer Charles M. Young:

> *There have been various interpretations of the rape in your play. Did Monty's punishment fit Janie's crime?*
>
> I don't know. That's just what he did. It was a phenomenon. It started with the nonviolent integration movement and ended with the separation of blacks from white European culture. Blacks have always been the property of their masters, in a sexual as well as economic sense. Monty was expressing his own imperative to reach self-determinism. Janie was very dishonest. She knew what he wanted; he never disguised his intentions. But she still was trying to keep him as her own little slave or eunuch. The theme of the play is the destruction of illusion.[45]

By making the rape Monty's "imperative to reach self-determination," or his "act of supreme liberation from white oppression," as the critic Barbara Mackay put it, Bullins kids even himself. Mackay believes that Bullins's play reinforces the notion that black men so covet white women—either as sexual ideals preferable to black women or as symbols of class and power—that they will stop at nothing to possess them. Mackay feels that this notion is based on a sense of black inferiority, a belief that black leaders have tried to counteract for years. Mackay believes that Bullins hurt everyone's cause by making this the heart of his play. She wrote that, had Bullins stressed Monty's willingness to use force to get what he wanted, Monty might have been a more accurate portrait of modern black pride and determination. She believes that Bullins, instead emphasizes the importance of the prize itself, not the means his hero uses to get it.[46] Mackay's argument breaks down not because it does not have merit, but because she ignores Monty's "willingness [—even plan—] to use force":

MONTY

(Rises and stalks her.)
Shut up, bitch! You phoney, whining white bitch!

JANIE

(Hurt and tearful.)
Don't call me that . . . Please don't say that, Monty.

MONTY

Shut up, I said! I've wasted too much love and caring on you already. From the first moment you met me, you knew it would come to this. . . . And you've got the nerve to cry and act like this.
(Pulls her to him and kisses her and "dry fucks" her until he begins arousing some response against her will.)

Whether or not Mackay approves, Monty is simply cashing a check signed by Janie, a promissory note that Janie has always known would be called in. More importantly, Mackay, like so many other critics, confuses Bullins with his anti-hero.

The critical reaction to *The Taking of Miss Janie* shows the danger of permitting people to believe that the public presentation could speak for the private playwright. The irony of Bullins's insistence that the public and private be one is that critics, violating what Jervis Anderson calls good critical etiquette, attacked him for his characters.[47] Julius Novick, for example, wrote that *Bullins* used Janie as a punching bag: "Like his hero, he seems to enjoy humiliating her, and he creates her exclusively to be humiliated. . . . This does not mean that the humiliation of women should not be shown on the stage, but I wonder if it should be shown as an eminently satisfying and rewarding kind of behavior—which is the way Mr. Bullins shows it, gloating and licking his lips."[48] The critic Richard Cohen said, similarly, that *Bullins* took special pleasure in "beating up on" Jewish characters, that he reserved a "real contempt" for Jews:

There is the Jewish girl who tries to steal a black's manhood by marrying him; the marriage fails, of course. And there is the stock character ex-beatnik Jewish poet who tries to steal the black man's pleasure (drugs) and turns into a loathsome addict begging his black buddies for a fix; to complete the picture, this wretched and repugnant creature is a Zionist.

Ed Bullins, "promising playwright," promises plenty, all right, but it is not a very pleasant prospect; for what he offers is nothing less than racial and religious war. . . . At the end of this road lies Auschwitz, and we have had enough of that. And quite enough of Ed Bullins, [the director] Gilbert Moses and [the producer] Joseph Papp, too.[49]

Bullins struggled publicly to distance himself from his characters, stressing that they in no way represented his personal views. He justified the separation by explaining that characters are but inventions, things made up of elements of the human psyche, from human experience, from a transactional intercourse with humanity, from figments of the imagination, and from selective samples of subconscious bias. The playwright chooses traits for a character, he stated, in order to reflect a point of view—not necessarily the author's.[50] Monty's rape of Janie, indeed, does not mean that Bullins himself advocates such mistreatment of women—notwithstanding his clowning about rape: When a feminist in Buffalo asked him if he glorified rape, he answered: "Not really. You've got to understand the phenomenology of the act." "The what?" the woman asked. After laughing, Bullins assured her that he would never glorify rape.[51] He appears not to understand that some subjects are too humiliating and dehumanizing to be taken so lightly. It is, then, Bullins's love of "stirring things up" with both subtle and outrageous words and actions that might cause some to confuse him with his characters.

Some feminist critics, however, might have welcomed the mistaking. Even seven years after the Bullins novel *The Reluctant Rapist* (1973) appeared, influential feminists still had it in for him. *Village Voice* editor Erika Munk reportedly told her critic, Lionel Mitchell, that Bullins "was proud to be a rapist."[52] This supposedly happened when Mitchell submitted a favorable review of Bullins's *Leavings*, which Mitchell viewed as an indictment of "the growing psychological totalitarianism of white feminists."[53] Munk allegedly refused to run the review, sparking what Mitchell called a "minor civil rights battle" between himself and Munk. She denied that she ever told Mitchell that Bullins was a proud rapist. She said that she had merely referred Mitchell to her stinging 1976 review of Bullins's *Jo Anne!!!* Mitchell said, however, that this denial was the first time he had ever heard of that review. Nevertheless, Munk had *Leavings* re-reviewed by the feminist critic Thulani Davis, who wrote what Mitchell called a "superficially hostile review." Mitchell felt that this played right into the hands of the ongoing feud between Bullins and Munk: "Munk and Bullins had worked together back in the sixties on various projects, but neither was willing to tell what their feud was really all about. Bullins professed to hold no grudges against Munk, and Munk covered herself with a series of samurai-like moves that concluded with Bullins being allowed to answer Davis's review in the pages of the *Voice*."[54]

What Mitchell did not know is that Munk apparently had a conflict of interest when she wrote the *Jo Anne* review, which was as much a brief against Bullins as it was a putdown of the play. Her thesis was that Bullins was a sexist con man. She quoted from his novel: "It was nice, so much better than I had imagined. The firmness of her box surprised me. She was so drunk she couldn't handle the strength of my attack, so I had my way with her like I wanted." Munk said that Bullins never distanced himself from or disapproved of his "rather autobiographical" narrator's ideas and actions.[55] She quoted from the foreword to his anthology, *New Plays from the Black Theatre* (1969), in order to break his alleged confidence about having written *We Righteous Bombers* (1969), attributed to Kingsley B. Bass Jr., a twenty-four-year-old "Blackman murdered by Detroit police during the uprising":

> Bullins told me he himself had actually written the play. . . . This is the unconscious speaking, and not of an unknown Detroit rioter. And who was the joke on? The audience who saw the play at the New Lafayette? The students and theatre people who use the anthology? In a 1972 interview with me in *Performance,* Bullins said, "Should we try to make a truthful history, or not deal with truth or falsity at all, but try to create a history, a collective unconscious?" His answer is still "living historical theatre of the mind"—half truths, manipulated to create a history which is anti-history.[56]

Munk's review might be considered anti-criticism because she does not let the audience know that she has an ax to grind: Bullins alleges that he and Munk had once been secret lovers. The supposed affair began in 1968, when they were working on the Black Theatre issue of *The Drama Review.* Bullins claims that she tired of the secrecy and wanted him to go public with their romance. He refused. Bullins states that his friends told him that she then began an underground whispering campaign to ruin him with the word that he had raped her.[57] On 7 November 1976, the day that Munk's scathing review of *Jo Anne!!!* appeared, Bullins wrote in his journal:

> Erika Munk just wrote a big put-down of me in the *Village Voice.* Funny. Somehow I was very flattered. At least she's looking for something, and most critics and others think they have me pigeonholed. I've always taken Erika too lightly; I always thought she had a second-rate mind, so I have dismissed her or put her on. She didn't tell how I screwed her. And how she got mad at me when I wouldn't go to LaMama's with her. Women do things for very tacky reasons. But it's better to be notorious than not known at all. I've wanted to make it with her again, for the past several years, but she's gotten so strange. And now this feminist thing and the yellow journalism. A female John Simon/Carl Tucker. I guess working with the *Voice* has gone to her

head. Would answer that piece, if there were any reason to. I could really devastate her, if I wished. But I mustn't be ungentlemanly.[58]

When I asked her about this, Munk angrily denied having had an affair with Bullins. She wondered, in fact, how anybody would dare ask her questions about her personal life.[59] The only significance of this grade Z soap opera is that it offers perspective on how represented action in a play often gets assigned to its author, and how the alleged ulterior motives of some critics might shape that assignation.

How ironic that Bullins was critically raped because he wrote against sexual abuse—notwithstanding Munk's view that he did not distance himself from his "rather autobiographical" creations. Based strictly on the textual evidence in *Miss Janie* and *Jo Anne!!!*, Bullins made rapists into losers. Monty's loss of power—under the delusion that he is exercising it—is no less tragic than All Goode's loss of his life. Bullins highlights Monty's spiritual and political deaths by showing the monumental discrepancy between Monty's promise and his achievement. The gifted poet becomes sloganizer, turning song into noise. His clear view of history, which once motivated a people to know and love themselves as they plotted their political paths, is now clouded by marijuana. His liberation is not economic equality but a white vagina. His spiritual death is less merciful than All Goode's because Janie's choice of weapons is ever so much more painful than Jo Anne's ice pick. Taken together, both deaths might serve as metaphors for the demise of Bullins's public persona. His image—and, more importantly, his place in theatre history—suffered almost irreparable damage because, among other things, he deluded himself into believing that being notorious was better than not being known. He ignored the Harry Overstreet notion that image is more powerful than reality because how one behaves toward people is chiefly determined by images one has of them.[60]

Bullins felt comfortable with a slough of negative reviews he received in the mid 1970s because he dismissed the critics: "In regards to Gloria Steinem and the Women's Movement mounting a writing campaign against my novel, *The Reluctant Rapist,* and turning it into a rare book in America, I never burned up too many brain cells about it. Maybe I'm one of those who haven't gotten it yet. They haven't the foggiest notion of what my writing is about, so what can I say?"[61] He took this same laissez faire attitude about the scowling photographs of him in what he called his "post-revolutionary urban peasant wear: dashiki, beard, wild hair, worn denims, and sandals."[62] He was unconcerned because he knew that this was but costume and makeup to ensure he got time and space in the media. It did not matter to him what was said, so long as *he* knew who he was and what he believed. When he read that he was anti-woman, for example, he simply dismissed it as "strange": "I have for years kept my brain buzzing about what seemed to me the two most beautiful things in the universe—better to me than the sun rising and setting, [than] volcanoes exploding, meteors falling, waterfalls doing likewise, critters and pests droning through emerald tinted jungles, etc.—the two most beautiful creations are a woman and a baby."[63]

Bullins was not solely at fault for his misrepresentation in the media, however. Either through conditioning or design, the critics totally missed his love of irony, subtlety, and jest—his adherence to the Lockean tradition of substituting satire and sarcasm for wailing and appealing. Locke contended that race relations would be improved by these new kinds of calming analyses. How ultimately ironic that the new ways backfired, turning into a monster a craftsman who refused to get so buried in or saddened by social dilemmas that he lost control of the necessary perspective of art or of social and self-criticism. Granted, Bullins shook things up while he carried on the traditions of Randolph Edmonds and Willis Richardson of character and plot development. Significantly, his imposition of radical themes and characters ultimately improved racial harmony by forcing whites to repair their own damaged group psychology. Inverting Locke, Bullins wanted whites to be known for who/what they were—shortcomings and all. Munk's view that Bullins relished being mirror more than advocate overlooks mirroring as advocacy.[64] The critic Lionel Mitchell perceived this, saying that Bullins's plays hold up a mirror to the audience: "And if you don't like what you see, too fucking bad!"[65] It is important to Bullins that people know that accepting their mirrored selves will be painful and costly—notwithstanding the fact that images are "only an imperfect reflection of our imperfect perception of what reality is."[66] Perhaps it was Bullins's recognition that his subtle pictures were not effective enough that caused him to change tactics from the quiet putdown in *Malcolm: '71, or Publishing Blackness* and the humorous pranks in *The Man Who Dug Fish* and *The Theme Is Blackness* to the psychological and physical rapes in *The Helper, A Minor Scene, It Has No Choice, Leavings, Jo Anne!!!* and *The Taking of Miss Janie.* Although Bullins feigned surprise at the maelstrom that these race plays created, he knew quite well that in them he had gone for the jugular.

Bullins somewhat naively surmised that in the end people would appreciate his tough stand because his heart meant no harm. He believed that somebody, somehow, would make the public know that every time he appeared to be a raging ingrate, it was because—as shall be shown—some official had treated him like a worthless dog. He expected somebody to show one day that while he popularized back-street lifestyles in theatre, he was the one who had forced a new generation of playwrights to find other images to portray black lives. He hoped that the "black bourgeoisie," whom he often put down along with whites, would someday know that it was he who got young playwrights to phase out the "kill whitey" noise. He thought that nobody would ever believe that he hated white people, even as Peter in *A Minor Scene* and Rick in *Miss Janie,* along with other characters, tapped into race-baiting sixties rhetoric. He imagined that astute spectators would see that he was putting down all racists by making them into clowns: Peter and Rick, for example, are comic relief. Bullins presumed that people would know, as Erika Munk said, that he really distrusted politics.[67] The irony is that the man who most loved honesty allowed—even fostered—a dishonest public persona by turning reality into plays, by playing games, seeking notices, as well as by obsessing over his own contrariness. The latter, in fact, ultimately almost robbed Bullins of his prized honesty—as might be seen in his Black Revolutionary plays.

2

BLACK REVOLUTIONARY CLASS OF THE BLACK ARTS SCHOOL OF DRAMA

Just as Bullins's female characters often got him into deep trouble with feminists, his Black Revolutionary plays offended black revolutionaries of every stripe and model. *We Righteous Bombers* (1969), for example, seared so many raw nerves among the New York City revolutionary Marxists and black cultural nationalists that after opening night at the New Lafayette Theatre on 18 April 1969, several told the artistic director, Robert Macbeth, that they wanted to talk to him. With pistol butts sticking out from under their dashikis, the men told Macbeth that he had done the community a "great disservice" by producing the play, that he had "tampered with our revolution," and that they were considering "moving" on him. Macbeth asked them if they wanted him to close the play. They replied that closing was not enough, that he would have to suffer the consequences of failing to be "more cooperative with the brothers." They cited his not having done any plays by revolutionary blacks. "If this is supposed to be the black theatre of Harlem," they told him, "then these brothers' plays should be done. And you are going to do them." To make their message clear, they reminded Macbeth that he had already "lost one theatre."[1] Macbeth suggested that he sponsor a symposium on the play and that the comments be published in the *Black Theatre* magazine. The revolutionaries agreed, but they told Macbeth that they were going to "preach very harshly about what you have done here. And know that you cannot walk alone by yourself while our revolution is going on."[2]

The question must be asked why Bullins's revolutionary plays made these and many other "revolutionaries" so angry. Could it be because that Bullins believed these plays, like the race ones, were "fun and action," designed to expose "truth and hypocrisy"?[3] Although Amiri Baraka, the creator of the Black Revolutionary class of drama, might have gone along with the "truth and hypocrisy" business, it is doubtful that he would have viewed as "fun" any of the seven subclasses of Bullins's plays in this genre, named after the Seven Principles (or *Nguzo Saba*) of Ron Karenga's cultural nationalist doctrine of *Kawaida: Umoja* (Unity), *Kujichagulia* (Self-Determination), *Ujima* (Collective Work and Responsibility), *Ujamaa* (Cooperative Economics), *Nia* (Purpose), *Kuumba* (Creativity), and *Imani* (Faith). These principles call for a total commitment to cultural nationalism; getting this from Bullins in 1965 was about as likely as getting blood from a pickled pig foot.

Bullins was the man, after all, who only two years earlier had written the highly conservative essay, "The Polished Protest: Aesthetics and the Black Writer," in which he attacked all protest literature for its "hard scolding, embittered denouncements of whites, the South, the aloof North, and the overall tragedy of being a black man in America."[4] The essay disparages those "tiring multitudes . . . who achieve minor recognition in exploiting the plausible by claiming conclusive answers for the Negro problem in the same standard generalities and cliches."[5] He called for multi-dimensional black characters doing the routine but difficult job of living out their "anguish-filled lives in their ghettos." He wanted to put an end to analyzing the hate that existed between the races, to commenting upon the unsavory aspects of random—and certainly taboo—miscegenation, to exposing the circumstances of misunderstood homosexual love, and, incidentally, to examining the inequalities that confront black Americans. He wished for more "objectivity" and "aesthetic distance." Without these, "New-Breed writers remain as self-deluded as their cotton-patch brethren, *and as irrational as their black nationalistic kin who race into the arena of ideas in a chariot of emotional slogans and incredible panaceas.*"[6] Bullins concluded by admonishing the serious writer—whatever his color—first to seek *honesty* with himself concerning his work, and then to decide if he honestly wished "to make art of his writing, or facile craftsmanship for money, recognition, glamor, or proselytizing for a cause."[7]

What happened to these views after Bullins and Baraka became fast friends in 1966? Baraka—of all people—fit completely the negative bill outlined in Bullins's essay. How could these men have ever become friends? Baraka attributes it to the fact of Bullins being closer to Baraka's own type, each having been hooked up to and having stepped past white bohemia.[8] Bullins attributes it to his own honesty and Baraka's generosity. Shortly after they met in San Francisco, Baraka bailed Bullins out of jail in San Jose. Bullins and the poet/dramatist Marvin X had been arrested outside of the Black House for a series of traffic violations. Baraka probably had little choice but to put up the $1,400 bail because Bullins and Marvin X were the backbone of Baraka's Black Communications Project, which was co-sponsored by the Black Student Union and the Experimental College at what was then San Francisco State College. As local black community theater people and as cultural organizers, Bullins and Marvin X were vital to the project, especially since Baraka was new in town and, according to Bullins, "didn't know who was friend, enemy, or informer."[9]

Bullins proved his honesty by stopping "some black revolutionary types" from stealing Baraka's bail money. Shortly after Bullins and Marvin X were released, the charges were dismissed. The Eldridge Cleaver faction in Black House planned to keep Baraka's check as a payback for his having muscled his way into the Northern California revolutionary scene. Cleaver really wanted Bullins and Marvin to stay in jail because they had included Baraka in Black House activities, thereby strengthening the hands of the cultural nationalists. Bullins somehow "Bogarted" Baraka's money and returned it to him.[10] Bullins's act and Baraka's presence, significantly, frustrated Cleaver's early plan to turn Black House into a full-blown Marxist center.

The differences between Cleaver and Marvin X might be viewed within the context of cultural nationalism versus Marxism: As a nationalist, Marvin X held the view that liberation would result from African Americans' becoming an African-based cultural nation with no ties to white people. On the other side of the issue, Cleaver believed that the freedom of African Americans was tied to an armed socialist revolution by all oppressed people, including poor and working-class whites.[11] White youth, he felt, repudiated their "heritage of blood" and took people of color as heroes and models.[12] They, in fact, used techniques learned in the African American struggle to attack problems in the general society.[13] Cleaver developed careful alliances, therefore, with the Socialist Workers Party, as well as other white leftist groups. He consolidated with the leftists late in 1967 by accepting Huey Newton's advice to kick the "reactionary" cultural nationalists out of Black House.

From the outside, this appears to have worsened considerably Bullins's attitude toward Cleaver. However, Bullins claims that this was not the case:

> Cleaver and Emory Douglass appointed me the first minister of culture for the Panthers, [a post] which I used to raise money and get media attention. Later, I took a trip to Algeria to meet with Cleaver under the auspices of the First Pan African Cultural Festival, sponsored by the Pan African Congress. I usually took the mediating ap-

proach among various activists and revolutionaries. Therefore, I retained most of their friendships for many years.[14]

Yet, the notion of Bullins as a political revolutionary dramatist in 1966 is a bit strange. Even Bullins as a cultural nationalist dramatist seems out of kilter in light of his mistrust of politics and politicians. Bullins remained close, nevertheless, to Baraka, the hardcore politician, who began speaking out in favor of cultural nationalism throughout the country.

This friendship appears odd because, when Bullins moved to New York City in 1968, his mentor became Robert Macbeth, who disrespected Baraka's art and politics. Macbeth descended from the upper class in Charleston, South Carolina, where for generations certain African Americans protected their culture and privilege. They made sure that they were connected nationally to the likes of the singer/musician Cab Calloway and the jazz musician Fletcher Henderson, along with concert artists Dorothy Maynor and Roland Hayes. Macbeth's schooling at the prestigious Avery School, at Morehouse College in Atlanta, and at City College of New York prepared him well for moving comfortably among the elite of all races. His brief stays in public school, moreover, helped him to understand and respect rough street life. A four-year stint as a basketball player in the air force stationed in Korea further toughened him, forcing down his young throat the knowledge that "real war" was "a hellish and heartless sacrifice." His theatre training differed radically from that of the Barakaians: After studying at the Actors Studio in New York, he understudied Billy Dee Williams in Shelagh Delaney's *A Taste of Honey* (1958) on Broadway; Macbeth appeared in Peter S. Feibleman's *Tiger, Tiger Burning Bright* (1962) opposite Diana Sands; and he traveled throughout Europe with Judith Malina and Julian Beck's Living Theatre (1948). So, when Macbeth brought Bullins to New York in 1968, and when he shared an apartment with him and hired him as writer-in-residence, Macbeth possessed a theatre knowledge and practice shaped by the traditional American theatre.

It might have been predicted, then, that Macbeth would refuse continually to produce any of Baraka's plays at the New Lafayette Theatre: Macbeth felt "that they had no substance. They were not even plays."[15] Yet, at the time, Bullins credited Baraka for "creating me as a playwright" and for being "one of the most significant figures in American theatre."[16] Consequently, Bullins appears to have had an identity crisis. To whom—or what—was he committed? He was probably sworn to nobody because he was not the committing kind. He had often observed fights of all kinds without taking sides, as, for example, when the nationalist leaders and organizations vied for supremacy in Southern California during 1960–1964. Bullins's relocation to Northern California in 1964 was probably motivated in part by his indifference to both the US organization of cul-

Ed Bullins's maternal grandfather, Samuel Queen.

Ed's mother, Bertha Marie Queen Bullins.

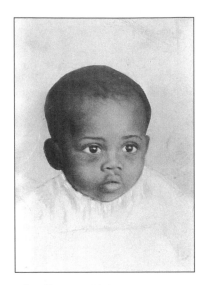

Ed Bullins, c. 1936.

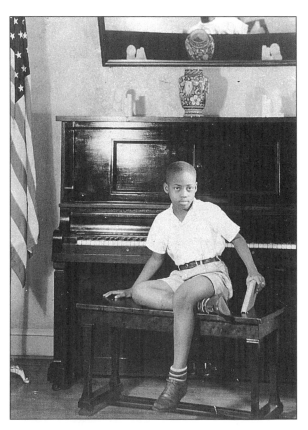

Ed Bullins, music student, c. 1945.

Ed Bullins (second row, second from right) *with classmates at Ludlow Elementary School, 1947.*

Ed Bullins, Easter, 1940s.

Ed Bullins at the Celebrity Club in Providence, Rhode Island, listening to Sammy Davis Jr. and the Will Masterson Trio, 1953.

Ed Bullins's U.S. Navy days, 1952–55.

"Buller" Bullins (left) fighting "Slugger" Johnson during a smoker held aboard the USS Midway CVA-41, *c. 1953.*

Bullins, student at Los Angeles City College, 1962.

Left to right: *Ameena Bullins, Cousin Florence Garrison, and Sun Ra Bullins, Easter 1976.*

"Bullins and children," c. 1976. Back row, from left: *Eddie Jr., Ed Sr., Donald;* middle row, from left: *Ronald, Darlene, Patsy, Diane;* front row, from left: *Sun Ra, Ameena.*

Ed Bullins's daughter, Catherine Room.

Ed's mother, Bertha Bullins, 1975.

Ed Bullins, Marva Dorsey Sparks, 1986.

New Lafayette Theatre, 1969.

Clara's Ole Man, *American Place Theatre, 1968.* From
left: *Kelly Marie Berry, Roscoe Orman.*

We Righteous Bombers, *New Lafayette Theatre, 1968.*
From left: *Roscoe Orman, Bill Lathan, Kris Keiser.*

Ed Bullins, Sonia Sanchez, August Wilson, 1994.

Clara's Ole Man, *American Place Theatre*. From left:
Carolyn Caldwell, Kelly Marie Berry.

From left: *Bernard Gersten, Joe Papp, Ed Bullins, Gilbert Moses, and Woodie King Jr., 1975.*

Reverend Michael Duke, 1995.

Ed Bullins, 1975.

From left: *Ed Bullins, Ishmael Reed, Cecil Brown,*
Berkeley, 1988.

Bill Lathan, Ed Bullins, 1969.

New Lafayette Theatre Company. Back row, from left: George Ford, unidentified, Peggy Kirkpatrick, Yvette Hawkins, Wayne Grice, Gordon Watkins, Roberta Ryso, Ed Smith; front row, from left: Gary Bolling, unidentified, Helen Ellis Macbeth, Carl Lee, Estelle Evans, Betty Howard, Ed Bullins, Roscoe O'man, Robert Macbeth.

Ed Bullins, 1995.

tural nationalists and the opposing Slauson gang of five thousand, led by the fearsome Slauson Renegades, which later became the nucleus of the Black Panther party. Even as the Panthers and the nationalists were warring in Black House in San Francisco in 1966, Bullins admitted that although he sided with the nationalists, he tried to remain on good terms with Cleaver—principally so that he could put on his plays. Similarly, he was not really obligated to either Macbeth or Baraka in their feud in 1968—notwithstanding the fact that Bullins viewed Baraka as a revolutionary brother and Macbeth as an arts brother. Both Macbeth and Baraka returned Bullins's friendship: Baraka and his wife Amina had dinners and parties with Ed and Trixie Bullins. Baraka highly respected Bullins as an artist, calling him "one of our most powerful playwrights." Significantly, though, Baraka never once directed a Bullins play nor ever produced one in Baraka's Spirit House in Newark.[17] This indicates that whereas these men greatly admired and defended each other as men and dramatists, they accepted the wide—and defining—differences between them as both men and dramatists. What did these distinctions make of Bullins, however? How did his political peculiarities manifest themselves in each of the four subclasses of revolutionary plays that he attempted—especially the *Umoja* (or Unity) subclass, which instructs people about the need for and the means of maintaining oneness in personal, family, and community relationship?

Bullins wrote three Unity plays, all of which, needless to say, are unlike those written by the Barakaians, which include plays as varied as Baraka's own ominous warning to the older generation that his is not a war of words (*Arm Yrself or Harm Yrself* [1967]), and Ron Zuber's poetic call for stronger man-woman ties to themselves as insurgents (*Three X Love* [1972]). It would seem that Bullins would have little new to add, especially in the area of his speciality, the family drama. The Baraka advocates penned such plays as Ben Caldwell's *Family Portrait or My Son the Black Nationalist* (1967), in which a son leaves home after he tires of his parents' trying to make him into "a middleclass white boy"; and Marvin X's *Flowers for the Trashman* (1968, also known as *Take Care of Business*), as well as Jimmy Garrett's *We Own the Night* (1968), which shows that young revolutionaries are willing to kill counterrevolutionary family members—even their own mothers. Bullins's Unity plays, nevertheless, find something new to say in a quite different way. For example, his *Black Commercial #2* (1973), which calls for African Americans to replace self-annihilation with brotherhood, takes place in a "pigfoot emporium" that overflows with whiskey, beer, and wine. A chanting crowd delights itself with the fight of two men bent on killing each other.[18] The crowd eggs the men on until a soft-spoken and neatly dressed young man steps out of the crowd:

BLACK MAN

Brothers.

(The Two stop fighting.)

RUFUS

What you say, man?

BLACK MAN

Brothers.

RUFUS/BLUE

(Together)

Huh???

BLACK MAN

Brothers.

BLUE

You mean you think him and me is brothers?

BLACK MAN

Brothers.

CROWD

BROTHERS! BROTHERS! BROTHERS! BROTHERS! BROTHERS! BROTHERS! BROTHERS! BROTHERS! . . .

RUFUS *(to BLUE)*

If we brothers, man . . .

BLUE

(Perceiving)

Yeah . . . then . . .

RUFUS

(Recognizing)

Why . . . brother . . .

(RUFUS helps BLUE up. BLUE begins brushing his brother off)

BLACK MAN

Black.

CROWD

(Chants)

Black brothers. Black brothers. Black brothers . . . Black brothers.

(BLACK MAN steps back into the CROWD.)[19]

This short is a mixed-bag. The first half is influenced by Alain Locke's Art-Theatre philosophy, which shows life as it is, thereby espousing the art-for-art's-sake philosophy found in Bullins's 1963 conservative essay. Although the aristocrat Locke would never have approved, Bullins depicts low-income people doing their Saturday night thing:

> The CROWD *watches* RUFUS *and* BLUE *as they occupy the dance floor.* RUFUS *and* BLUE *are killing each other.* RUFUS *has a broken beer bottle and is trying to gouge* BLUE's *eyes out.* BLUE *holds his friend's arm with one hand and is kept from driving his bone-handled switchblade into* RUFUS *by the man's tenacity to remain alive.*

The second half of the play, however, embraces the W. E. B. Du Bois Protest School of Theatre philosophy, which shows life as it should be: Black Man steps from and back into the crowd—persuading the squabblers to stop the killing. Equally as important is the fact that the change occurs not because some self-annointed "black nationalist" leader races into Bullins's "arena of ideas in a chariot of emotional slogans and incredible panaceas" designed to build a cultural nation or a poor people's alliance. There are no obligatory monologues that state, re-state, and summarize the "point" or "message," but, rather, an aesthetic distancing that reveals the message by simply showing the low-income people doing "the routine but difficult job of living their anguish-filled lives in their ghettos."

This half-and-half milkshake satisfied neither nationalist nor Marxist appetites. To spoil further already barely tolerable conditions, Bullins went public with the private squabbling among the revolutionaries in his second Unity play, *A Street Play* (1970). An actor—of all people—questions a Black Panther as the latter sells the *Panther* newspaper:

ACTOR 1

Say, brother . . . you Panthers sell papers just like the Muslims . . . don't cha? You learned to do that from them? Naw . . . ya didn't? . . . Then where did you learn it from?

Now, look, brother . . . I ain't tryin' to hassle you . . . I think that brothers should learn from brothers.

But I just heard that your boss, Eldridge Cleaver, said that the Muslims were counterrevolutionary . . . or somethin' like that . . . and I was wonderin' . . . if you patternin' your newspaper methods after the Muslims because you want them to become real revolutionaries like you. . . .

(ACTOR 2 comes up)
ACTOR 2

(To Panther)
Say, man . . . I just read Cleaver's Manifesto . . . wow . . . man. What do you think of that?

ACTOR 1

Of what?

ACTOR 2

Didn't you know? . . . Cleaver's callin' for a race war between black people and whites.

ACTOR 1

Wow . . . man . . . we can get the shit on now.

ACTOR 2

Maybe you can, Home . . . but it seems to me that Cleaver's doin' the writin' 'n talkin' . . . and my ass is over here doin' the fightin' in this race war. . . .

ACTOR 1

Damn . . . hey, Panther . . . is the Muslims, SNCC, CORE, The NAACP, The Cultural Nationalists, The Urban League, The Preachers and the other Black people in this too?

ACTOR 2

War is war . . . brother.

ACTOR 1

Damn . . . why ya have to go an' call it now . . . I just about got mah short paid for . . . I was gonna cool it this summer . . . now I gotta take me out a loan to get me some guns . . . Hey, man . . . give me another one of those papers. I gotta show this mess to mah ole lady.[20]

By airing the intra-Panther complaint that Cleaver created wars for others to fight, Bullins not only settled a score but also voiced a till then unspoken call for the Panthers to win other groups over to the struggle. That this position was eventually adopted (in 1971) by the Black Panther party, which called for an alliance between the Panthers and the church and business communities, shows how right Bullins was in *A Street Play* to make revolution appear absurd if it does not first consolidate all African American groups and ideologies.[21] Although Baraka's *Madheart* (1966) broaches this subject by suggesting that counterrevolutionaries might be redeemed, Bullins advances that notion with the belief that without such a redemption, any struggle is but playground revolution. Bullins's play smirks, in other words, that a Cleaver-called revolution between the races is laughable—especially when placed within the context of ordinary African Americans going about their daily routines.

Bullins's final Unity play, *Death List* (1972), threatens the sixty-four prominent African Americans who signed a statement supporting Israel. First performed by Theatre Black at University of the Streets in New York

City, this piece, too, angered revolutionaries. In the play, a warrior cleans his high-powered rifle as he gives the names and positions of his intended victims, along with his grounds for killing them: Congresswoman Shirley Chisholm, because she "is a Super Nigger woman traitor to the Black Nation and [an Arthur] Goldberg lover"; the president of Freedom National Bank, William R. Hudgins, because "he is a so-called black capitalist"; Gardner Taylor, president of the Progressive National Baptist Convention, simply because he is a "Nigger preacher"; the NAACP executive director, Roy Wilkins, because he "has been a Tom too long"; and the publisher John H. Johnson, because "he is a dangerous and resourceful stooge" who has "poisoned Black People's minds for decades with skin-whitener-straightened-hair-bad-body-odor ads." It pains the assassin, however, to have to kill Morehouse College president Hugh M. Gloster, "one of the first to hip me to Afro-American literature"; or Martin Luther King Sr., because of the memory of "your deluded, dead son . . . The Peace Nigger"; or AFL-CIO vice-president A. Philip Randolph, because he is one "of the shining colored hopes of the left, the lost left"; or Jackie Robinson:

> ### BLACKMAN
> I had a teacher once in a school that I long ago went to in another life, a teacher named Miss Cohen who I was uncontrollably in love with, being that I was very young, years before puberty, and love was a fresh experience with me. A teacher named Cohen with white white skin, who said that the day was special, in fact, was the greatest in my young negro life because Jackie Robinson had been admitted into the major leagues of baseball. Cried, she did. I won't lie to you. My greatest day, she said. And I remembered that day . . . for years, for centuries of altering life I remembered . . . even though I hated baseball . . . but that had been my greatest day, hadn't it? Miss Cohen had cried for me. . . . Then on another day, when I was older, but still innocent, when I was centuries away from Miss Cohen with her white white skin, almost long forgotten, and in another place, one day I met Jackie Robinson . . . and found he was a nice man, not someone who should make anyone cry, however sensitive their nature. . . . So now I have learned that those painful, tragic days in which you discover some wisp of truth and reality, that those painful unbearable days are truly your great ones.
>
> And today reality demands that I destroy you and your kind, Mr. Robinson.

Had the play consisted simply of this liturgy, it would have been but another Barakaian Unity piece using the scare tactics first popularized by Langston Hughes's communist-menace play, *Scottsboro, Limited* (1932).

Bullins adds depth to *Death List,* however, with the inclusion of a woman character who tries to persuade "my man, my Black lover/husband/warrior" not to kill the people. Her reasons, which riff his dirge, cry out to the warrior to forgive the "uninformed" in order to save not only them but also himself and the race. Her concern is that the present revolution has no strategy for ever stopping the killing cycles:

> BLACKWOMAN
>
> Is there not another way? A way that we might see the end of this revolution in our lifetimes, or else win some concrete goals that the following generations can build a foundation for the future upon? A way that points to the East, that points to the future and not toward the vast cemetery of the West?

Since there are no realistic and concrete plans and goals, she reasons that killing is not only a revolutionary means to an end but also an end in itself. This translates into suicide—and, more importantly, into the deliberate and systematic destruction of the race by the race. This, then, makes the revolutionary savior "the true enemy of Black people . . . the greatest threat to survival." Logic, however, loses out to emotion:

> BLACKMAN
>
> Whitney M. Young, Jr. . . . Executive Director, National Urban League . . . Last on the list . . . I might be sorry when I finish with you, Whitney . . . But I'll try and make it painless.
>
> (*BLACKMAN exits. Sounds outside rise; gunfire, scream. Lights return to red, with the BLACKWOMAN standing over the table with head lowered, fingering and tapping to the beat of the music the lone shell left by the MAN.*)
>
> BLACK VOICE OFF
>
> (*Half screaming*)
> NO . . . NO . . . IT CAN'T BE . . . IT CAN'T BE!
> (*A single shot.*)
>
> BLACKNESS[22]

To some, the fault in this Unity piece is that the play encourages diametrically opposed interpretations—made by equally compelling arguments presented on the same scale. Some critics legitimately read Blackman as a fantasy revolutionary, therefore, whose naive utopianism leads him to believe that murder solves an inherent social malaise. Although Blackwoman lends credence to this view, Bullins's dedication of the play to the Palestine National Liberation Movement (Al-Fatah) and its striking military wing (Al-Assifa Forces) shows that he disagreed. Through Blackman, Bullins calls for an international alliance between Arabs and African

Americans—no doubt influenced not only by his several working trips to the Middle East but also by his 1969 participation in the Pan-African Cultural Festival in Algeria with Julia Wright, who, according to Bullins, "got into lengthy arguments. As a Marxist, she was an ideological enemy to all nationalist groups."[23] Through Blackwoman, nevertheless, Bullins implicitly demands that the Cleaver faction of the Black Panther party in New York City stop the random assassinations of other Panthers.[24] Such dual—and apparently contradictory—calls are what made Bullins's brand of Unity plays different. The plays speak with forked tongues to "the uninformed" as potential Panthers and to "the informed" as latent fools.

Bullins's *Kujichagulia* (Self-Determination) plays, which show the need to help people define, name, and speak for themselves, made black revolutionaries even angrier. These Barakaian-type plays argue that in order to stop whites from controlling African Americans, they should sever *all* ties to "devil whites" and their "black stooges." To force the issue, the black revolutionary school painted whites and middle-class African Americans in their worst colors in such plays by Baraka as *A Black Mass* (1965), which dramatizes the Nation of Islam myth of the Creation; *The Death of Malcolm X* (1966), which uses Malcolm's life to accuse whites of conspiring to assassinate him; and *Slave Ship* (1967), which shows that slavery was not only genocide but also parenticide. Bullins expanded these issues by turning his Self-Determination pieces toward the revolutionaries themselves, asking them in the unproduced screenplay, *Night of the Beast* (1972), for example, if they are emotionally equipped for the horror and sacrifice of a real war in urban America. In the screenplay, a black Vietnam veteran (Brother) goes out for a drink, after having relaxed and "turned on" alone in his room for three days. He finds himself in the middle of a full-scale race war:

> *A large white car with oversized American flags painted on each side nearly runs him down, as it swerves around the corner. The car passes him and screeches to a halt down the street, its huge rear lights casting a crimson glow back in the brother's face. Doors on each side of the car spring open and two black-uniformed negroes leap out, pulling at their holstered pistols.*
>
> *Instinctively, the brother runs. Gunshots bang out behind him as he flees in terror of his life. His radio explodes in his hand, the bullet passing through the plastic box and ricocheting off a metal light pole on the far side of the street.*
>
> *At a full run, the brother lunges through the bar door.*

While hiding in the basement of the bar, he kills a revolutionary field commander in self-defense. Sensing that Brother is a valuable recruit and is not a "plainclothesman," the Leader recruits Brother by filling him in on past events: The rebellion started when revolutionaries joined Harlem University students in retaliating against the police for shooting a coed. The community joined the rebellion, the first day of which the rebels won. Because the revolt spread nationwide, President Richard Nixon ordered all black communities sealed, and all rebellious residents "rounded up and taken to prepared concentration camps. Or killed. Exterminated." The results burn unforgettable images into the spectator's mind:

> *Black families being taken away to unknown destinations by trucks, buses and freight trains. Large groups of Blackmen being herded into fenced enclosures.*
>
> *Street-to-street and house-to-house fighting between the army and die-hard pockets of resistance.*
>
> *Blocks upon blocks of gutted buildings and desolate, deserted city streets.*
>
> *Tanks rolling down wide, spacious urban boulevards with no movement in sight, except the early morning fog.*
>
> *Public executions by hanging, firing squad and pistol shot to the head. Large white signs bearing bold black lettering reading CURFEW, RE-STRICTED, OFF LIMITS, etc.*
>
> *Expanses of hungry Black children's faces begging for food and water.*

Brother agrees to be drafted "into the service of your people" just in time to blow up a column of tanks and armored carriers. Although the insurgents win the battle, Brother is killed. The warriors move on to the next battle. A breeze blows a sheet of a newspaper down the street, into the bar, and onto the face of Brother: "*Close-up of headline of the June 13, 1969 issue of 'Muhammad Speaks' newspaper . . . announces 'AMERICA IS FALLING.'* "[25] This screenplay, significantly, is one of the very few revolutionary pieces that shows the hero dying. Because of the inspirational nature of other Self-Determination plays, revolution became a romance and, as claimed by some, a death-wish. The result was that audiences were robbed of seeing the horror of the losses of John Huggins and Bunchy Carter in the US-Black Panther shootout at the University of California at Los Angeles; or of Fred Hampton, victim of an alleged state police assassination in Chicago. Unseen as well was the horror of the end of seventeen-year-old Bobby Hutton, the first Black Panther to die, with bullets tearing into his face and chest and arms.[26] Unless these images become part of the stage picture, Bullins argued, bright and brave young men would continue dying.

Bullins reinforced this unpleasant message by challenging the plethora of "kill-whitey" playwrights with two plays that say, "Put up or back out." In *It Bees Dat Way* (1972)—first produced at the Ambiance Lunch-Hour Theatre Club in London—a predominantly white audience of twenty-five gets physically and verbally assaulted by six black characters (a drunk woman, a thieving junkie, a professional mugger, his violent partner, a half-drunk quarreler, and a female hustler). These "characters" steal wallets, insult mothers, and rub their own crotches. To rising and falling music, along with sirens, police radios, blinking lights, and moving shadows, the audience is blasted by revolutionary rhetoric: "Shoot the President . . . He's cuttin' off welfare and puttin' people out of work and tryin' to destroy you with birth control pills and worms in yo' water . . . and sendin' your boy to Vietnam! Get your gun and join the revolution, brothers . . . and change, change this shit!" After being warned that they had "better get out while you can," the audience is allowed to leave in twos and threes. It is telling that the verbal bombast is fired by the half-drunk quarreler, who, at the very end, is surprised: "AIN'T DIS A BITCH, MAN . . . I'M STILL ALIVE!!!" The historic significance of this play is that it was the first Revolutionary play to physically assault the audience. Although the beasts in Baraka's *A Black Mass* (1965) kiss, lick, and slobber on the spectators, Bullins directed his actors to do *"whatever is most unlikely and threatening, even into physical abuse: scuffling, rape, strong-arming, and beating the audience."*[27]

The white audience in the final Self-Determination play, the unproduced *A Short Play for a Small Theater* (1973), was not so lucky. The people were calmed by psychic music, incense, and colored lighting before being surprised:

> *At a small table, a tall* BLACK MAN *methodically applies colored face paint. The stripes and circles and dots make brilliant contrast to his dark skin.*

> *Upon completion of this ritual, the* BLACK MAN *carefully wipes his hands upon a towel, then places soft, black leather gloves upon his hands. He then picks up a large hand gun and deliberately goes to each white person in the audience and shoots him in the face.*

> *If there is need, He should unhurriedly reload as many times as necessary and complete his assignment.*

> BLACKNESS[28]

Such an outlandish action calls the bluff of the "kill-whitey" dramatists: If you are at all serious about killing white people, the play says, then here is a perfectly sane way to do it. If, on the other hand, *A Short Play* appears utterly absurd, then, perhaps, it matches the very "kill-whitey" rhetoric itself.

Revolutionaries no more wanted to hear this argument than that of Bullins's *Ujima* (Collective Work and Responsibility) plays. These plays question the middle class's obsession with appearance, class, and individualism—instead of helping to solve individual, group, and community problems with positive assessments of the impact that historical events, personal decisions, and rites-of-passage have on people's lives. In lieu of using middle-class leaders as bad examples—as in Sonia Sanchez's *Sister Son/ji* (1969), Salimu's *Growin' into Blackness* (1969), and Roger Furman's *The Long Black Block* (1971)—Bullins turns on the so-called revolutionary leaders. In his *Dialect Determinism (or The Rally)* (1973)—first produced by the San Francisco Drama Circle at the Firehouse Repertory Theater in San Francisco and directed by Robert Hartman—Bullins warns people—especially the low-income—that they had better stop looking for messiahs because any who appear are but false prophets motivated by materialism and martyrdom. In the play, a hypocritical Boss Brother, wearing a black woolly wig on a bald head, calls a meeting of his followers in order to urge them to help him "take over." He preaches that the people must accept their "common experience, future, aspirations, and destinies." They are—like it or not—"a brotherhood," a "nation." In order to persuade this nation that he is the ordained leader, Boss Brother claims the historical magic and importance of Hitler, Karl Marx, and Malcolm X. When the Spirit of Malcolm challenges Boss Brother, he hides as his followers attack the Spirit, who breaks one attacker's neck, backbone, and hipbone with a nifty judo chop before the Spirit is dragged outside. Boss Brother resumes his "communion," becoming the resurrected "Martin Luther, Butterbeans without Susie, Uncle Tom, Fred Schwarz, Emperor Goldwater, Lumumba, Castro, all the L.B.J.'s, Lincoln Rockwell, the Birds' Turds":

BOSS BROTHER

Now, yawl knows dat I's goin' to take ov'va, so let me tell ya how's I's goin' to do it so you can help me.

(HE walks to the blackboard and in bright chalk writes large letters, then reads them aloud:)

DIALECT DETERMINISM . . . YAWHL!

(Rustles stir within the BROTHERS' and SISTERS' ranks and grunts of cleared throats are mingled with the squawks of parrots and farts of zebras.)

FIRST BROTHER

Dialect . . . what?

SECOND BROTHER

Ummmmmmm . . . ???

BOSS BROTHER

REMEMBER THOSE WORDS, BROTHER.

VOICES
We'll remember.

BOSS BROTHER
Now, to bind us closer together, we needs a martyr.

LOUD BROTHER
YEAH, DAT'S WHAT WE NEEDS IS A MARTYR![29]

The followers stomp Boss Brother, who, before dying, salutes and instructs his disciples: "SING RIGHT." This response, significantly, was slogan uttered by the Los Angeles revolutionaries during the early sixties to show support for their leaders. The title, "Dialect Determinism," like the play itself, burlesques the Marxist theory of dialectical materialism, which holds that the material basis of a reality constantly changes in an intellectual investigative process that gives matter priority over mind. The play might be interpreted as a farcical slap in the face for some of the Panthers, who considered themselves dialectical materialists.[30]

In his second Collective Work and Responsibility play, *The Electronic Nigger* (1969), Bullins explores the consequences for those who turn cotton-stuffed ears toward his warning about false prophets in the black community. He contends that African Americans are extremely dangerous when they are wired to white values and devices. In the play, which was first performed at the American Place Theatre and directed by Robert Macbeth, A. T. Carpentier (a sociological data research analysis technician expert who insists that his name be pronounced with a "silent T") takes—and takes over—a creative writing evening class. The teacher, a Mr. Jones, has been described by the critic Toni Cade as having "first-night nerves and first-novel failure, [and is] anxious, earnest, cultivated, well-read, square, co-opted."[31] Mr. Carpentier overthrows Mr. Jones first by establishing high-sounding credentials: "Penalogy is my field . . . and I have been in over thirty-three penal institutions across the country . . . in a professional capacity, obviously." In order to show his expertise in creative writing, he announces that

> My good friend J. J. Withertorn is already dickering with my agent for options on my finished draft for a pilot he is planning to shoot of *Only Corpses Beat the Big House*, which, by the way, is the title of the first script, taken from an abortive *novella narratio* I had begun in my youth after a particularly torrid affair with one Eulah Mae Jackson.

Then Mr. Carpentier undermines Mr. Jones's authority by making the students doubt his pronouncements and accept Carpentier's. This relentless process works, even when Carpentier admits to wiretapping everything from "a con pacing his cell" to Alcoholics Anonymous meetings. Not only does he defend the practice ("Crime is a most repetitive theme these days. . . . The primary purpose of we law enforcement agents is to help stamp it out, whatever the method"), but he also deflects Mr. Jones's reprimand:

MR. JONES

But, sir, speaking man to man, how do you feel about your job? Doesn't it make you uneasy knowing that your race, I mean, our people, the Negro, is the most victimized by the police in this country? And you are using illegal and immoral methods to . . .

MR. CARPENTIER

Well, if you must personalize, that's all right with me . . . but, really, I thought this was a class in creative writing, not criminology. I hesitate to say, Mr. Jones, that you are indeed out of your depth when you engage me on my own grounds . . . ha ha . . .

When Mr. Jones finally musters the courage to demand that his "Black brother" Mr. Carpentier stop using large words to hide having been "whitewashed" into not accepting his obligation to remove some of the intellectual, political, moral, and social tyranny that infects the African American community, Mr. Carpentier parades his colors:

Sir, I am not black, nor your brother . . . There is a school of thought that is diametrically opposed to you and your black chauvinism . . . You preach bigotry, black nationalism, and fascism! . . . The idea . . . black brother . . . intellectual barbarism! . . . Your statements should be reported to the school board—as well as your permitting smoking in your classroom.[32]

Mr. Jones surrenders, leaving his students to Mr. Carpentier's wiles.

Whereas the play is among Bullins's funniest, he labeled it a tragicomedy because of its critical subject. The historic importance of the play, in fact, is that it is the only Revolutionary drama that deals solely with spying in the community—although several pieces, notably Jimmy Garrett's *We Own the Night* (1968), warn about reporting networks. Many people believed during the sixties that these caveats were gross paranoia. Bullins sensed, however, that intelligence was the most efficient means of destabilizing Collective Work and Responsibility. This intuition has been confirmed by revelations that as early as 1917 the United States military had developed spy units consisting of African American church members, businessmen, and educators.[33] Bullins's condemnation of these people is so effective because instead of being a strident diatribe, the play is hilarious, thanks to his use of some language and action common to the Black Experience School. The classroom as metaphor teased some into believing, however, that the play principally dealt "with modern schools and schooling, with 'computerized' thinking and teaching, with the force, attraction, and horror of mechanized education."[34] Bullins said at the time, however, that the electronic nigger is a black man who has fully accepted white values and become a "gross distortion of what a black man should be." He is what white people call a nigger, but he helps whites keep tabs on his own people by letting "them train him in wire-tapping and other snooping methods."[35]

In his final Collective Work and Responsibility play, *The Gentleman Caller* (1970), Bullins invites the "revolutionary leaders" to see what a *real* revolutionary is. In the play, a quiet war rages between a longtime maid and her employer. The battle is over place and order. Madame believes that because Maid is so uppity, she needs to be put in her place:

MADAME

Mamie! Mamie, come here at once!
   (*The MAID enters.*)

MAID

Yas'sum?

MADAME

You're fired.

MAID

Yas'sum.

MADAME

Get your things and be off at once.

MAID

Yas'sum.
   (*MAID turns to go.*)

MADAME

Is that all you have to say?

MAID

Yas'sum.

MADAME

Why?

MAID

'Cause I didn't want to upset lil Missy anymo'.[36]

Touched, Madame endows the Maid's "innocence" with a two-dollar raise. The Maid announces a spurious decision to quit, nevertheless, allegedly because she must deal with such new-order things as Madame carrying on with an African American gentleman in the front parlor, with Madame's refusal to answer a persistent telephone caller, and with the hours Madame's husband spends clipping his beard in the bathroom. Instead of quitting, however, the Maid slits the husband's throat, and drags his flag-wrapped body into the parlor. She shoots Madame in the head and pumps bullets into the twitching corpse. She orders the apparent Gentleman Caller to help her slide the bodies into the hallway, where she then blasts him. Dressed in an "exotic gown" and an "Afro hairdo," she then answers the continually ringing phone:

MAID

(*Black and correct*) Hello. Yes, you wish to speak to madame? Yes, she is speaking.

(*Pause*)

Yes, father . . . the time is now. It is time for Black people to come together. It is time for Black people to rise from their knees and come together in unity, brotherhood and Black spirituality to form a nation that will rise from our enslaved mass and meet the oppressor . . . meet the devil and conquer and destroy him.

(*Slow curtain as the* QUEEN MOTHER *speaks into the phone passionately.*)

Yes, we are rising, father. We are forming the foretold Black nation that will survive, conquer and rule under your divine guidance. We Black people are preparing for the future. We are getting ready for the long war ahead of us. DEATH TO THE ENEMIES OF THE BLACK PEOPLE! All praise is due to the Blackman.

The historical importance of this play, which was first directed by Allie Woods for the Chelsea Theatre Center at the Brooklyn Academy of Music, is not that it turns a stereotype inside out in order to freshen up an ancient theme. William Wells Brown pioneered this device in *Escape: Or a Leap for Freedom* (1858), where—at the last moment—the contented slave Cato gets hit with the sense to skip to Canada. William Branch dusted off the gadget almost a century later in *A Medal for Willie* (1951), which has an ample Negro Mama throw away a medal posthumously awarded to her son for bravery in Korea. This practice of turning stereotypes into positive symbols gained currency during the sixties not only in theatre, but also in art. Most memorable might be Murry DePillars's untitled painting of the traditional Aunt Jemima on a box. With her naps tucked underneath a bandanna, she raises high her black-gloved fist in salute to John Carlos and Tommy Smith's act at the 1968 Olympics awards ceremony.

The importance of *The Gentleman Caller,* then, is that it was the first full-blown and mature blending of substantive elements from Alain

Locke's Art-Theatre and W. E. B. DuBois's Protest schools of theatre. Whereas playwrights S. Randolph Edmonds and Willis Richardson started such mixings, which were upgraded by Langston Hughes, Bullins purifies the blend by substituting more fully developed plots for static ones. He exchanges, as well, better developed characters for ideational ones. Because the typically short Revolutionary play does not permit full development of leading characters, Bullins tailors popular stereotypes into distinct personalities. The Maid, for example, is Murry DePillars's Aunt Jemima: "*large, heavy, black, sometimes though seldom smiling, mostly fussing to herself, but always in her place, at least for the moment.*" The Madame and the apparent Gentleman Caller, too, are respectively the typically pampered person of means and the young, black, well-dressed, and well-mannered up-and-comer. The Maid is individualized not only by her atypical final act but also by such small insurrections throughout as drowning out Madame's singing of "America" with a vigorous chorus of a Negro spiritual.

This back talk was quite atypical of the stereotype:

MADAME

But you can't [quit], Mamie, dear.

MAID

Yes I can.

MADAME

But what about all these years you've spent with me? With us?

MAID

I dunno, ma'am.

MADAME

What about my suckling your big flabby breasts?

MAID

They dry now, ma'am.

MADAME

. . . and you raised me as one of your own?

MAID

Dat's 'cause I's never had time fo mah own, ma'am.

By combining the expected and the unexpected, along with making sure that the latter reveals vital background information about the character, Bullins creates a protagonist who is anything but a walking idea. These same combinations keep the plot moving. When Madame propositions the handsome Gentleman Caller, for example, he surprises her by picking up a book. His longing for her husband's beard because it symbolizes "ecclesiastical rank" (or power, as with Sampson) so startles that the plot leaps as it unfolds one ambush after another. Tying together all of this action and activity is the ironic title, which makes clear that the Gentleman Caller is the spy Maid's revolutionary leader, not a status seeker, whom the Maid is nice enough to shoot offstage—probably in order not to wash dirty racial laundry in plain daylight. What makes this play something special is the neat fashioning of the art-for-art's-sake Art-Theatre and the highly political Protest School conventions into seamless finery. The only prominent feature of the latter school is the *epilogos* monologue, which, although as predictably preachy as monologues in other Collective Work and Responsibility plays, grows entirely out of the action.

Not even Bullins wrote plays in the *Ujamaa* (Cooperative Economics), the *Kuumba* (Creativity), and the *Imani* (Faith) subclasses of Black Revolutionary Drama. The reason that he, like most other dramatists, avoided Cooperative Economics plays is that his experience did not then include the concept of profit sharing in community-owned shopping and financial organizations. The need to watch out for the commercial piracy of talents and businesses, instead, is shown in such representative works as OyamO's *His First Step* (1968) and Ben Caldwell's *The King of Soul or The Devil and Otis Redding* (1967). Baraka warns in *Junkies Are Full of (SHHH . . .)* (1972) that the first order of Cooperative Economics is to rid the community of the white-controlled drug business. The importance of this emphasis is that few good or bad examples were given of investing the little money there was in the black community into cooperative ventures, organizations, and endowments in order to ensure the long-term health of communities and theatres. The result was that as soon as the federal, state, and private grants dried up, the theatres and other community organizations closed.

The scarcity of plays in the *Kuumba* (Creativity) class should not be attributed to an experience vacuum but rather to Ron Karenga's early dicta that blues be avoided in the arts. Although Bullins and Baraka ignored Karenga, during the sixties and early seventies neither wrote revolutionary mixed-media musicals like those of The BLKARTSOUTH Poets, the Sudan Poets of Houston, the Last Poets of New York, and Chicago's Organization of Black American Culture in Chicago (OBAC). Bullins used most media—especially music—in most of his plays. Even in *A Short Play for a Small Theatre,* the last thing that the whites hear before being assassinated is "psychic" music. The reason that Bullins did not write *Imani* (Faith) plays is more puzzling. His longtime disdain for the hypocrisy of ministers should have inspired him to add to the plethora of plays by others designed to undermine the church. Examples of these are Ben Caldwell's *Mission Accomplished* (1968), which shows Christian missionaries subverting African religions and customs in order to loot their minerals and

94

treasures; The Last Poets' *Epitaph to a Coagulated Trinity* (1968), which questions the Church for failing to declare slavery a sin in the sixteenth century; and Ben Caldwell's *Prayer Meeting, or The First Militant Minister* (1967), which demands that ministers stop being agents for the status quo. Whereas Bullins was an "alleged agnostic" during the sixties, he somehow remained very respectful of the church.[37] He later wrote many nonrevolutionary New Spirituality rituals, patterned after Robert Macbeth's *A Black Ritual* (1969).

Most of Bullins's Revolutionary plays belong to the *Nia* (Purpose) Subclass, which deals with values, as well as with problems concerning delivery systems for goods and services. Bullins wrote four types of these plays. Again, he did not follow the prescribed line. The Education Type, for example, generally argues that the lack of African-centered curricula and teachers in the school systems turns African Americans into "niggers in the window."[38] Bullins sings a different tune, however, in *How Do You Do* (1968), which Robert Hartman first directed for the San Francisco Drama Circle at the Firehouse Repertory Theatre. In the play, Dora and Roger, two street stereotypes, regale each other about their possessions and capabilities:

DORA

Do I know you? I had assumed as much. That suit fits you so well. How much did it cost?

ROGER

One hundred-and-fifty dollars. One of my cheaper numbers. I have sixty-two of them. All exactly like this one. I only wear them on Wednesdays. They were made especially for me. I look so beautiful in my clothes.

DORA

You sho' does.

ROGER

It's nice that you know. You have a fine . . . uhhh . . . intellect.

DORA

I'm president of three clubs!

ROGER

Really!

DORA

And I have color TV!

ROGER

How grand!

DORA

How much do you make?

ROGER

I have a very good job. I'm classified very highly. I'm a G-0000. And my credit rating is magnificent.

DORA

How magnificent!

ROGER

Are you married?

DORA

(Clutching between his legs)
Would it matter?

These wannabes look down on another character, Paul, who instructs them on how to become guerilla warriors able to hide their intentions behind the racial stereotypes they already inhabit. The play hypothesizes the real reasons for the characters' being what they are:

DORA

I got to percents in school, and shit, dat's all I could do to pass. Nex' year I was pregnant.

ROGER

Read a book? Sheet! Ain't gonna be wastin' mah time readin' some fuckin' book. I read one once in school. Just sat up dere and finished it to see what it was all about. Found out dat readin' ain't shit. Ain't gonna be wastin' mah time.

PAUL

Kill him in the mind—the age of the body is done; imitate the State, it kills its questioners in the cerebrum. Become a guerilla warrior of ideas.[39]

This argument differs significantly from that in Marvin X's *The Black Bird* (1969), which contends that school curricula are responsible for socializing children into being status quo "niggers" incapable of distinguishing power from its trappings. Ron Milner's *The Monster* (1969) blames educators, whom he shows being murdered by revolutionary students. Although Bullins did not dismiss these notions, he blames principally African Americans themselves for being as "dumb as Dora." This revisionist slant apparently did not disturb Amiri Baraka, who included *How Do You Do* as part of his traveling repertory for the Black Communications Project.[40] These touring shows went to schools and halls throughout the San

Francisco Bay Area in 1967, as well as to Los Angeles, and even to the convention of the Congress of Racial Equality.[41] The Panthers acted as security during these shows, with "armed brothers flanking the stage in a symbolic gesture, showing the links between black revolutionary art and political struggle."[42] The artists tried to maintain this bond. Even after Cleaver ousted them from Black House, the cultural nationalist artists did benefits for the Black Panther party.[43] The Panthers undermined these artists, however, because the party valued white youth. This made all the more paradoxical the productions of the Values type of the Purpose plays, which aim to destroy African Americans' trust in whites.

Such plays as Baraka's *Home on the Range* (1966) and *Great Goodness of Life* (1966), along with Ben Caldwell's *All White Caste* (1969), assert that whites have no values worth imitating. Bullins's Values play, *One-Minute Commercial* (1973), a radio commercial for the New Lafayette Theatre's performance of his *A Ritual To Raise the Dead and Foretell the Future* (1970), accuses not whites but African Americans themselves of mindlessly valuing the superficial. A person (1st Man's Voice) asks a member of the New Lafayette company (2nd Man's Voice) what is being performed. The 2nd Man plugs repeatedly the ritual, the date, time, place, and theatre address. Then comes the clincher:

1ST MAN'S VOICE

Say, brother?

2ND MAN'S VOICE

Yes, my brother?

1ST MAN'S VOICE

You gonna shave your head again this time?[44]

Governments need not ever worry about falling, the play implies, with such people in the "revolution." The most interesting thing about this humorous short is how well Bullins mixes advertising and statement, hammering home the essential information, but laughing home the need for people to learn what is and is not important.

Bullins continues this theme in his Criminal Justice type of Purpose play. This type usually accuses the police and correctional officers of targeting African Americans for brutality, of covering up complaints from African Americans, of compelling African American police to be especially inhumane toward their own people, and of corrupting and raping prisoners. Bullins's Criminal Justice play, on the other hand, blames the victim as much as the perpetrator. *Next Time . . .* (1972) is a tribute—and reprimand—to the revolutionary poet Henry Dumas, who was killed in a Harlem subway station by a transit policeman on 23 May 1968, leaving behind a wife and two sons. In the play, which was first performed at the Bronx

Community College and directed by Nicholas Gilroy, Poet happens upon a police officer, who is arresting a young man for ducking under a turnstile. Poet tries to persuade the officer to let the young man go. This angers the officer, who tells Poet to empty his briefcase:

POET

My bag . . . Naw . . . I can't do that. I can't open my bag to you.

PIG

You can't huh? Well, you can die then, can't you?
(The PIG cocks the hammer of his revolver.)

PIG

I begin counting . . . and when I get to three, there's one more dead nigger we don't have to worry about.

POET

You may kill me . . . but you cannot destroy what I have in this bag.

PIG

One . . . you've forgotten Hiroshima already, haven't you? What's one more dead nigger to me . . . or a dozen . . . or a whole nation?

POET

Your days are coming to a close, beastman. Six thousand years you have been allotted to reign in evil . . . but now the East is rising to engulf you.

PIG

Two . . . you sound almost brave, nigger. But you forget that I lynched your fathers, uncles and brothers since you were brought to these shores, the cattle you are. You forget Attica, Sharpeville, Martin Luther Coon, Malcolm X, which stands for nothing now, and all the thousands of niggers runnin' down the street a hundred feet ahead of my bullets zinging at the backs of their nappy heads.

POET

Your next number is three, devil.

PIG

Yeah . . . it is . . . and my first shot after I call the number will tear off the chin of this little sambo here.

The Poet throws his briefcase at the officer, which allows the youth to escape. The policeman kills the Poet. While dying, the Poet recites a poem that is in his bag: "Listen to the sound of my horn, my people. / This rhythm of years long past. / Listen to the sound of my horn, I say. / Music and I . . . have come at last!" He brags that the message has gotten through, causing the policeman to empty his gun into the Poet. This play went beyond Ben Caldwell's *Riot Sale, or Dollar Psyche Fake Out* (1968), which accuses the police of orchestrated genocide. *Next Time* even extends the charge in Baraka's *Police* (1968) that African American police are especially vicious toward their own people. *Next Time* indicts African American victims for allowing themselves to be fair game. The theme of the play, interestingly enough, has less to do with the policeman's act of murder than with the Poet's sacrifice of himself in order to save a petty offender. As indicated by the title, the play, in fact, reproaches the Poet:

PIG

Huh, you died for poetry . . . didn't do you much good, did it?

POET

It wasn't for me . . . but for the people, the Black people. I was only an instrument.

PIG

Not much good . . . long dead instrument.

POET

The message was delivered . . . it got through . . . the little young brother . . . he has the word now. He'll always carry the word to the people now. And he and his brothers wait for you outside when you leave this hole.

PIG

Stop dreaming, nigger. You're already dead. Next time try a pistol instead of poetry.[45]

This reproof is even less kind in Bullins's three plays in the Government type of purpose plays. These plays usually accuse the government of committing genocide against African Americans, of frustrating people with bureaucratic red tape, and of invading people's privacy. Bullins's plays put the revolutionaries in the blame by showing them their neglect of duty. His scenario, *State Office Bldg. Curse* (1973), for example, calls the bluff of the "podium revolutionaries" who rail against the construction of the New York State Office Building at 125th Street and Seventh Avenue in Harlem. The scenario shows African Americans enjoying the opening day ceremonies. After listening to speeches by Governor Nelson Rockefeller, Mayor John Lindsay, and Senator Jacob Javits, along with the "artificial integration political machine," the blacks tour the building. They do more than sightsee, however, as they wander through the tunnels, caves, and restrooms. At three o'clock the next morning,

Explosion rips the whole State Office Building apart. Fire. Torn out windows. Total destruction through explosives.

Fire engines. Police. Harlem crowds. TV camera man. Photographers. Silent brothers and sisters standing on far side of the street looking knowingly at each other.

And the Black crowd senses the moment in Revolutionary Black History and begins a festival to celebrate the emerging Black nation of Harlem.[46]

The message in *The American Flag Ritual* (1973) was no less comforting to those who only mouthed revolution. In this short, a young black man unties a bundle and slowly unfolds a large American flag. He stands just a bit southeast of the field of blue.

He reaches into his pants fly, pulls his penis from his pants, and upon the initial tones of the American National Anthem, begins to urinate on "Old Glory."

As he relieves himself, the music plays and finally dies down and stops as his last drops dribble to an end. . . .

He shakes himself, puts his joint away, zips his pants up, wipes his feet on the "Stars and Stripes," then exits.[47]

No other playwright dared go so far in descecrating the emotional symbol of patriotism in order to pay back the government for pissing all over African Americans. Other playwrights were more civil in charging that the government plotted to control and frustrate the black population through birth control (Ben Caldwell's *Top Secret, or A Few Million after B.C.* [1968]), through bloated bureaucracies and complex guidelines (Caldwell's *Run Around* [1968]), and through the invasion of people's privacy (Caldwell's *The Job* [1966]). Bullins went for the raw nerve, especially in his devastating *We Righteous Bombers* (1969).

First produced by the New Lafayette Theatre and directed by Robert Macbeth, *Bombers* paints revolutionaries as slogan-spouting romantics who are totally unprepared emotionally or intellectually for an urban guerilla war. Bullins later commented that "I have learned through experiences in San Francisco, New York City, London, and Algiers that the first ones these types of 'revolutionaries' try to shoot are their less-than-equal comrades."[48] The play centers on a New York City revolutionary unit's determination to eliminate "by any means necessary" all "loyal negro mercenaries" who fight to stop the insurrectionists from overthrowing the repressive government. At the top of the hit list is the Grand Prefect, the Negro leader responsible for keeping African Americans in encampments. To the revolutionist Murray Jackson goes the honor of throwing the bomb to kill the Grand Prefect. After completing his mission, Jackson is captured, imprisoned, and tried. He is sentenced to be hanged. He meets his executioner, Foster, a prisoner who gets a year off of his seventy-five-year sentence for each hanging. After killing Jackson, Foster will have but five more before being freed. Foster's unconsciousness bewilders Jackson, but not so much as does the discovery that he has not killed the real Grand Prefect but a stand-in. The real Grand Prefect, who masquerades as Chief of Security Smith, propositions Jackson: either be portrayed as a turncoat who tells all, or become the state's new executioner and save his comrades' lives. Jackson reluctantly agrees to become the hangman. His first job is to execute the betrayed Foster, who doubles for Jackson himself. As the drugged Foster goes to his televised hanging, Jackson's comrades praise (Foster as) Jackson for giving his life for the revolution.

The play demands that black revolutionaries take a hard look at themselves and their activities. That look would make them see how much of a joke many of their beliefs and leaders had become, too many of whom were like the revolutionary leader in the play, Elton "L" Cleveland (an Eldridge Cleaver surrogate). Cleveland dooms the "revolution" in pursuit of his own personal agenda: he assigns Murray Jackson as bomber because he wants to have sex with Jackson's girlfriend. Cleveland encourages others to "meet death like the Black heroes we are," but he hides behind his rhetoric: "I have to stay here while others are on the firing line. It's tough, but discipline must be maintained."[49] His hapless followers are deluded, suicidal, and unintelligent. They crack under fire, they run from blood, and they recoil from reality. These portraits seem forged from life: from the real struggles within the Black Panther Party, from the allegations concerning Eldridge Cleaver's deceptions, and from Huey Newton's alleged wish to die.[50]

The play's historic importance lies in the symposium that resulted from the revolutionaries' angry response to its initial production. That debate updated the W. E. B. Du Bois-Alain Locke controversy of the twenties concerning art for art's sake versus protest art. The insurrectionists of the late sixties and early seventies charged that *We Righteous Bombers* pretended to be both, but that the play was really a fraud because it failed to distinguish the fool from the true revolutionary. More importantly, the revolutionaries said that by projecting the wrong image, the play was but a "hymn to death as escapism."[51] The symposium was about more than this, however. It was first a forum for settling scores. The revolutionaries, represented on the panel by writers Askia Muhammad Toure and Ernie Mkalimoto, obviously wanted to impale the New Lafayette Theatre artistic director Robert Macbeth not only for having produced this "counterrevolutionary" play but also for turning the theater into his fiefdom. What is so paradoxical about their purpose is that they were fighting to get Macbeth to produce plays by Baraka, who was leading the team that defended *Bomber*, composed of the critic Larry Neal, Baraka's ally, and of Macbeth, with whom Baraka strongly disagreed philosophically. Baraka's delicate tasks, then, were to defend Toure and Mkalimoto's aesthetics, to assail their politics, to protect his friend Bullins, and to attack Macbeth.

Baraka vigorously supported Toure and Mkalimoto's concern that the revolutionary cause must inform all art. Baraka attacked these Cleaver supporters, however, for violating the cause of cultural nationalism by bringing "violent integrationist whites back into the liberation movement." Not yet a full-blown Marxist, Baraka espoused cutting all ties to whites. However, the man that Baraka was defending disagreed with Baraka's position on this issue: "What?" Bullins later asked. "You mean I can't be friends with whomever I want?"[52] Yet, Baraka supported Bullins by separating the playwright's gifts from his attitude and from this particular play. Whereas he pronounced Bullins "our most powerful playwright," Baraka agreed that the play was "ambiguous" because it presented "negative examples." He attributed this to Bullins's use of "the Western form," which, of course, Baraka knew Macbeth preferred. By continually slamming Macbeth about this form, Baraka succeeded both in avenging having been shut out of the New Lafayette and in defending his friend.

In addition to accommodating these personal agendas, the symposium, more importantly, served as a platform for denouncing the old order in both society and theatre. Bullins faced a dilemma. He had earlier subscribed to the precepts of the old order in theatre, as seen in his then five-year-old essay, "The Polished Protest." It was only after having been rebuffed by the Bay Area theatre old order that he adopted the Barakaian dramaturgy and politics. Having been recently embraced by Robert Macbeth, a bastion of the old order, Bullins now danced to whatever tune happened to be on the Victrola. Understandably, Bullins disagrees with this "unfair" characterization: "I artistically collaborate in the theatre. It's a give-and-take proposition at its best. For example, working with [the director] Gilbert Moses: We didn't collaborate on *Duplex*. We did with *The Taking of Miss Janie*. Measure the results."[53]

Collaborator Bullins had been only too happy to comply with Macbeth's request in January 1969 that he write a "real revolutionary play" that would give its actors something to do and say besides shout slogans. Macbeth had given Bullins a copy of Albert Camus's *The Just Assassins* (1949). He returned three weeks later with *Bombers*. Bullins later said that he had "turned each of Camus's philosophical tenets upon its head because ideology doesn't drive my art. My art frames ideology as part of humanity, history, and story."[54] Interestingly, Bullins asked that his name not be used on this work because he knew that there would be political and theatrical repercussions.[55] The latter came in the form of critic Larry Neal's introduction to the published symposium on the play:

> Brother Bass, whoever he was or is, is a poor literary thief. The whole play is abstracted from Albert Camus's *Les Justes*. . . . In many places,

Brother Bass has stolen Camus's play word for word, situation for situation, conflict for conflict; in short the whole thing. If we wanted to get academic about it, we could lay both texts side by side and compare them, but the textual correspondences are too numerous to illustrate. You can check for yourselves by comparing the texts of the two plays. This is serious shit. What we have on our hands is the first literary hoax of the Black Arts Movement. Bad scene. We have all lost something.[56]

As editor of *Black Theatre,* the magazine in which Neal's reprimand appeared, Bullins quipped that what had been lost was "our innocence"—again borrowing from Camus.[57] Macbeth, too, dismissed Neal because the play was really a joke gone bad—one extended when he and Bullins invented the Harriet Webster Updike Theater Award for Literary Excellence and bestowed it on *Bombers.* Although they had planned to reveal their mischief, they kept quiet so as not to offend the audiences, who really loved the play. They gave each performance a standing ovation. Many returned with friends and family, who shouted encouragement to the actors. One person told Macbeth that this was the Lafayette Theatre's most talked-about production.

Neal was correct, however, because plagiarism—joke or not—is serious. *Bombers* was the "first literary hoax" not only in the Black Arts Movement but also in twentieth-century theatre history. No reputable modern playwright had ever rewritten another person's play, changed the title, and not given the original author credit. Although other playwrights had rewritten and retitled plays (Eugene O'Neill's *Mourning Becomes Electra* from *The Oresteia* by Aeschylus, Larry Gelbart's *Sly Fox* from *Volpone* by Ben Jonson, and Joshua Logan's *The Wisteria Trees* from *The Cherry Orchard* by Anton Chekhov), each author acknowledged the source. Macbeth's later defense that Shakespeare borrowed freely is correct, but Shakespeare's sources were narratives and chronicles, not other plays.[58] Shakespeare left outright plagiarism to such nineteenth-century Englishmen as Thomas Holcroft and to Americans like William Dunlap, who "borrowed" the German playwright August Friedrich von Kotzebue's melodramas.

Bullins's "hoax," interestingly enough, is better than Camus's original—notwithstanding the latter's intelligent theme that justice is all that matters in life. Bullins improves on Camus by using an absurdist rather than Camus's linear plot, by opening with Camus's Act IV, by replacing Camus's sometimes melodramatic exposition with film footage, and by bringing the spectator into the action. More importantly, Bullins makes the play his own through substantive changes in the plot: the bomber's discovery that he has not killed the real Grand Prefect but a stand-in; the real Grand Prefect's masquerade as Chief of Security Smith; the bomber's becoming the State's new hangman in order to save his comrades' lives; and the bomber's hanging the betrayed former hangman. These changes alter Camus's theme from the pursuit of justice justifying all to the pursuit of justice deceiving all. As hoax, then, the play itself is a metaphor. What appears to be a cheap imitation, therefore, is probably as valuable—and as valid—as the original.

As a writer of Black Revolutionary Drama, Bullins maintained his honesty and contrariness. Rather than being merely contradictory, he had simply evolved from the 1963 ultraconservative author of "The Polished Protest" to become a staunch Baraka defender. Bullins spanked the sports columnist A. S. (Doc) Young, for example, for saying in the *New York Times* how much he resented Baraka's presuming to speak for "millions of American Negroes":

> I speak as a Black Nationalist Artist when I deem the occasion to speak; when I speak it is through that Black consciousness that makes me what I am; if my voice and vision carry the intellect and soul presence (consciousness) of one of the great races in human history, then that is the universal phenomena of my being Black. That is my reality. That is Black Art. If Imamu Baraka speaks and millions of American Negroes receive a bad headache, it may be because his truth touched and awoke a responsive nationalistic nerve in their collective Black mind. And the Black mind is there no matter how dead the Negro mentality is that enslaves it. Thus is the power of Black Art to raise the dead.[59]

This defense shows that these men's political divide—Baraka was now a Marxist—was not so important as their artistic gap. That difference—as viewed by Bullins—lay in his belief that, as "a revolutionary artist," he had to create concurrent revolutions in the people's streets and in their minds (their "spiritual and conscious centers").[60] His Black Revolutionary plays, therefore, had to forge a thinking people capable of weighing situations before committing themselves. It is not surprising, then, that *Death List* encourages diametrically opposed interpretations—presented on the same scale and scope. Neither is it startling to see in *We Righteous Bombers* revolutionaries made into fools, and in *Night of the Beast* potheads turned into accidental—and dead—war heroes. By showing the principal characters' strengths and weaknesses on an equal scale, Bullins reduces the characters from demi-gods to people who are at least as real as the plays' spectators. People would see themselves in the characters, therefore, not paper saints. This places on the viewers the extraordinary burden of doing something, of committing themselves—faults and all—to the revolution.

What Bullins wanted was for people not only to do something but also to make intelligent choices about what they do. To ensure this, he teaches through the negative example of his characters' faults. By so doing, Bullins aimed not to denigrate revolutionaries, as the New York City Black Panthers charged, but to stick a mirror in front of them and other spectators both in order for each to compare their professed and practiced beliefs and activities. It is understandable that most firebrand revolutionaries objected when he replaced their neat slogans with troubling questions. It is equally comprehensible that so many insurrectionists grew uncomfortable when Bullins pushed issues and slogans as far as their logical and bloody extensions permitted. This meant that the revolutionary street-shout, "rise up and destroy your enemies," had to be weighed against the high probability that the young person who shouted the words would, like seventeen-year-old Panther Bobby Hutton, have bullets tearing into his or her flesh. Such wrenching thoughts forced playwrights, too, to choose carefully their images and words—as Bullins said in *It Bees That Way* and *A Short Play for a Small Theater*. This refocusing for artist and audience bred a full-blown and matured thinking in Black Revolutionary Drama. It led to peace.

3

BINDING RELATIONSHIPS CLASS
OF BLACK EXPERIENCE DRAMA

The peace that Bullins brought to Black Revolutionary Drama never existed in any of his Binding Relationships plays. Perhaps this is because this class, according to Alain Locke, shows folks under extreme conditions.

> All classes of a people under social pressure are permeated with a common experience; they are emotionally welded as others cannot be. With them, even ordinary living has epic depth and lyric intensity, and this, their material handicap, is their spiritual advantage. So, in a day when art has run to classes, clique, and coteries, and life lacks more and more a vital common background, the Negro artist out of the depths of his group and personal experience, has to his hand almost the conditions of a classical art.[1]

Transposed into plays, Locke's notion became a class of drama that represents African peoples to be so bonded together in nuclear, extended, and assembled families that regardless of how miserable their relations become, they simply cannot walk away.[2] This causes never-ending games and battles, which Bullins just loved recording—and starting. For example, once he and his girlfriend Marva were at the meeting of some of her high class friends, who were planning a covered-dish benefit. When the chairwoman asked Marva if she would bring a quiche Lorraine. Bullins blurted out: "Marva? The only thing she knows how to make is quiche pig's feet."

107

Most people would just laugh off the embarrassment, but not Professor James Lacy, the chair of Black Studies at Contra Costa College in San Pablo, California. The occasion was the celebration of black history month. As chairman of events, Lacy, without having read the play, let Bullins talk him into presenting *In the Wine Time* (1994), which shows low-income people doing low-income things. The distinguished interracial audience had its brains fried. Professor Lacy fired off a seven-page letter to Bullins, complaining that the characters were shallow, the language vulgar, the point missing, and the event humiliating.

> I was embarrassed for myself because as I identified myself with the evening, I just didn't feel that the message brought by this depiction of a portion of Afro-American life was appropriate for an audience . . . of younger children, ministers and their wives, and more refined members of the community. [The play] didn't say anything to me that justified my continued feeling of embarrassment—not, mind you, because of the Europeans in the audience. That would be another analysis. I saw my colleagues embarrassed. They looked so humiliated. This was an affair that educators were sponsoring. Black educators. We do have our sense of appropriateness. . . . Had I read the script beforehand, I would not have approved showing it to Saturday night's audience on the occasion of celebrating Afro-American History Month.[3]

Were this not representative of so many responses to Bullins's Binding Relationships plays, it could be dismissed as a typical reaction of middle-class African Americans to seeing low-income people's lives dramatized. Such negative feedback dates from W. E. B. Du Bois's attacks on Alain Locke's Art-Theatre in 1921 up to Langston Hughes's blasts at NAACP executive director Walter White in a New York City taxi cab over Arna Bontemps and Countee Cullen's *St. Louis Woman* (1946).[4] Lacy's letter is somehow different, though. The full letter, which will be analyzed throughout this chapter, shows a man wrestling with a play that simply hits too close to home. The play questions the effects of the intraracial socio-economic barriers erected by middle-income African Americans not only to ward off the lower class but also to keep such people from getting their "shot at the world." This is the theme of *In the Wine Time*, one of four plays in the Rites of Passage subclass of Binding Relationships plays, which show people going through certain stages of life.

In *In the Wine Time*, which premiered at the New Lafayette Theatre and was directed by Robert Macbeth, a low-income extended family (Cliff Dawson, his wife Lou, and her nephew Ray) finds itself in a neighborhood that tries desperately to be "respectable."[5] The Dawson people simply do not fit because of their lifestyle. They and their friends drink and cuss on the front steps. Navy veteran Cliff, furthermore, refuses to get a steady job. He chooses to take classes under the GI Bill, instead, and to let his pregnant wife work at the laundry to support the family. The neighbors see that he sets the wrong example for sixteen-year-old Ray, who lives with Cliff and Lou because his own mother has drunk herself to death. Ray himself is already a heavy drinker, thereby continuing a family tradition. Cliff wants Ray to break this tragic cycle, to join the navy, to see the world, and to "claim it." Lou fights this because Ray is the only family she has left. She is about to lose him, however, because in defending his emerging manhood, he kills a man, Red. When the police come, Cliff takes the blame in order to give Ray a chance in life.

What James Lacy disliked most about this apparently simple play is what the critic Edith Oliver calls its "surface action," the talk and behavior of the characters.[6] "The vulgar and unacceptable language," complained Lacy, "was gratuitous . . . gross, tasteless, and too disgusting for mixed company. . . . The dialogue and conduct of the characters were brilliantly trite, nauseating, lurid and graphic."[7] Lacy had much to bemoan. Seldom before in African American theatre had there been as much profanity on the stage—from the very start of the play:

> (MR. KRUMP enters and stands at the streetlamp. He is very drunk.)

MRS. KRUMP
(Strident, over the radio)
Krumpy! What cha doin' on da corner? Hey, Krumpy! Hey Krumpy!
. . . *Krumpy!* . . . *Get the hell on over here!*
(Lights on third doorstoop.)

CLIFF
Hee . . . heee . . . look a ole man Krump work out.
(BUNNY GILLETTE and DORIS enter Derby Street at the corner and see MR. KRUMP)

LOU
Hush up, Cliff.

CLIFF
Sheet.

BUNNY GILLETTE
Look a' there, Doris!

LOU
Be quiet, Cliff. Will ya, hun?

DORIS

Awww, shit, girl. That's nothin' . . . it just that goddamn Mr. Krump again . . . drunk out of his fucken' mind.

This life, filled with what James Lacy called "Catfish Row antics," appeared so out of place on the African American stage in 1968 because it had been banned from theatrical representation since 1946. Political and theatre leaders agreed that negative images of African Americans had been infecting the American body politic. When Arna Bontemps and Countee Cullen's *St. Louis Woman* closed, therefore, the frolicking of low-income black people was thrown offstage. Bullins dared bring back the pimps, whores, and hustlers, along with the black working class.[8] Endowed with "a wonderful ear" for their language, he refused either to compromise or to cartoon it.[9] There is not even any sensational spooning up of filth or sentimentality in the play—only the searing eye of analysis.[10] Bullins is not, however, so sure of himself in *In the Wine Time*, which is the first play in his Twentieth-Century Cycle of plays.[11] He couches the return of low-income characters in qualifiers, making them call attention to their misbehavior.

LOU

Fuck you, Cliff! . . . Ohhh, just listen to that. You make me say bad things, man. You think you so smart and know all them big words since you been goin' to school. You still ain't nothin' but a lowdown bastard at heart as far as I'm concerned.
(*CLIFF takes a drink. LOU is wary but defiant.*)

CLIFF

(*Smiles*)
We do cuss too much, don't we?

LOU

(*SMILES*)
And we drink too much.
(*He pulls her over and fondles her; she kisses him but pushes him away.*)

CLIFF

Like sailors?

LOU

Yes!

CLIFF

(*Amused*)
I thought we cussed like sailors.

Lou

We do.

Cliff

(*Raises voice*)
Make up yo' mind, broad. Now what is it . . . do we cuss and drink like sailors or cuss like sailors and drink like . . . like . . . like . . . what?

Lou

Like niggers.

This self-analysis offers the spectator a full view of back-street people. These characters, like George Broadus in Willis Richardson's *The Chip Woman's Fortune* (1923), possess and consciously exhibit both good and evil. Although, viewed externally, they might seem wicked, some characters are sterling. Cliff confesses to Ray about Lou: "She's got character. Your aunt's got principle and conviction and you have to be awfully special for that. . . . Now don't tell her, your aunt, I said these things, but she's special in that way." Sometimes Bullins makes one character into what the poet/critic Sterling Brown calls a "plaster saint."[12] In *In the Wine Time* the part of plaster saint falls to religion fanatic Miss Minny: "You and your friends shouldn't all the time be usin' that kinda language, Cliff . . . gives the street a bad name. We got enough bad streets and boys around here without you makin' it worse." In order to make sure that the rebuke counterbalanced the "catfish Row antics," Bullins backs up Miss Minny, who had earlier led a petition drive to keep the Dawsons out of the neighborhood, with Beatrice, an old-order—and better off—neighbor who refuses even to speak to the Dawson crowd. This morality business is but a device for character and plot development. In developing Cliff, Bullins uses the S. Randolph Edmonds model in *Bad Man* (1934), in which a brutal and bullying sawmill worker ultimately reveals his noble spirit. James Lacy felt that the change in Cliff, which carries the play's message, is overshadowed by the "antics": "I anxiously waited for the play to take off, to pull together a statement that had depth and understanding and would bring reason and insight into the picture."

Such waiting periods are so long in coming—and common—to Bullins's works because of his expert use of irony, subtlety, and trickery. Lacy might have gained immediate insight into the action of the play had he known to look not at Cliff but at Ray. The play really tells Ray's story about his final ritual before "going into the world." The key to understanding this is Ray's prologue, "a lyrical recollection of a sultry summer in the fifties, when a black youth waited at dusk each day for a glimpse"[13] of an older woman, whom he wanted—not sexually, according to Bullins, "but as a mother/sister/spiritual figure":[14]

She passed the corner every evening during my last wine time, wearing a light summer dress with big pockets, in small ballerina slippers, swinging her head back and to the side, all special-like, hearing a private melody singing in her head. I waited for her each dusk, and for this she granted me a s mile, but on some days her selfish tune would drift out to me in a hum; we shared the smile and sad tune and met for a moment each day but one of that long-ago summer.

The woman confessed on the last day of summer that she loved him. In order for Ray to have her, however, he had to give up drinking wine, which was too much of a sacrifice. Electing to search for her later sets Ray up for her fantasy intrusion upon his drinking, trying to pull even his hard-drinking buddies away from the avenue. Failing this, she haunts Ray, causing him repeatedly to tell Cliff about her smiling and "dancing, along with her little funny walk." This woman obviously symbolizes the world that awaits Ray, a world poetically painted for him by Cliff:

In some ports you can get a quart of the best imported whiskey for two bucks, and in some ports you can get the best brandy for only a buck or so.

And the nights . . . ahhh . . . the nights at sea, boy. Ain't nothin' like it. To be on watch on a summer night in the South Atlantic or the Mediterranean when the moon is full is enough to give a year of your life for, Ray. The moon comes from away off and is all silvery, slidin' across the rollin' ocean like a path of cold, wet white fire, straight into your eye. Nothin' like it. Nothin' like it to be at sea . . . unless it's to be in port with a good broad and some mellow booze.

Although this "dramatic high point of the play" motivates Ray to come of age, his movement through the maze into the world requires the final communion of sacrificial blood.[15] There must be the killing of Red, the lamb on the altar, ironically because the drunk Ray has assaulted Ray's own ex-girlfriend Bunny, who had tried to stop him from drinking a bottle of urine given to him by Red. Instead of being a melodramatic shift in the play, as the critic Lindsay Patterson suggests, the violent death is Ray's price of escape.[16] The sacrifice is set up well by Bullins's use of suspense. The spectators know that blood will be let as soon as Cliff, Ray, and ole Silly Wily Clark return from their drinking contest. Bullins feeds the suspense by exposing Cliff's past affair with Lou's best friend, Tiny, whose drunken presence among the supplicants heightens the tension. By the time the unholy trinity returns from "drinking each other into next week," the audience—even Lacy admits—longs for the showdown, a longing made even more unbearable when Cliff goes inside the house without having beaten up anybody. The battle finally erupts so rapidly that it catches the spectators completely by surprise. To top everything off, the final murderous deeds, like those in Greek drama, occur offstage—this time in an alley. The audience sees only the tragic results, as well as the insight.

It is not entirely Lacy's fault that, as he admitted in his letter to Bullins, he could not get the point. He believed that the play's theme "was not clearly demarcated from the insanity and the mindless conversation," causing, therefore, "confusion as to what to take as unacceptable and what as positive." The demarcation is Ray's seminal prologue, which is often dropped from performance, or, as in the case of the New Lafayette Theatre's premiere production, simply printed in the program. The prologue, as the critic Sandra Mayo urges, "should be read by a narrator prior to the beginning of a performance in the theatre—Bullins did not give directions on this."[17] If not read, the absent prologue could cause the play to be mistaken as Cliff's story, and spectators might give undue importance to Cliff's railing against the fate that has left him swilling cheap wine to wash away the thought of a dreary existence with no tomorrow and a fading yesterday.[18] Additionally, without the prologue, Ray becomes Cliff's surrogate. This, then, confuses the ending, turning the needed sacrifice into a poorly motivated "outburst of violence."[19] Instead of sharing a vision of the world with Ray, it appears that Cliff simply "indoctrinated Ray into the mysteries of man's estate, drinking, and sex."[20] More importantly, the prologue's absence from the main action opens the play to interpretations that could be impositions—critics have called the play everything from "a serious indictment of white society" to a treatise against oppression.[21] Cliff's heroism at the end has even been seen as "a suicidal gesture, an abdication of his life [and] manhood."[22] Cliff has been viewed, as well, as an "oppressed man," made so by his "empty idleness." These readings violate Cliff, turning him into a profane man who feels compelled to affirm and give life, to share paths and make sacrifices. This is far from who Cliff is. He, in fact, has only recently gone through his own rite of passage from the streets, as is demonstrated in *The Corner* (1973), the second play in this subclass.

The Corner, a "sulphurous one-acter," questions whether facing the plain and painful truth is the only bridge to real manhood.[23] In the play, Cliff's buddies drink wine and await him, their leader. It is soon clear that this wait will be unlike any other. The "crew" relishes the idea that Cliff will break a member's head for having threatened Cliff's half-brother Steve. That excitement causes them to abandon the custom of leaving Cliff some wine. The coming thrill emboldens one even to insult Cliff's "corner" woman. Another fellow dares to get a "hard-on" for her. They "play" insult games, until they tire of waiting. They leave. When Cliff shows up, he dismisses the fight between Steve and the member; he barely complains about not being left any wine; he makes love to his woman in the usual backseat of a car; he invites the members to gang-bang her; and he announces that he is giving up the "corner" in order to spend more time with his pregnant woman, Lou.

This piece, first performed at the Theatre Company of Boston and directed by David Wheeler, would have made James Lacy feel even more "demoralized"—caused by the same "languishing" people's drinking, swearing, and bluffing. Lacy might have gotten the point earlier, however, that what he was seeing was to be taken as "unacceptable." He would have reached this conclusion with the clear knowledge that what he was seeing was Cliff, not from his own perspective, but from that of his corner buddies. Their "antics" are clear signals for—not symbols of—the meaning of the play. The difference approximates that of the action before and after Cliff's arrival in *The Corner*. Meaning for Lacy might have come with the knowledge that he was being set up by all of the "before" action, whether it humored or disgusted him. Bullins had little choice, frankly, but to make the "before" into deterioration at its best:

SLICK

(*Angry*)
I hope Cliff don't come. I hope Lou don't give him no fucken money to spend on you.

STELLA

(*Breath*)
He'll come. He knows I'm here.

SLICK

You here? Sheet . . . woman, he don't care if you here or on the moon.

STELLA

(*Drains bottle*)
Yes, he does. He's only with that little bitch cause she works and gives him money. But he spends it on me.

SLICK

(*Coldly furious*)
Spends it on you? You mean he buys you a bottle of wine to drink with him before he screws you?
(*Mocking*)
Spends it on you? . . . He don't even buy you a hotel room at night . . . ha ha ha . . . Spend it on you? . . . How many times you've spent in the back seat of Silly Willy's broke-down Buick that don't run no mo'?
(*Names her*)

Spends it on you . . . you weak-minded bitch! How many times you been on my couch . . . in *my* front room . . . with him?

(*Cruel*)

Spends it on you . . . Ha ha ha . . .

(*To* BUMMIE)

Man . . . I can hear those old springs just'a squeakin' . . . "Squeak'a . . . squeak'a . . . squeak'a" . . . Spends it on yo. I hear Stell here sayin' from through the wall in the other room: "Don't you love me, Cliff, baby? . . . Don't you care 'bout me some, Cliff, huh?" . . . ha ha . . . Spends it on you?

(*SHE throws the empty wine bottle at* SLICK: *it misses*)

STELLA

Punk! Faggot!

As depressing as this scene might have been for Lacy, it is necessary if Stella's discovery and Cliff's epiphany are to be convincing enough to carry the theme. Stella's awakening to the truth of Slick's vicious attack makes it essential. This degrading display prepares as well her testing for truth: "Please . . . Cliff . . . please. Take me to a motel, Cliff . . . just once." It also gives her irrefutable proof of what she really means to Cliff: "I ain't got no money to be wastin' on that foolishness, woman!" Even more important to the "before" of *The Corner* serving the "after" of *In the Wine Time* is Cliff's understanding that his corner-days are over. The former helps the spectator better appreciate that this "letting go" is a supreme— and surprising—sacrifice, at least to Cliff's buddies:

BUMMIE

Cliff . . . is there anything really bothering you, man? You don't . . .

CLIFF

(*Annoyed*)

Awww . . . man . . . it's just one of those goddamn days, I guess.

BUMMIE

But somethin' had to happen, man. This ain't like you, Cliff.

CLIFF

What's like me, huh? To be a bum? To drink wine and fuck bitches in junky cars? To stand half the night on some street corner that any fucken cop can come up and claim? . . . Is that like me? . . .

Nawh . . . nawh . . . Not any more. . . . I'm a family man now.

Although this "affecting moment," as the critic Mel Gussow calls it,[24] might have caused Lacy to applaud Cliff, the importance of the moment is wholly defined by Bullins's showing what Lacy called the "too graphic displays" of the "spiritual deterioration" of a "dying community." Importantly, Lacy—among others—did not wish to come to Cliff's noble transformation by way of "the misery and hopelessness of ghetto life, the ways in which people prey on one another and seek release in drink, drugs and . . . music."[25] Cliff's conversion might have seemed to Lacy to have been overwhelmed by the "before" because of its scale and spectacle. This is not the case, however. Whereas the rebirth occupies only one-fourteenth of the total action of *The Corner*, the scene's placement at the end, along with its being continually foreshadowed, makes Cliff's action pivotal. Only the very cavalier mistaking of signals for symbols could have caused the view that Cliff's change showed a pimp's "manliness or nobility," unworthy of admiration.[26] Such misreadings were so disturbing to Bullins that he analyzed them in the final two pieces in the Rites of Passage subclass.

In the short film scenario, *The Box Office* (1969), Bullins asks if some people (read, critics and the middle class) misunderstand a play because they too often view characters as symbols of truth, rather than as signals of lies and joys. In this work, an old black drunk, along with some girls, watches four members of the New Lafayette Theatre place a box office outside of the newly renovated Renaissance movie theatre. The old man focuses on the box office. The girls play and pose, hoping to have their pictures taken by the publicist, who stands around waiting for candid shots. The old man hopes to enter the theatre to see a movie. He puts his money in the box office window, and he waits. When nobody takes his money, "the weary man backs away. He stares at the empty box office, then at the children." When told that "the movie's closed," that movies "won't be shown here anymore," he is confused. He walks back up the street, where he merges into "the thickening crowd." The girls' attention wanders as they stop playing. The publicist takes their picture.[27]

This scenario illustrates characters' actions (or "antics") as but signals that point to how the characters feel, what they believe, when and where they live, or what bedevils their dreams.[28] These signals might or might not be the truth either about real feelings or imagined situations. Bullins enjoys engaging his spectators by making them decipher the truth in his plays. This search is most often successful when observed language and behavior are compared with objective reality, a sense of which is gleaned by studying the entire situation from several perspectives. The most effective way of doing this is by separating language and behavior—which simply call attention to something or someone that deserves clear and objective thought—from the thought itself, represented by a symbol. The language and behavior (signals) often have absolutely nothing to do with the thought (symbols). To the drunk, for example, box offices signal movies. To the young girls, a man with a camera is a call to pose. They do not realize that neither box offices nor cameras guarantee seeing movies or taking photographs. The man's confusion stems from his belief, in other words, that the box office, the signal (or language) of going into a movie, is a one-to-one representation of movie-going. His experience, as well as that of the children, has taught him this lie. Only experience, then, can teach them that signals are most often not symbols, and that signals are often lies.

This in Bullins is especially true when the signal is behavior. In calling attention to themselves, Bullins's characters do humorous things that cause great confusion when people take them to be serious. The important question must be, then, why are the very same things so funny to some people and so serious to others? Nowhere in Lacy's letter, for example, is there any mention of a single funny line, incident, or character in *In the Wine Time*. Had the audience at the African American History Month observance included pimps, whores, and low-income working people, the audience might well have collectively shouted and screamed pains into its sides. The street people might have told Lacy what they had often said to Bullins elsewhere: "Man, that was boss. When are you going to do another one like that?"[29] The play is funny to backstreet people because they accept the representations for what they are: lies about "everyday insanity." Neither Lacy nor his "refined" friends can laugh, according to the theorist Henri Bergson, because they feel threatened.[30] They fear that others might believe that the language and behavior represented on stage are not correctives but accurate portrayals of a predominant reality.

The middle-class African Americans would not have had any such fears had the whites in the *Wine Time* audience seen on the same bill Bullins's short, *Dirty Pool* (1985), the final play in the Rites of Passage subclass. A man at poolside sees a policeman handcuffing and shackling a little old lady, who wears a sedate 1920s bathing suit. The old woman looks resigned. The man finds out from the officer that she is being arrested for having urinated in the pool. The man defends her:

MAN

But . . . but . . . everyone has peed in the pool. Everyone! You, me, your children, your mother even. It's a fact of life, officer. Everyone has peed in a swimming pool.

OFFICER

Yes I know, sir. But not everyone does it from the high diving board.[31]

Lacy's audience at the African American History Month celebration would have granted the whites the intelligence of knowing that this behavior (or signal) is only fun, from which truth might be derived. Had this same fun, which is gained from what Bergson calls "inversion" and "surprise," been applied to the people drinking and cussing on the porch, then the African American History Month spectators could have laughed as freely as the whores, pimps, and the workers. The laughter would have come from being sufficiently "freed from the worry of self-preservation."[32] Only this freedom from personal threat could have prevented any misunderstandings about *In the Wine Time*, or the other plays in the Rites of Passage subclass.

When there is no such freedom, characters and spectators alike lie to cover themselves. These are not teeny-weeny untruths but violent expressions of moral reprobation. The liars are so artful—and bewitching—that Bullins poses revealing questions about them in the five plays making up the Lies subclass. For example, he inquires in *Michael* (1978), how consciously untrue statements can be rendered venial or praiseworthy. The play, which premiered at Northeastern University and was directed by James Spruill, tells the story of Michael and Candy. Michael is a highly successful musician, composer, and arranger. As the play opens, he relates war stories about the Newark black ghetto, topped by his sexual marksmanship. His earliest conquest was Jackie, mother of his four children, whom he abandoned in order to move on to new brawls. While playing a concert in the South, he spotted Candy, the nineteen-year-old daughter of the local college president. He seduced her. After he breaks her in, he discovers her to be a liar and manipulator.

Interestingly, this difficult and unfragmented one-act, which Bullins called a "dramatic fragment," is itself a lie. Like Candy, it presents itself as innocence—encouraging the spectator to know already Michael's rambling opening monologue, which takes up almost one-fifth of the playing time. Michael gains little sympathy as he composes and talks—casting the obvious as profound: "My music expresses my creative spirit, my soul, and my background, my vision of life and existence, and it satisfies most of my intellectual and artistic urges." He paints himself as walled-off music, allowing nobody into his "inner creative reality." He claims none of his cultivated mysticism for himself, only for his music, which completes his life. He admits to feeling guilt—not for having abandoned his children, but for having survived a "truly miserable, mean time." His family responsibilities are but "negative circumstances" that are wrong for him. He shares a self-image that was fathered by Southern nineteenth-century authors in order to influence the body politic: "I was a predatory male animal, stalking the female pussy creatures through the slum jungle. So many conquests I had at such an early age that I soon lost count. On couches, upon overstuffed chairs, on kitchen and dining room tables, and under those tables, and in hallways, stairwells, alleys, backyards, parks, and sometimes even in bed."[33]

The familiarity of this path leading to Jackie (a "wild, hot, fast little mama" whose "fabled cherry" he burst) encouraged people only to *hear* of his becoming a parent at fifteen, a married father of six at nineteen (two of whom died), and an army veteran at twenty-one or so. Audiences could not possibly care about his blaming his feeling of being trapped on Jackie, who, not having gone on sex tours throughout the Mediterranean, Africa, the Orient, and Europe, simply cannot understand his "new dream of a life outside the ghetto." Sealing the audience's dismissal of him is repudiation of Jackie as "a thirteen-year-old mind in a woman's hot, insatiable body," along with his fishing for sanction through "reading and studying and working and saving . . . and drinking"—all attributed to his unhappiness with Jackie:

> But I found my music, and played it as a shield, as a disguise, as a salve to my soulfelt wounds, and soon I lived more and more for my music, and everything else became impermanent and unimportant. . . . I gave up everything for my music; for it was my life; it was my salvation; it was my future, and I know I was right to do it, for my then wife had degenerated into a ghetto strumpet. I use that archaic term for her because "whore" leaves such a bitter taste in my throat.

No such "egotistical, self-centered stud" could possibly cause anybody to pity him for his lost and recouped mind.[34] Not one heart would bleed for his loneliness—not even for his alleged "guilt" for having abandoned his "helpless ones." Audiences were glad that he could not forgive himself. This contempt for Michael was so widespread that critics called for doing away with the monologue because it was only "cumbersome exposition" that was "unrelated to what followed."[35] This interpretation fooled people into believing that the play was "simplistic."[36] Bullins tricked people into such judgments by attaching to the monologue the seduction concert, presided over by a giggling conductor:

CANDY

> I'm not even supposed to be out here. In fact, I'm not supposed to be at this party. My parents would have a grit fit if they knew that I was here with you. But the night is so so sweet. Magnolias hang from the trees and their fragrance hovers in the air like the wings of night-birds—warm, soft, smothering, complete. I wish I understood you. And you me. But I'm not used to big city ways. I've been down here all my days. And even though I'm educated from a classical black perspective, I don't know my buns from a huckleberry bush. Really. And you're so nice. . . . You know, when you play your music, it's like you're speaking to me, you know. Not that you know me. Goodness, we just met. And haven't even been properly introduced, yet. But it seems as if I've always known you and that you've spoken to me before, from far away in my dreams, from some long ago fancy place. Is the north a romantic place? I want to know because when I hear your

119

music, it touches me where my dreams come from, and these are such romantic dreams. That place could never exist in this world, I guess, but you must have seen something, you must have visited some place to be able to sing to me with your music the way that you do. Because I don't understand music much except for spirituals and the blues.

These fragrant sounds pretend to be nothing more than what they are: recognized, offered, and accepted packages wrapped to convey false impressions. Michael and Candy understand this:

CANDY

Oh, yes. About the drinking. Wow, I have drank some at our sorority and things, but that was different.

MICHAEL

How was it different?

CANDY

It wasn't with you, Michael.

MICHAEL

And don't forget because you love me.

CANDY

It means the same thing, Mike. Hey, you don't believe me, do you?

MICHAEL

Naturally not.

CANDY

Look, Michael, I'm not in the habit of telling lies.

MICHAEL

You aren't? Well, how did you get to be so above the likes of we mortals, pussy . . . cat?

CANDY

Probably it was the way I was raised. Perhaps, because I'm the daughter of the President . . .

MICHAEL

You're the President's daughter?

CANDY

Righto! In the flesh . . . and I'm all yours, sweet daddy. Tee hee. Don't I sound so terribly gauche, Mike?

Since Candy admits in *Daddy* (1977; on which *Michael* is based) that her father is only the college chaplain, this exchange shows how unprepared Michael is for battle with this lying teenager. The audience admires her, however, because she delivers poetic justice to an absent and selfish father. Her lying might be considered praiseworthy, consequently, because it mirrors Michael's own contemptible past behavior. Her importance, then, is that she is his own spit being blown back into his face, a point missed by any who believe that, with Candy, Bullins was only playing to "stereotypes long since abandoned even by the Hollywood dream factory."[37] It was not for the fun of it that Candy was created a stereotype: this matches Michael's stereotypical past, which means that when Michael has sex with her it is nothing more than masturbation. Therefore, this is no "battle between the sexes" nor is it a look at another "vital man" being dragged down by his "girl."[38] Bullins is far too subtle and mischievous for such triteness. The play is a look at a man being forced to know intimately through continual re-plays the repulsive and damaging past lies he has repeatedly told to and about himself.

The second Lies play, *A Sunday Afternoon* (1987), which Bullins co-authored with the director Marshall Borden, might be deemed a rather simpleminded soap opera. The authors inquire about man's search for peace from family fuss through ignoring what he knows. First produced at San Francisco City College and directed by Borden, the play tells the story of Jake Robinson, the kind of football fanatic who watches on television three games on a Sunday afternoon. He presides over these viewings with family members and buddies. He looks at little else, especially not the games between his wife, Lora, and his white buddy, Nick, who is the route inspector for the city bus transit, where Jake also works. Jake makes his not knowing so disturbingly obvious that his father-in-law Arthur shoots out the television set between games. Jake then throws out everybody. Alone, he watches the third game.

The importance of the play, on first appearance, is only that Bullins's name is connected to it. The linear plot, along with the well-made-play elements, demonstrates that he had only minimal input in the script. Bullins's hand shows only in the subtle and ironic ending, which is foreshadowed by Jake's reaction to being force-fed the truth:

NICK

(Angry)

Jake, it's you, man! All your bullshit!

(Forcing HIMSELF to calm down)

Look, Jake, try to understand. Lora ain't walkin' out on you. She's been driven out, man. Jake you drove her out.

JAKE

Since it was so good, you can enjoy each other in hell!

(HE pulls the gun from HIS pocket, aims at NICK. JAKE's trigger finger tightens.) (The following lines overlap)

LORA

No!

ARTHUR

Jake, no!

JERI

Daddy!

WILLY

Jesus!

ARNIE

Holy fuck!

> (*There is a tense silence as the gun moves slowly back and forth between LORA and NICK. Finally, the gun begins to tremble and then shake. The weapon ultimately falls from JAKE's hand and HE collapses on the floor. There is a collective release of tension.*)

After everyone leaves, Jake picks up the weapon on the table:

> (*Slowly HE, brings the gun to HIS temple, and we hear a resounding "CLICK" HE smiles as HE removes the bullets from HIS pocket. As HE flips each bullet in a different direction, HIS smile grows into a satisfied laugh. HIS focus then returns to [a portable] TV. HE picks up a beer from the table and takes a drink as HE sits on the sofa. The sound in the portable comes up.*)

ANNOUNCER

Welcome to ESPN and game number three on Sunday Afternoon.

JAKE

(*Smiles broadly and kicks back*)

Yeah.

That Bullins would have anything to do with a play in which a white man steals a black man's wife and daughter opens more than surprised eyes. Just what is he saying—or letting someone else say for him—about African American women? Even here, however, Bullins has swords up his sleeves. He apparently wanted to see how a white playright would handle Bullins's own real-life experience of having lost his second wife to a white man, whom she later left to be herself.[39] This recent revelation makes the play into something other than a cartoon of a black Ralph Cramden: The play offers to a black man a white man's unique analysis of a white man taking a black man's wife. However, the white author elected to ask the wrong question: Why does Lora—a play on Nora in Henrik Ibsen's *A Doll's House*?—leave her husband? The answers, taken within the context of the life of a bus driver and sports addict, are hackneyed: He is crass, selfish, impatient, manipulative, anti-education, paranoid, overbearing, and unbelievably rude:

JAKE

Goddamn it! I knew it! I knew it! I knew that lo som'-bitch would screw up my game!
(*HE slams down HIS beer and starts in on [HIS father-in-law] ARTHUR*)
Same ole song 'n dance! Same ol' same! I ask for one simple thing out o' life—a Sunday afternoon, one afternoon, my afternoon, nothing else. An' you fuck it up every time! I love it! I just love it! Now, you been told, and you been warned. So get out my face, ol' man! Hike yo ass up stairs and stay there!

LORA

Jake, no, please.

JAKE

And you shut your trap! I got my nose full o' this ol' dude.
(*Points to ARTHUR*)
UP! Get up the goddamn stairs!

ARTHUR

(*As HE starts to go, HE gestures at the TV with HIS cane*)
It looks like C.B.S. has won again.
(*JAKE grabs ARTHUR's cane away from HIM and breaks it over HIS knee, hurting HIMSELF. HE throws the cane pieces down and hops about.*)

JAKE

Aaaaagggg! Damn! Shit! Jesus! God!

ANNOUNCER

. . . Unquestionably a broken pattern . . .

The sum of such outbursts justifies the white author's answer that the black man "drove" his black wife between the sheets with a white man. This answer could not have been totally satisfactory to the black co-author because sex and self-worth are involved, served up by the historic love of sexual prowess and superiority: The black character Jake, after all, is another Michael, a "predatory male animal, stalking the female pussy creatures through the slum jungle." The black man's loss to a white man of his prized "pussy creature" is, therefore, a complicated and troubling experience, one which the white author only demonstrates through the other characters' surprise that Jake could hide anything.

LORA

You knew?

JAKE

(Making it rhyme.)
Ol' dumb Jake know more than you thank. If you ain't sure 'bout gettin' fucked, go see one o' your friends.

NICK

Jake, it wasn't like that, man. Believe me! Lora and me, we never intended it to be. It was just there, man. It just happened.

JAKE

So, we finally gonna get some honesty out o' the honkey and the vanilla queen. Le'me tell you just how much ol dumb Jake knows. Nicky boy come on as my route inspector and suddenly I got me a lot o' time on my hands. I'm latchin' on to the easy routes with the forty-five minute naps at the end. I'm sure it's jus' 'cause we old friends. Right? I mean, he one o' the bloods. He did his march to Washington. He eat soul, he hip, and his boots on my coffee table every Sunday. But then ol' dumb Jake start wonderin'. So, durin' one o' my nap times, I drive back here to the hood and park a block away. I do my Mike Hammer routine and watch this place from behind a tree. Holy Africa! Ain't the revolution ever gonna end? Who come walkin' outta my house but my route inspector, my boss. My good friend. Wow! ol dumb Jake finally realize, Nicky boy be in my house doin' my some-time wife.

LORA

Ooo, Jake . . .

JAKE

(Vicious, to LORA)
Did you like the honkey action better than mine?

Whereas the white co-author might have unknowingly posed this unanswered question for his black co-author, neither might have wanted to hear the answer. Otherwise they would have asked the far more interesting question: What is there about the black man's nature that makes him withhold such devastating and defining knowledge? Is it that with this information, power shifts to him, allowing him to throw darts throughout the play at Nick and Lora? What satisfies the black character when, for example, he says—after Nick offers "to give Lora a hand" with serving the brew: "*(Laughing)* You sure that the only thing you wanna give her, boss"? Whatever makes Jake throw such darts remains so mysterious that it takes over the whole play, rendering everything else petty. This makes the end even less satisfactory, the part which was apparently designed to assuage the black character: By throwing out everybody, Jake does not have to face his possible sexual inferiority or, more importantly, his ravaged self-worth.

Jake's need to lie in order to hide knowing also informs the unpublished and unproduced *Teacup Full of Roses* (1985), which was adapted from Sharon Bell Mathis's novel of the same title. In this full-length play, disaster looms over the Burns family, comprised of domineering mother Mattie, sickly father Isaac, prophesying Aunt Lou, artist/addict son Paul, dreaming son Joey, and scholar/athlete son Davey. The principal cause of this disaster is Paul's drug addition. The mother lies to herself that he will recover; her exclusive devotion to him causes the others to feel neglected. The family—minus the mother—finally has a showdown with Paul's supplier, who has intentionally given Paul an overdose. While Paul is dying, his quite ill father blows off the supplier's head, which causes the father to have a fatal heart attack. His example nourishes his sons.

The fact that *Teacup* has never been performed speaks to a clash of wills and visions between author and adaptor. When Bullins finished it in 1985, he sent it to Mathis for her comment. She never even acknowledged receiving it. Neither did she respond to producer/historian Ethel Pitts Walker, who sent Mathis two letters in 1992 requesting permission to publish the play. Walker emphasized that Bullins "was willing to make *any* changes she wanted. She would have complete control over the project." Walker explained further that the play, which many "theatricians felt was one of Ed's best works, spoke to this generation," and that "it made a significant, positive statement." This was undoubtedly the reason, Walker concluded, that "several people had expressed an interest in producing it."[40] Only after a mutual friend of Walker's and Mathis's interceded did Mathis deign to reject the offer, and then in terms that reportedly cast the play as a personal insult.[41] Mathis informed her publisher that the play did "not—in any way—reflect the Black community—as I see it, or the characters in *Teacup Full of Roses*."[42]

Comparisons of Mathis's and Bullins's views on the African American community and of their writings raise serious questions about Mathis's conclusion. The authors' beliefs, interestingly enough, are quite similar, notwithstanding their different classes and tastes. Like James Lacy, Mathis is a middle-class educator. Although an award-winning author of children's books and a librarian for an elementary school, she closely identifies, nevertheless, with the poor people of the urban black ghetto.[43] Unlike Lacy, however, Mathis has never disowned ghetto lifestyles as "tangential" events that so "very many of us only read about, heard about, and went to funerals about." She prefers, in fact, real black characters: "The Black child is usually portrayed as lacking street wit in books written by whites. I

125

teach—and I see textbooks that have painted a few faces brown. But they still haven't added any facts about Blacks. Parents, teachers, and librarians primarily are responsible for the books children read. And it's their duty to inspect these books more carefully and not buy or order them just because the faces are black."[44]

This sensibility, along with the characters in *Teacup,* matches Bullins's. Both authors use Aunt Lou, for example, as a choric seer designed to create mood, foreshadow action, develop plot, and emphasize theme. Looming over the play more than the novel, Aunt Lou strengthens the former without altering whatsoever Mathis's character. Neither did Bullins's rendering of the mother Mattie make her any harsher than Mathis had done: Mathis has said that Mattie "loved her oldest son [Paul] above the rest of her children," and that he "was his mother's dream of everything good in the world." This unshared adoration stands out because Mattie shows not even gratitude toward her other sons, even when Joe buys her a dress to wear to his graduation:

> He hung his mother's dress on a hanger and took it in the kitchen and gave it to her. He winked at his father and aunt. "For you, Momma," he said. David was grinning.
>
> Mattie turned the dress around and around, never smiling. "You know I don't wear no color like that," she said finally.
>
> Joe saw the smile leave David's face and his mother looking for a price tag.
>
> "When do I ever get a chance to wear a new dress? Don't nobody around here take me nowhere!"
>
> With that, she walked out of the kitchen with the dress and down the hall to her bedroom. Joe heard her open the closet door. Then she came out, put dinner on the dining-room table, and sat down to eat.[45]

Bullins simply lifted the scene:

> (*JOEY presents dress to* MATTIE. SHE *looks at it suspiciously.* ISAAC BURNS *looks on.* DAVEY *enters to look.*)
>
> (JOEY *winks at* ISAAC)
> For you, Mama.
> (*MATTIE turns the dress around and around, never smiling.*)
>
> MATTIE
> You know I don't wear no color like that.
> (*The smiles leaves the* MEN'S *faces.*)
>
> MATTIE
> When do I get a chance to wear a new dress? Don't nobody around here take me nowhere!

(*SHE goes into her room, slamming the door.*)

Such close adaptations are so typical in Bullins's play that his changes in character complement Mathis's design and theme. Joe, whose name Bullins changed to Joey, is, for example, a real dreamer in Mathis's novel. He works hard for his school diploma so that it might "open doors to higher education, security, success—a magic life with his girlfriend, Ellie, in a place "where trouble never comes . . . in a teacup full of roses.' "[46] Bullins expands Joey's dreams to include a nightmare:

I wake up and find myself in strangely colored surroundings. . . . Suddenly, a crowds of junkies and crack heads are all about me. I have to push my way through their zoombie-like mass. Somehow, I know I am looking for Paul. And I see him . . . But then he disappears. And I see another figure ahead of me that looks like Paul. But this time the figure stands still, bending slightly at the knees and waist, like a junkie gone into a deep nod . . . When I am close enough to it, I see its face. The thing's got the face of Warwick. . . . Oh, God! Please let me wake from this nightmare! Oh now Paul laughs strangely at me, and now he's throwing the ball at me hard . . . I shoot out my hands and catch it . . . But it's warm and slimy and almost slips out of my hands. But I hold it. And when I look at it . . . aahhhhhh! I see that the thing is the shaven, decapitated head of my . . . my brother DAVEY!!! AAAHHHHHHHHH!!!

This dramatic license effectively uses Mathis's suggestions to motivate Joe's determination to get Paul off drugs. Mathis might have objected, however, to Bullins's drastic change in her concept of the father, Isaac. He is last seen in the novel encouraging Joe before the commencement:

"I guess I'm about ready to go, Pop."
Isaac Burns got up and held his son as tight as he could. . . .
Joe saw tears in his father's eyes for the first time in his life.
"You look good, Joseph. That beige suit laying on you perfect."
Grasping Joe's hand tightly, his own hand was trembling. "Joseph," he said, wiping away his tears.
"Yes, Pop."
"I'm proud of you not just tonight but all the time. But you got to keep moving on. That's what makes you a man. It don't have nothing to do with schooling—it's deeper and harder than that, and you got to do it by yourself. You think you up to it?"
"Yes. Sir."
"That's what I want to hear."[47]

In the play, Bullins takes Isaac to the showdown between Joey and druglord Warwick, which occurs immediately after Joey's graduation:

(WARWICK aims at JOEY in the doorway.)

WARWICK

YOU DEAD, JOEY!!

(At that moment, ISAAC BURNS enters and blows off the top of WAR-WICK's HEAD) Then ISAAC is struck by a heart attack and dies.) LIGHTS CHANGE. JOEY cradles ISAAC's dead body. HE cries uncontrollably.) . . .

JOEY *(tender)*

Thanks, Pop. Thanks. You not only gave us life . . . you raised us to be men. Thanks, Pop. For giving us something we can never repay.

Mathis had these lines delivered by Joe to his dead brother David. This marks the principal difference between the play and the novel. Not only does druglord Warwick survive in the novel, but he also kills David, who jumps in front of a bullet intended for Joe. Could Mathis have resented David's survival in the play, along with Warwick's death, and Isaac's heroic sacrifice? If so, she failed to recognize that the play presented an even stronger, more hopeful, and greatly sustaining image for black children, whom she said that her work salutes.[48] The strong and positive male image, additionally, could not have violated the importance that she put in her relationships with the men in her own family. Bullins's Isaac, in fact, is quite similar in many ways to Mathis's descriptions of her grandfathers.[49]

Because Bullins's and Mathis's characters are from the very same stock, could it have been Bullins's dialogue that caused Mathis to reject the play? Unlike James Lacy, Mathis has no aversion to profanity. Although *Teacup* targets children from ages twelve to fifteen, the novel is sprinkled with the language and behavior common among some low-income urban African Americans:

> Joe fought two more [of Warwick's henchmen] before everything happened. He was fighting the third when another one jumped in and hit him. In a second Phil was beside him. Things were moving well when Joe heard Ellie screaming and police sirens.
> "Davey! Get away! Get the hell out of here! I'll beat your ass if you don't get away from me!"[50]

Except for "shit," Bullins does not use a single curse word that does not appear in the novel—an incredible feat in light of his depiction of the drug culture. Language, then, could not have been the cause of Mathis's rejection.

Some people have speculated that Mathis had "a personal sense of loss, which she did not wish to share with the world. She must be undergoing a continuing personal mourning."[51] If true, this would make more comprehensible her view of the play as a desecration. What makes this doubtful, however, is that she sold the film rights in 1975 to the producer/director St. Clair Bourne. Bourne hired Bullins to write the screenplay, which was never made into a film because of lack of funding.[52] This is unfortunate because the film, like the play, could have been an incredibly forceful tool for steering the young away from drugs. The hope now must be that Mathis will change her mind so that Bullins's planned workshop production of the play can become a professional one that will travel throughout urban America.[53] Seeing this powerful work would undoubtedly save lives because of the play's connection to the young through the use of familiar words, styles, and characters.

In the last two plays of the Lies type (*C'mon Back to Heavenly House* [1977] and *City Preacher* [1993]), Bullins moves from praiseworthy to venial lying. Both plays question whether deceit—for saving a job or a lifestyle—is worth the eventual losses of jobs, as well as esteem. First performed at Amherst College and directed by Pat Golden, *C'mon Back to Heavenly House*, which was adapted from Bullins's teleplay, *The Home* (1974), tells the story of Roy, a new hospital relief clerk, who unintentionally exposes the deceit of four of his coworkers. All subsequently lose. Roy's immediate supervisor (Mrs. Odell) gets reassigned because Roy's output shows how much of a goldbricker she is. His amoral department head, Robert Jefferson, loses his rest/guest home—called Heavenly House—because Roy refuses to appease Jefferson's hypocrisy. Roy's married lover, a maid named Dorothy, gets beaten up by her husband. Roy's would-be lover, the two-timing maid Queenie, loses Dorothy as a best friend. Roy leaves town. These losses pale in comparison to those in *City Preacher*, which loosely uses the life of the Reverend Adam Clayton Powell Jr. to pose questions concerning deceiving oneself in order to avoid having to give up the good life. The well-off Aaron Jackson Price Jr. deceives himself into believing that he can escape his calling to replace his father as the pastor of the family church. Aaron answers God's call only after he loses his father and his sister.

In terms of structure, characterization, and dialogue, these plays show how Bullins's contrariness works against him. He abandons his signature absurdism for the traditional structure, complete with linear plots, cause-and-effect episodes, and well-defined beginnings, middles, and ends. Interestingly enough, however, he remains "a scorner of most dramaturgical rules, recipes, formulae, and plans."[54] This means that he obeys only select rules governing inciting actions (or incidents), climaxes, and characterizations. In *City Preacher*, for example, he delays the inciting action, a device that alerts the spectator to the central conflict. In order to grasp and keep audience attention, convention dictates that this incident occur as soon as possible. It is not until the sixth scene, however, that the audience understands Aaron's dilemma:

AARON

(To his SISTER)
Look, I'd like your advice about something.

BETH

(Mild surprise)
You do? Well, you've seldom confided in me, since you've been big enough to put your pants on.

AARON

Beth, please . . .

BETH

Okay, okay . . . I'll try and do my best.
(HE takes a drink, then looks BETH in the eyes.)

AARON

Beth, I don't want to take over for father. I don't want to be a minister.
(SHE drops her teacup.)

BETH

(Startled/whispers.)
Aaron, please don't say that.

AARON

But why?

BETH

It's just . . . just that you've made an impossible decision.

AARON

But how is . . .

BETH

You've been groomed to be father's successor, even before you were born, Aaron.

AARON

I know, but I never wanted it. I was never right for it.[55]

The spectator might have been entertained by the five scenes that precede this one, but he or she would have no context for Aaron grabbing center stage in a Spanish nightspot, turning down a business proposition, seducing a gypsy, hearing the call, or not knowing about Harlem's bad times. In fact, Bullins has argued that the call in Scene 2 is the inciting incident:

> (*AARON leisurely saunters to the mirror and drinks and chuckles with satisfaction at his bare-chested reflection in the candle-lit mirror.*)
>
> (*Suddenly, the window behind him is pushed open by a strong gust of wind. The candle blows out, but the room is not dark, for the moon is tropical and full.*
>
> *From somewhere outside, though inside too, a man's soft, insistent voice whispers*):

VOICE

(*Eerie*)
Aaron . . . Aaron . . . Whom shall I send? Who will go for me?
(*AARON spins around in the semi-dark room.*)

AARON

(*Frightened*)
Who's there? What do you want? Who's there?

VOICE

Aaron . . . Whom shall I send? Who will go for me?
(*AARON rushes to the window. HE sees only the full moon. HE stares into the moon, then clutches his head and falls backwards into the room, fainting at the foot of his bed.*)

Although captivating, this episode mystifies more than it clearly identifies some idea, commitment, or resolution on Aaron's part. Whereas the inciting incident might have been an external force such as the Voice, the spectator should have seen Aaron's reaction. If Aaron had said to the Voice, "I don't want to be a minister," not only would the inciting incident have complied with the rule, but also it would have done away with the criticism that the play was slow to get off the ground.[56] Bullins's picking and choosing his rules explains, as well, the trouble with the middle of both plays, the episodes that were to be so selected and shaped that they gradually climaxed. The criticism was that his middles appeared "shapeless and unfocused."[57] The middle in *C'mon Back to Heavenly House* consists of too many episodes presented on the same scale, whether or not they develop theme or character. The same criticism applies to *City Preacher*, where, as one critic complained, the characters blend into a monochromatic backdrop, each an exemplar of temptation or trusting devotion behind the hero's private communion with the devils inside: gin, women, gambling, and "in a page borrowed from *Hamlet*, his father's ghost. But Bullins does not shape or modify these potentially powerful [and] elemental building blocks."[58]

Equally as damaging is the predictability of the action of each play.

This problem in *City Preacher* is challenging, in light of the fact that it is what Bullins accurately described as a historical piece about a man who was larger than life. It is well known that during his youth, Powell, later a member of Congress and pastor of the Abyssinia Baptist Church, enjoyed chasing fun. Aaron's "transformation," as one critic complained, is, therefore, "pre-ordained."[59] The question, then, is how could Bullins have made Aaron's known conversion something other than "dramatically vacant"?[60] Other writers of historical drama have solved this problem not by simply detailing the many events in the protagonist's life but by focusing every event through a single conflict between two equally powerful and determined combatants. Although the spectators might have known the outcome of the battles between Aaron and his sister Beth, his mother, or the Voice—just as the audience knows how the conflict between Frederick Douglass and John Brown will end in William Branch's *In Splendid Error* (1955)—the all-out escalating battle itself would have been a satisfying and cleansing spectacle.

This problem of predictability in *C'mon Back to Heavenly House* might have been solved by using less heavy-handed foreshadowing, which telegraphs most of the action. Because of her continual threats, for example, when Queenie eventually tells Dorothy's husband that Dorothy is having an affair with Roy, it is unsurprising. Such foretelling is not the main problem in *City Preacher*, however, which premiered at the Magic Theatre in San Francisco and was "sensitively and resourcefully directed by John Doyle."[61] The difficulty is the development of characters who are "so two dimensional that their speeches were predictable at every appearance."[62]

This is a surprising flaw because character development remains the same regardless of structure. By 1984, Bullins had so mastered character development that his principals are among the most memorable in American drama. Why he shows repeated examples of the same traits in Aaron indicates, perhaps, that he might not have cared enough about Aaron or his struggle—as might be surmised by his failure to give Aaron a single monologue full of Bullins's signature prose poetry. Although he was challenged to reproduce the language of the thirties, what evolved was "moribund and earthbound."[63] Even the dialogue in the non-period piece *Heavenly House* is not par Bullins: The twelve-year-old Ella Mae, for example, talks like an adult:

ELLA MAE

(Angry)

Lucy's not my mother! The state adoption service boards me out with her. She keeps threatening to adopt me . . . that's why she calls me her daughter. But she can't adopt me. She's not married. And Mr. Jefferson's not going to divorce his real wife across town and give up

132

his kids for Lucy Brown. He just stays with her so he can use this house.

ROY

(Confused)
I don't think I understand.

ELLA MAE

You don't huh? That's no mystery. Everything that comes out of Robert Jefferson and Lucy Brown's mouth is a lie. Don't believe one word they say to you, about nothin'.[64]

This dialogue problem, along with the faulty structures and characterizations, is indeed "a far cry from Bullins at his best."[65] It is, instead, Bullins at study. He simply wanted to see a production of the play that he had written while he was in New York in 1981. He had delayed showing *City Preacher* in New York because everything there was "packaged for bigtime success." He evidently believed that he could be "far more daring and experimental" in San Francisco without so much close scrutiny.[66] He forgot that his very name would draw critics from throughout Northern California to see him experimenting with—and learning in public—what he called the "epic" structure. The critics gave him hell, telling him what he had already concluded from the rehearsals.[67] Some critics seemed delighted to ravage him: Steve Winn violated the rules of good criticism by calling the play a "simplistic medieval morality play" in need of help from "the Most Holy Magic Church of God."[68] *City Preacher* is historically important, nevertheless, because it and *C'mon Back to Heavenly House* are Bullins's only full-length experiments with realism and traditional structure.

Bullins is "at his best" in the third subclass of Binding Relationships plays, those dealing with Gay and Lesbian Relations. In three short plays, he poses complex and unprecedented questions about gay and lesbian ties. In the first two plays, Bullins argues that people are not necessarily what they refuse to condemn. He poses brilliant questions in the first draft of *Snickers* (1985) about gay life as a microcosm of prison life. The unpublished and unproduced short tells the story of a teacher's brief stay in jail for not paying his traffic tickets. There he meets three people: a female guard, who propositions him; a cellmate called Animal, who makes a sexual advance toward him; and an inmate called Ghost, who has been raped by Animal. The guard finally gets the teacher to agree to date her. The teacher rejects Animal's overture and his Snickers candy bar. He later savagely beats up Animal for having raped his "jailhouse wife," Ghost, a marriage sealed when Ghost ate Animal's offered Snickers bar. Animal, it turns out, is doubly beaten: Ghost reveals that he has AIDS.

The dramaturgical significance of this play is that it shows Bullins's mastery of dramatic irony, first seen in the title. Snicker is what the female guard does to let the teacher know that she knows—"From computers, buddy"—that he is not what he seems, notwithstanding his well-rehearsed lines. The second meaning is that the candy itself has the laugh on all givers and takers. The play, as a statement on gay life, indicts prison life. Animal, as metaphor for prison, controls, exploits, and coerces Ghost. In order to do this, Animal, like prisons, turns every desire against Ghost. By denying conjugal visits, prisons turn men—gay or not—into creatures who, according to the Black Panther Huey P. Newton, "lived largely for the next sexual encounter. To them, sex was all."[69] The purpose of enhancing these cravings is "to undermine prisoners' normal yearnings for dignity and freedom. The system was the pusher in this case, and the prisoners were forced to become addicted to sex. Love and vulnerability and tenderness were distorted into functions of power, competition, and control."[70] As lieutenants of these functions, the guards seldom interfered with gay life, "content to look the other way as long as things stayed cool."[71] In fact, some guards themselves were gay, which is important only because they used their positions for favors. "Often, as I showered," Newton reported, "a guard would stand in the doorway, talking, looking not at my face but at my penis, and say, 'Hey, Newton, how you doin' there, Newton? Wanna have some fun, Newton?' I laughed at them."[72] Sex (or "pseudosexuality," as Newton calls it) translates into ownership. When Teacher tries, therefore, to save Ghost from Animal's thrashing, Animal lets Man know that Ghost belongs to Animal.

MAN

Nobody belongs to anybody else.

ANIMAL

You don't know where you're at, stupid. But you'll find out before you're carried out of here. When Ghost came in here, I helped him.

MAN

You helped him?

ANIMAL

Yeah, I give him my last Snickers.

MAN

So what?

ANIMAL

He ate my Snickers and I later asked for it back. . . .

I told him I wanted the same Snickers that I gave him, not a new one.

MAN

But I don't know what you're getting at.

ANIMAL

What I mean is that if I couldn't have my own Snickers back, then I'd have the hole where my Snickers came out. And I did. I took it! And took it! And took it![73]

That Animal (again, prison) commits suicide by raping his love slave warns "correctional institutions" that rehabilitation has nothing to do with destroying will, with policing thought, or with coercing obedience. Prisons exist, in part, because of the low self-esteem of inmates. The notion that anyone—short of God—can remake the human personality so that it conforms to societal expectations probably explains the reason that, since 1971, the United States has embarked on the largest "social experiment in punishment in the history of the world" without any "appreciable drop in the crime rate."[74] Punishment advocates still consume 85 percent of the nation's criminal justice resources, with "budget crumbs" going into sending young criminals to drug, literacy, and employment programs while they clean up parks and perform restitution short of cell time.[75] *Snickers* endorses none of these solutions because, as playwright, Bullins always observes and seldom preaches.

One more significant answer to criminal and sexual behavior can be found in *Hunk* (1980), another unpublished and unproduced work of the Gay and Lesbian Relations type of Binding Relationships plays. This is the slight story of three people who wait out a heavy thunderstorm in an east side New York tenement stoop. There is the reefer-smoking Blackman, along with two women, Hazel and Woman. Hazel looks like any woman. The Woman, however, "dresses like a man—overalls, sneakers, and rolled-up sleeves." Blackman ignores both. Woman offers the man a cigarette, some Colt '45, and conversation. He accepts none of it. Woman pointedly lets Blackman know not only that she has a son and granddaughter, but also that she knows that the news surprises him. Blackman says nothing. She asks him for a match. He gives her a book of them, and then he leaves. Woman says that he is "one of the nice people in the world."[76] This short play, significantly, poses simultaneous questions. The most obvious concern is with jumping to conclusions about people's sexuality. The lesbian-looking woman's continually, though subtly, making overtures toward Blackman plays off of the irony of the title "hunk." The two women initially use the word with its connotative meaning in mind, a sexy man. Other meanings gradually take over, making "hunk" mean everything from "sex" to "truth" to "forever." The truth is that "hunk" means one, none, and/or many of these things. Truth is not the important issue, however; and therein lies the significance of Blackman's lack of interest either in Woman's sexuality or in her fixation on his opinion about her sexuality. Blackman's wish only to get out of the storm speaks to the need to depoliticize sexuality.

It is the politics of gay and lesbian life—not necessarily the scriptures—that have caused African American churches to condemn homosexuality, according to theologian Cornel West. Because white America has made sexual orientation a tenet of "the subversive and transgressive," and because black institutions believe that "black survival required accommodation with and acceptance from white America," homosexuality became an "abomination."[77] The Black Liberation Movement, too, bought into the idea that gay is subversive because the struggle against racism required "real men," meaning only those whose very presence intimidates, whose sense of power knows no bounds. Gays, therefore, were "by nature in contention with being not only a man" but also a politically astute freedom fighter.[78] African American theatre even characterized the gay as a threat to the black community.[79] Some African American studies made gay and lesbian life into a "deviation from Afrocentric thought because it makes the person evaluate his own physical needs above the teachings of national consciousness." The studies, then, were "redemptive" for those not wishing to be "controlled by European decadence."[80] The importance of all of this is that if an individual can make people buy into his or her definitions and arguments, then that person can seize control by making people measure their own self-worth on others' terms. This applies to both gays and anti-gays. The apparent lesbian in *Hunk* is obsessed with introducing her apparent sexuality only because it is her sole hope of engaging Blackman in some activity or dialogue. Blackman avoids both, thereby indicating that for him one's sexuality is not grounds for passing either judgments or time.

The final play of this type, the Bullins classic, *Clara's Ole Man* (1969), tells how a low-income lesbian, Big Girl, fends off a male caller in order to save her marriage to a passive but curious partner, Clara. The caller is Jack, whose courting of Clara is "forestalled" by the presence of Big Girl, who, having stayed home from work, turns the occasion into a drinking party. Jack wears a jacket and tie, and he uses big words to express "earnest liberal sentiments." Clara is quiet, agreeable, and nervous. Big Girl is butch, foul-mouthed, and domineering. With the addition of Baby Girl, Big Girl's spastic younger sister, it is an "odd, unbalanced quartet." They drink and pass the time. They are visited first by the pleasantly tipsy Miss Famie, who daily calls on Big Girl's shut-in Aunt Toohey to drink gin. A trio of young toughs, having just stolen a bottle of gin from a drunk, later stops by to hide from the cops. The young men nearly start a fight with Jack, who has drunk more than he is used to, making him increasingly unsettled by something that he cannot quite grasp. Groping to understand, he finally explains that he has come to visit Clara because she said that her old man would be at work that afternoon. He is stunned by the revelation that Big Girl is the old man in question. Big Girl's young friends take him outside for a beating.[81]

The historic importance of this play is that it was the first scripted non-homophobic play in African American theatre. Traditionally, the theatre reflected the anti-gay public stance of the African American community: Churches preached that homosexuality was "abominable" (Leviticus 19:22), "wicked" (Genesis 19:4–7), "shameless" (Romans 1:26–27), "wrong-doing" (1 Corinthians 6:9, 10), and "lawless, disobedient, godless, sinful, unholy, and profane" (1 Timothy 1:8–10). So ingrained was this view that Langston Hughes hedged his introduction of the first non-improvisational gay characters (Masculine Woman and Youth) in African American theatre in his hilarious *Little Ham* (1935):

(Enters an effeminate YOUTH)

YOUTH

Can I get a polish?

HAM

You mean your nails?

YOUTH

I mean my slippers.
   (Mounting the [shoeshine] stand.)

HAM

Well, . . . er, are you . . . er, what nationality?

YOUTH

Creole by birth, but I never draw the color line.

HAM

I know you don't. Is you married?

YOUTH

Oh no, I'm in vaudeville.

HAM

I knowed you was in something. What do you do?

YOUTH

I began in a horse-act, a comic horse-act.

HAM

A who?

YOUTH

A horse-act. I played the hind legs. But I got out of that. I've advanced.

HAM

To what?

YOUTH

I give impersonations.

HAM

Is that what they call it now?

YOUTH

I impersonate Mae West.

HAM

Lemme see.

YOUTH

Of course.
   (Begins to talk like Mae West, giving an amusing impersonation of that famous screen star.)

HAM

You a regular moving picture!

YOUTH

Indeed I am.[82]

Gay characters were subsequently banished from African American theatre for almost thirty years, until Amiri Baraka dragged Homosexual into *The Baptism* (1964) to play the devil, aiming to seduce a boy. This set the tone for the Black Liberation Movement, in which Eldridge Cleaver's celebrated attack became characteristic:

It seems that many Negro homosexuals, acquiescing in this racial death-wish, are outraged and frustrated because in their sickness, they are unable to have a baby by a white man. The cross they have to bear is that, already bending over and touching their toes for the white man, the fruit of their miscegenation is not the little half-white offspring of their dreams, but an increase in the unwinding of their nerves—though they redouble their efforts and intake of the white man's sperm.[83]

Significant segments of the African American community joined Cleaver in his belief that homosexuality was a "sickness equal to baby-rape."[84] Some people asserted as late as 1991 that instead of "coming out," gays and lesbians "should be 'going back in' as a way of making a positive contribution to black liberation."[85] Although Bullins, as early as 1963,

138

warned that writers and thinkers might be misguided in "exposing the circumstances of misunderstood homosexual love,"[86] he, too, represented anti-gay sentiments. In his short story, "Travel from Home," church people condone the beating and robbery of an innocent white man when the narrator lies that the man is "a fag."[87] Although this view is offset by the short story, "The Drive," in which the narrator "admitted secretly that queers and dikes weren't so bad if they knew where you stood,"[88] Bullins uses homophobia to motivate several actions in his plays. In *The Corner*, for example, Bummie breaks off his lifelong friendship with Slick when Slick implies that Bummie might be like a woman. Tootsie in *The Duplex* wants to kill his friend Marco because he invites a gay guy, whom Marco hustles for reefer without sex, to sleep on the sofa where Tootsie sleeps. O. D. in *The Duplex* slashes his wife Velma's arm because she calls him a faggot. Nevertheless, it was a daring move on Bullins's part to allow Robert Hartman to direct the San Francisco Drama Circle's premiere of *Clara's Ole Man* about lesbian love at the very outset of the Black Liberation Movement in 1965.

This "well-constructed play that deliberately revealed itself with an engaging and diverting energy,"[89] interestingly enough, is not about lesbianism but power. Bullins depicts an all-out war over the transgression and cleansing of a space, which just happens to be the home ("*The Lower Depths* of the South Philly") of lesbian lovers Big Girl and Clara.[90] That a cultivated postal worker is the unwitting transgressor heightens the combat to terrifying proportions, all shaped and measured for exorcising by high priestess Big Girl. This expurgation, like the Crucifixion, must happen: Jack, in other words, must pay. The liturgy calls for him to know, repent, and sacrifice, a sequence of events to be achieved as cleric Big Girl subtly lays claim to Clara, as Clara initially deflects that claim, as Big Girl declares war, and as Clara obliquely warns Jack about the ensuing fight. Things are frustrated, however, when Jack misses each warning because of his blind pursuit of a wife. He assumes that bowing and kneeling and sucking up to Big Girl are but maneuvers necessary to outlast what he perceives to be but a simple delay in having Clara. The resulting dramatic irony lifts to laughable heights this ultramodern tragedy, which critic Edith Oliver called a "funny and frightening horror comedy."[91] Bullins exploits the irony with chess moves that make double entendres explode like candle wax:

BIG GIRL

Do you know why I taught [Baby Girl] to cuss?

JACK

Why, no, I have no idea. Why did you?

BIG GIRL

Well, it was to give her freedom ya know? Ya see, workin' in the hospital with all the nuts and fruits and crazies and weirdos, I get ideas 'bout things. I saw how when they get these kids in who have cracked up and even with older people who come in out of their skulls, they all mostly cuss. . . . But when the docs start shockin' them, puttin' them on insulin, they quiets down. That's when the docs think they're gettin' better, but really they ain't. They're just learn'n like before to hold it in . . . just like before, that's one reason most of them come back or are always on the verge afterwards of goin' psycho again.

JACK

(Enthusiastic)

Wow, I never thought of that! That ritual action of purging and ca-tharsis can open up new avenues in therapy and in learning theory and conditioning subjects . . .

CLARA

(Struck)

That sounds so wonderful . . .

JACK

(Still excited)

But I agree with you. You have an intuitive grasp of very abstract concepts!

BIG GIRL

(Beaming)

Yeah, yeah . . . I got a lot of it figured out . . .

What Big Girl has not figured out is how to expose—without appear-ing to—the unaware sinner without forcing him and Clara into deflective dances. Their dances so anger the goddess that she feels obliged to remind Clara—and to inform Jack—that it was Big Girl who had purged Clara, who had cleaned a dead baby out of her, and who had pulled her off the night streets for holy communion of muscatel. To make sure that this blind Jack sees the picture, Big Girl draws her salvation-acts in loud and broad colors: Clara's soiled body had taken three water glasses of wine and had gotten "so damned sick" that holy mother Big Girl had had to put "my finger down her throat and make her heave it up . . . HAW HAW." This telling is the public renewal of their holy marriage vows: Clara said that she would "be my friend always . . . that we'd always be together." Jack, then, was not simply trying to score, he was tempting Clara to forsake her troth. Clara's eagerness requires that Big Girl stop circling her prey in order to go in for the slaughter:

140

BIG GIRL

That ole gin head [Miss Famie] tracked water all over your floor, Clara.

CLARA

Makes no never mind to me. This place stays so clean I like when someone comes so it gets a little messy so I have somethin' ta do.

BIG GIRL

Is that why Jackie boy is here? So he can do some messin' 'round?

CLARA

Nawh, B.G.

JACK

(Stands)
Well, I'll be going. I see that . . .

BIG GIRL

(Rises and tugs his sleeve)
Sit down an' drink up, young blood.
(Pushes him back into his seat)
There's wine here . . .
(Slow and suggestive)
There's a pretty girl here . . . you go for that, don't you?

JACK

It's not that . . .

BIG GIRL

You go for fine little Clara, don't you?

JACK

Well, yes, I do . . .

BIG GIRL

HAW HAW HAW . . .
(Slams the table and sloshes wine)
HAW HAW HAW . . .
(Slow and suggestive)
What I tell ya, Clara? You're a winner. First time I laid eyes on you I said to myself that you's a winner.

The arrival of Big Girl's disciple-thieves suspends the bloodletting, but their advent teases the audience's imaginations about what is to come. Bullins uses this to develop plot and character, further enhanced by inserting two other wayfarers: the closet drunk Miss Famie, and the out-drunk C.C., specializing in doxologies. The importance of Big Girl's thieves is that they free her to take off her partial mask and to show her raw and absolute power. That her every word is obeyed by all reveals to Jack that he is in the presence of something that he truly does not understand. As the critic Michael Smith indicated, Jack is totally confused "in the face of the fullness of life."[92] His disorientation is not sufficient, however, if he is to pay penance because it means that he is compensating for a sin that he does not yet know is one. The disciple-thieves, then, must make him understand and confess his wickedness. This ritual is taken over—without verbal cue—by Stoogie, the aptly named altar boy and leader of the police-dodging trio. Jack's need to please Stoogie dirties the ceremonial, forcing what is to come to begin over a simple insult about military service:

STOOGIE

What kind of a boat were you on, man?

JACK

A ship.

BIG GIRL

A boat!

JACK

No, a ship.

STOOGIE

(Rising, BAMA and HOSS surrounding JACK)
Yeah, man, dat's what she said . . . a boat!

CLARA

STOP IT!

BABY GIRL

NO! NO! NO! SHIT! SHIT! SHIT! DAMN! SHIT!

MISS FAMIE's Voice from upstairs
Your aunt don't like all that noise.

BIG GIRL

You and my aunt better mind ya fukkin' ginhead business or I'll come up there and ram those empty bottles up where it counts!

The terror of the threatened rammed bottles prepares Jack for absolution in this steadily tightening confession box, readied for his spilling: "Clara said for me to come by today in the afternoon when her ole man would be at work . . . and I was wonderin' what time he got home." The confessor is now ready for his own cleansing and penance. The cleansing comes when Big Girl baptizes him with the knowledge that "Clara's ole man is home now." Jack vomits, which cleanses his body for atonement—

142

the beating given him by Big Girl's thieves. Only because of this beating, which on the surface is about his "presumed uppityness," are power and order restored.[93]

This historic one act contains none of the pleas, apologies, or calls for a "solution" so typical of African American drama.[94] Bullins offers a simple picture of "a compassionate humanity."[95] His refusal to pass judgment must not be mistaken, however. One closeted gay minister/landlord in Los Angeles during the early sixties mistook Bullins's habit of silent observation and plied him with gifts and favors. When the actual sexual advance finally came, Bullins misbehaved so terribly that the minister hurriedly called the police. Bullins especially resented those who believed that his failure to condemn gays meant that he was one. When he misinterpreted a quote about him as an alleged gay-basher,[96] he fired off a letter: "Why have you passed along the lie that I'm a homo? I don't care what some ass hole thinks; it's not even worth repeating. What if any of my [eight] children or family read that? They might not be sophisticated enough to look at it as a lie. . . . With my boxing and martial arts background, you know whoever said that would not say it to my face."[97]

One must not underestimate the importance of the questions posed by Bullins's Binding Relationships plays—questions about the social pressures and the never-ending battles that so bind people that they simply cannot walk away. These plays excite deep—and often forgotten—animosities, loves, and fears, emotions that inform people's beliefs, attitudes, and actions. This unearthing is so significant because it is the buried—but not dead—inner life that puts people in touch with themselves. Bullins's plays are the fingers that go sliding down throats to make people "heave" up the past. Only with this cleansing can one gain—and maintain—total control over his or her life. Although this is the result that was sought, the purging itself is such a wrenching personal struggle that some people, such as James Lacy, bite down on those fingers: The problem with the plays is "the vulgar and unacceptable language" and the "gross, tasteless, and disgusting behavior" of Bullins's characters. Only after hours of post-purification reflection did Lacy accept the notion that the real problem was that the images were too close to reality, that they had profoundly rattled his self-image.

It was this that caused Lacy to resent so the public cursing and drinking and loud talking in *In the Wine Time*. What was startling was his thinking so hard about these during his ride home after the play. He tussled with the real reasons that this play angered him so. When he first got home, he wrote five pages of his seven-page letter to Bullins, allowing his frustrations with the play "to pour out of me." Then he cooled off. After several hours, he returned to the letter to write the final two pages, which admit that the play helped to reconcile him with his past, with his father,

143

"who had passed in 1960 because of cirrhosis of the liver." The play even put Lacy "in touch with his early fantasies" about calling women "bitches and beating up anyone who got in my way." He realized that a character like Cliff, who had held no fascination for Lacy since age eighteen, had been an important part of his own early experiences. Lacy had forgotten about "my days drinking wine": about calling a young woman "a stopper-cock whore," causing her not "to speak to me for more than twenty-five years"; about "playing pitty pat and tonk"; and about "masturbating in groups and having boys brag about the girls they had knocked up." He had left all of that behind when he was eighteen and had gone to Washington, D.C., where on his block there were only professionals, along with "one numbers runner." At his high school in D.C., over 70 percent of the graduates had gone on to college.

When Lacy returned to Oakland, he met again a few men and women "addicted to a low-income lifestyle," which by that time had lost its fascination for him. He was now, years later, grateful to *In the Wine Time*: "Whether I liked or enjoyed the play was one thing. Whether it was effective in its intent was another. Without question, the play was effective. Ed is a genius at what he does: It's like taking castor oil. The medicine might have tasted nasty, but it got me moving."[98] This Binding Relationship play got one person to call up the experiences necessary to take complete control of his life. This better empowered him to teach others in ways that were heretofore impossible. With full order restored in his own life, he could now help others to pose the right questions to find their own way through their rites of passage, through all lies, as well as through sexual politics in order to win their place and their peace.

4

THE FLOW CLASS OF
BLACK EXPERIENCE DRAMA

When asked at an unseemly early-morning hour if there had ever been an incident that made him so angry that he had wanted to bash somebody's face in, Bullins cleared his throat for what seemed like nineteen minutes. Then he said, "Give me a day or so. I really can't come up with anything right now." Then, after a pause, he added: "I seldom get that angry."[1] He was right—notwithstanding the fact that his children, Ameena and Sun Ra, had seen him "protect" them in California by fighting in the streets.[2] In fact, Bullins is considered such an easy-going human being that it seemed uncharacteristic when he closed down a performance of his *The Duplex* (1971) at Lincoln Center in 1972, two years after Robert Macbeth had directed its premiere at the New Lafayette Theatre.

The artistic director, Jules Irving (1924–1979), and Bullins had been going at it for weeks about the show. After the play opened on 18 March 1972, Bullins, along with some of his writer friends, cornered Irving outside of the theatre.[3] Irving hastily agreed to let Bullins talk to the audience during intermission. When intermission was over, however, Irving told Bullins that he could not speak because the second act had already started. All hell unfroze.

"You lied again," Bullins shouted.

"Liar! Liar!" the writers chanted.

"All right," Irving said. "We'll stop the show and let him talk for ten minutes."

145

Irving, dressed in a dark blue suit with a black turtleneck sweater, interrupted the show and announced that Bullins would make a statement. Bullins went on stage. He asked that the full cast come out. There was quiet.

"My play is about love," said Bullins. "The characters on this stage are savages."

Hisses came from offstage. Soon an actress emerged from the wings and paraded a sign around the stage: "Ed Bullins hates black women."

Bullins shouted at her. The audience cheered. Irving waved his hands for order.

The actors shouted for Bullins to go home and learn how to write.

The spectators cheered. Bullins called the spectators a whole host of dirty words.

Irving continued waving his hand, now as if he were making the sign of the cross. Fifteen minutes of this was all that he could take. "Get off the stage," he shouted at Bullins.

Bullins glared at him.

The actors eased off the stage to make sure that they were not in the line of ire.

"Start the second act," Irving commanded.

"And you can just act around me," Bullins muttered.

"All right, Bullins, you told us. Now go," somebody shouted from the audience.,

"Go. Go. Go," the audience chanted.

Bullins paced up and down, slightly out of step with the "Go. Go. Go."

Then he slowly sat on an ottoman. As his broad behind touched the naugahyde, something settled over the set.

"I can do two things," Irving said, breaking the spell as soon as he could muster the breath. He was determined not to be upstaged by this man.

"One is to have you, my good friends, to come back to see the show on another night."

Bullins watched.

"Or I can have Mr. Bullins here removed by the police."

The audience roared for the second choice.

"But I will not do that," Irving said.

Then he walked up the aisle and exited in front of the admiring spectators. One by one and two by four, they followed Irving.

Bullins sat.[4]

What made Bullins so angry? His announced reason was that Irving had turned *The Duplex* into a "burlesque show, complete with a 'Darktown Strutters Ball' kind of musical score and an over-all mood that's straight out of *Amos 'n Andy*. It's not the play I wrote, and it doesn't say anything about any Black people I know"—which, strangely, sounds like what Sharon Bell Mathis would say about Bullins's adaptation of her novel, *A Teacup Full of Roses*, some years later. Bullins added that neither the director Gil Moses nor the actors could really be faulted: "They're just paid mercenaries, they're doing a job. The person who condones this theatrical degradation of black people is Jules Irving, along with his staff."[5] What "they really want to do is sell to White people a negative image of Blacks as bestial types, fornicating all over the stage, acting like lustful clowns."[6]

Irving, a highly respected producer and director, could not let Bullins get away with this public rebuke. After all, Irving had founded, with the director Herbert Blau, the renowned San Francisco Actors Workshop (1952–64), which became known for its celebrated experimental productions. While at Lincoln Center from 1965 to 1972, Irving garnered considerable respect for his carefully crafted productions of the classics, as well as for his innovative presentations of plays by the German playwright Bertolt Brecht, the Irish dramatist Samuel Beckett, and the English playwright Harold Pinter.[7] And then along came Bullins. He cared nothing about the protocol that required upstart playwrights to show their gratitude for a major-house production by shutting up and letting the professionals put on a commercial performance that would guarantee investment-recovery and a hefty profit. If this meant using what Bullins called the "minstrel show format," so be it.

Irving did not realize, however, that he was doing more than changing Bullins's play, that, in fact, he was dynamiting Bullins's meticulously built bridge over a historic divide in African American theatre. During the twenties and thirties, the sociologist W. E. B. Du Bois had posed on one cliff and demanded that drama be used for protest and virtue. On the opposite shore danced the philosopher Alain Locke, cheering on the Broadway black musical comedies as "very intriguing American treasures," as well as "artistic possibilities for a new technique in the drama."[8] The men shouted insults: Du Bois scorned shows that were not political. Locke praised them as tools to help African American theatre "develop its own idiom, to pour itself into new molds."[9]

This gap, which Irving dug deeper, continued to divide the straight drama until Bullins wrote *The Gentleman Caller* (1970). The canyon was widened through musical theatre during the period 1900–49, when more than 622 black musical comedies splashed images around the world of the African American as jester and reprobate. This caused the musical to be unofficially banned by blacks throughout the fifties and the sixties. It was in 1970—in *Street Sounds*—that Bullins poured Du Bois's serious themes into Locke's fun forms. This same mix in *The Duplex* fooled Irving into so lightening this "tragic love story" with music and comedy that the violated Bullins's "intentions" and the play's "artistic integrity."[10] Irving had been deceived by the Flow Class of Black Experience Drama, which emphasizes Locke's views that drama must be a "delightfully rich transfusion of essential folk-arts":[11]

> The newer motive . . . in being racial is to be so purely for the sake of art. Nowhere is this more apparent, or more justified, than in the increasing tendency to evolve from the racial substance something technically distinctive, something that as an idiom of style may become a contribution to the general resources of art. In flavor of language, flow of phrase, accent of rhythm in prose, verse and music, color and tone of imagery, idiom and timbre of emotion and symbolism, it is the ambition and promise of Negro artists to make a distinctive contribution.[12]

Bullins's Flow plays, like those of other dramatists, might be divided into Musicals and the Forms subclasses. As seen in the Historical Type, the first of five types in the Musical subclass, Bullins massaged history into asking, What has historically motivated African Americans to develop distinctly different attitudes towards whites? Answers to this question might be found in five historic music plays. A quick review of the plots of those five plays, followed by analyses, will reveal four of the major influences shaping African American racial relations. The first factor might be found in *I Am Lucy Terry: An Historical Fantasy for Young Americans* (1993), where Bullins argues that African Americans should have forged a tighter union with Native Americans. *I Am Lucy Terry*, which premiered at the America Place Theatre with Robert Macbeth directing, is based loosely on the life of the abolitionist and author of the title (1730–1821): Lucy meets and falls in love with Abijah Prince, a former slave who has won his freedom fighting on the Spanish Main, and who has been hired by the Deerfield, Massachusetts, village minister, Reverend Ashley, to kill Native Americans. Abijah asks Ashley's help in getting Lucy's master to let Abijah purchase Lucy's freedom so that she can become his wife. Before this can be arranged, however, Lucy is abducted by the Native Americans, who want her to marry into the "Nation," thereby uniting African and Native Americans. When Abijah tries to rescue her, the Native Americans capture him, win him over, and marry Abijah and Lucy. Upon their return to Deerfield, they hear from Reverend Ashley that Lucy's owner refuses to sell her. Lucy declares her freedom and claims her husband. When the townspeople hear her heroic poem, "Bars Fight," they vote to free Lucy and Abijah.

This heroic story stands directly opposite the puzzle of a poet who rejects her own heritage and accepts white values, the second influence shaping racial perspectives. In *The Mystery of Phillis Wheatley: An Histori-*

cal Play for Young Americans (1993), which Elizabeth Van Dyke directed at the Henry Street Settlement's New Federal Theatre, Bullins depicts a misunderstood woman who is sold into a Massachusetts household. She is educated. She becomes a celebrity in Boston because of her poetry, allowing her to be baptized in Boston's Ole South Meeting House. When she becomes ill, her future husband, John Peters, a doctor, cures her. He prescribes a voyage to London, where she meets Ben Franklin, who gives her a message for George Washington. She returns to the United States because she feels that it is her duty to be with her mistress, whose death paves the way for her to marry John Peters and to deliver Franklin's message to Washington.

Sandwiched between these two poles of influence are other plots honoring successes in outsmarting whites—first through trickery. *High John Da Conqueror: The Musical* (1993) opened at the Black Repertory Theatre in Berkeley with Ethel Pitts Walker directing. Adapted partly from the works of the anthropologist Zora Neale Hurston and the folklorist Julius Lester, the play tells the story of how High John outfoxes his Massa in order to avenge the terrorism of past and present slavery. High John realizes that the roots of slavery are power and money. When Massa gives John a mule named Blackie, therefore, High John knows that the gift is intended to increase Massa's control over him. High John refuses to play Massa's game, which causes Massa to punish High John by killing Blackie. John bets Massa that even without the mule, he can beat Massa at making money. After Massa accepts the apparent sucker bet, John uses Blackie's skin to tell fortunes, which nets him more than $200. Not knowing how John has made his money, Massa kills his own mule, takes the skin to town, and sells it for almost nothing. Realizing that he has been made into a fool, Massa bets $30,000 that John cannot beat Uncle T., a "black bully boy" who can trounce "any darky in the whole country." At the fight, Uncle T. runs away after he sees John repeatedly slap the governor's daughter. John declares a worker's holiday by destroying all farm tools. An angry Massa threatens to kill John, who bets Massa that if he kills John, he will again beat Massa at making money. Massa puts John in a sack, shoots into it, and goes to find some weights in order to throw the sack into the river. Miraculously unhurt, John is rescued by the fair maiden Young Girl. When Massa next sees John, who has yet another pocket full of money from having told fortunes, Massa thinks that John is a ghost. Massa asks to be killed by John so that Massa, too, can make more money. John kills Massa and frees the slaves.

This use of trickery to gain freedom is replaced in the musical comedies *Storyville* (1977) and *Sepia Star* (1978) by stubborn determination to overcome all adversity—whether inspired by racism, sexism, or classism. Opening at the University of California-San Diego with Floyd Gaffney as director and Jaime Rogers as musical director, *Storyville* tells the story of the boxer-turned-jazz trumpeter Butch "Cobra" Brown. He comes to Storyville, Louisiana, which is America's first official red-light district. He meets Big Mama Little, the spellcaster and magic worker, who introduces him to the cabaret singer Tigre. Butch falls in love with Tigre, but so does her boss Hector Bonnot, who tries to seduce her and make her his queen in the Mardi Gras parade. After initially dismissing Butch and fighting off Hector's advances, Tigre falls in love with Butch, and, for professional reasons, consents to be Hector's queen. This angers Butch, who retaliates by sleeping with Tigre's friend Fi Fi. After Tigre discovers them in bed, she and Butch break up. Big Mama Little patches up the romance. Butch and Tigre start a band, and they live happily ever after.

Premiering at Stage 73 in New York City with Robert Macbeth as director, *Sepia Star* tells the story of the aspiring singer/dancer Star Mae Baker. A poet, she meets the pre-law student Jason at a coffee house in New York City. Although she falls in love with him, she allows her mother, Ruby, to manipulate her into rejecting Jason for an offer to sing and dance with Ramon, a hustler-cum-performer. Ramon uses Star's talent to advance his career. Ruby eventually sabotages that relationship in order to advance Star's career, which rises to make her a smash hit as a solo performer in Las Vegas. Yet, Star feels sad and unfulfilled. To correct this, Ruby, behind Star's back, invites Jason to visit. Although professing his love, he rejects the offer because of law school exams. Star realizes that she was wrong to have left him. Finally, Star finds the courage to stand up to her mother and leave show business. In her rush to get home, she is severely injured in an automobile accident, from which she, with Jason at her side, recovers. Together, they decide to rebuild her career because she now feels that her life has meaning.

Although the stories of *I Am Lucy Terry*, *The Mystery of Phillis Wheatley*, and *High John Da Conqueror* were chosen for young people, the plots of these music dramas and the musical comedies *Storyville* and *Sepia Star* are articulated by such sophisticated devices as flashbacks and dreams, along with parallel time. These tools might appear to be too difficult for children to handle, which explains Bullins's use of colorful narrators in all the works except *Sepia Star*. The narrators, typically, set the story, introduce the principals, develop plot, and reveal outcomes. These narrators are exotics, such as Mama Ju Ju (conjurer lady supreme) in *High John* and sorcerer Big Mama Little in *Storyville*. When there are two narrators, such as in *Terry* and *Wheatley*, the narrators themselves are usually at war—over whose perspective of Abijah and Lucy in *Terry* will prevail, and over whose powers over Wheatley will triumph: Lord Africa, "the spirit of African Liberation," for example, battles Captain Diabolical, "the symbol of slavetrading forces":

LORD AFRICA

It was a poem in memory of the Reverend George Whitefield who breathed his last at Newburyport, Massachusetts in September 1770. To many blacks, Whitefield, although he did not preach for the halt of the slave trade, was a friend to the slaves.

(*In an explosive flash of fire and smoke,* CAPTAIN DIABOLICAL *appears.*)

CAPTAIN DIABOLICAL

Enough of this! Enough of this . . . this poetry!

LORD AFRICA

What do you want around here, Captain Diabolical? Haven't you done your evil best? You stole Phillis, you enslaved her. . . .

CAPTAIN DIABOLICAL

I haven't even begun to make that little woman's life horrible. Her poems, her religious prayers, her sweet and humble ways . . . I hate and despise them.

LORD AFRICA

You fiendish fiend!

CAPTAIN DIABOLICAL

Call me what you will, Lord Africa, but you haven't any power to stop me. Didn't I come to your land and take your people? Don't I do what I want here in my own land, America? You are powerless . . . you weak story teller.

LORD AFRICA

I may not be able to stop you completely, Captain Diabolical, but I'll help Phillis as much as I can.

CAPTAIN DIABOLICAL

Help Phillis? Ha ha ha . . . you fool![13]

Such characterizations not only create poles that are familiar to young people but also keep the spectator engaged in very sophisticated plots and profound themes. One might conclude that the themes are far too serious for the young. How interested could children possibly be in the *High John* issue that Young Girl is refused a college student loan because of a "budget blight that has victimized the old and sick and young of this nation, while it builds Star Wars and world annihilation"? Bullins's priority, evidently, was to build an interest in connecting politics and personal strife, regardless of its nature. Even children, then, would see their troubles not through an emotional prism but as the result of historical forces that are manipulated by others for political or economic gain.

It follows, then, that *Phillis Wheatley* and *Lucy Terry* should demand that the young not only know their history but also know its uses in conquering fear and despair, in finding hope and courage, and in spreading laughter and peace. It is these, after all, that give meaning to the need to prepare well the mind in order to do one's duty, the central issue in *Wheatley*—notwithstanding the critic Carll Tucker's claim that Bullins never made up his mind what he thought about Wheatley.[14] With a subtlety that matches Wheatley's, Bullins takes his stance *for* Wheatley by helping children of all races gain a sympathy and respect toward others who might be different—and to do so, as attorney Charles Garo Ashjian pointed out, "without having suffered any personal humiliation or insult in the process."[15]

By respecting Wheatley, the children gain direction for their own lives. With choric repetition, Bullins carves for the children the image of Wheatley preparing and disciplining her mind for duty:

PHILLIS (*eight years old*)
I am a slave. A slave. A captive. Someone's property to be bought and sold and disposed of for profit. What a fearsome fate. How wretched can an existence be? How will I survive? How can I stand this?

LORD AFRICA
Use your mind, child. Use the genius that has been given you to escape this cruel prison.

PHILLIS
(*As if hearing a voice*)
What can I do? What . . . use my mind? Yes. That's it. . . .
(*Sings*)
There's a country
hereabouts
where you can escape
the fate
of being a slave

There's a region
that few
know its
whereabouts
but within its
borders you'll
surely know how
to behave

Raise anchor
Cast off

The Flow Class
'cause we're
heading for
the Kingdom
of the Mind
Yes, the Kingdom of
the Mind

Where all
wishes can
be created

Where each
desire is
abated

Don't be
left behind
not everyday
do you have
the chance
to enter the
Kingdom of the Mind

Shove off
Hit the
road
Batten down the
hatches
we're on
our way
To the Kingdom of the Mind
That's right
The Kingdom of
the Mind.

The benefit of this well-equipped mind, in Wheatley's case, is the discipline it generates to help her put duty before pleasure and to lure her enemies into underestimating her. They must have been surprised, for example, by her decision to return to slavery after an enjoyable visit to London:

This has been a wonderful summer for me. My spirits are high. My health is better than it has been for a good while. But I must return to America. My duty calls. Yes, my duty. For even though I am a slave, I have a duty of faith and loyalty to Susannah Wheatley, my mistress, my benefactress. The one who has raised me from the bottom of de-

spair after I was stolen from my homeland. I could stay here in England, I know, if I wished to. I could declare my emancipation and
refuse to return to the land of death and slavery from which I only
left a short while ago. But I have a duty. A duty to the woman who
bought me in slavery but never treated me as property. I have a duty
to another human that I cannot treat lightly. Not even for the sake of
my freedom. And I have a duty to myself and all the other black
people who will follow me.

What interested Bullins most about this return is "the question of
what could move a free woman voluntarily give up her freedom in order
to return to slavery. He rejected the easy answer of her having "preferred
slavery in America to freedom in Africa," which was introduced by the
scholar J. Saunders Redding in 1939 and trumpeted by some black revolutionary leaders and literary critics during the sixties.[16] Bullins aimed to
correct this. His use of the word "mystery" in the title refutes the critic
Mel Gussow's belief that Bullins saw Wheatley as being "unfaithful to her
roots, a black African who learned to write verse 'like a gentle English-
woman.' Manipulated by white values and aspirations, she abandons her
people and becomes something of the boxer Jack Johnson of poets."[17] The
play suggests—and her poems confirm—that Wheatley might have been
far more complex and duplicitous than Jack Johnson. It was the misread-
ing of her poems, in fact, that had led people to believe otherwise. It began
with "To the University of Cambridge, in New-England"—four lines
which Bullins used in the beginning of the play: " 'Twas not long since I
left my native shore / The land of errors, and *Egyptian* gloom: / Father of
mercy, 'twas thy gracious hand / Brought me in safety from those dark
abodes." Wheatley appears to have exhibited a low race-esteem, made apparently more obvious in "On Being Brought from Africa to America":

> 'Twas mercy brought me from my *Pagan* land,
> Taught my benighted soul to understand
> That there's a God, that there's a *Savior* too:
> Once I redemption neither sought nor knew.
> Some view our sable race with scornful eye,
> "Their colour is a diabolic die."
> Remember, *Christians*, *Negroes*, black as *Cain*.
> May be refin'd, and join the angelic train.[18]

Too many critics missed completely the fact that Wheatley ironically
whips white Christians over their hypocritical heads with their own beliefs
and attitudes in this poem. A careful reading of the poem shows that
Wheatley's negative references to Africa (e.g., Pagan land, land of errors)
are not her voice but that of the racists, whom she names "some" and
disparages as "*Christians*." It is with her expert use of irony, then, that she

won acceptance and high praise from the very people whom she had put down with such grace. Carll Tucker is wrong, therefore, in saying that the "problem with Wheatley, for a militant playwright like Bullins, was that she sold out."[19] Bullins's proposition is, as the character Lord Africa asks: "Was there more to Phillis than met the eye? Ahhh . . . now there lies the mystery." The play answers that not only was Wheatley "discovered and misused by civilization," as Gussow said,[20] but also that she was smart enough to fight that abuse by the means she knew best—an irony so "refin'd" that it prompted "*Christians*" to praise a "*Pagan*" from the "land of errors" even as she insulted them.

As if this mystery were not enough for young minds-at-play, *I Am Lucy Terry* shows children a multicultural world view—as seen in the formation of strong alliances with Native Americans through intermarriage. How optimistic it is of Bullins to believe that children would—or even could—respect the history and culture of "Injuns" so much so that future matrimony could take place, especially since African American attitudes toward Native Americans have been shaped by the entertainment media. These images make it all but impossible for African American youth ever to see the "braves" as the antidote to rampant American greed, power, and heartlessness. The play, nevertheless, depicts the evolution of an implicit hostility—much like the children's own—into a mutual defense pact. The conversation comes from the close interaction between strangers, from the discovery of similarities so overwhelming that the manufactured and manipulated fears are revealed for what they are. With the projected horrors erased, it is unsurprising how different the married Lucy is after she and Prince return from their stay with the "redskins":

ASHLEY (*pleads*)
This man be not thy husband, Lucy child. Are ye daft? Only thy, meself, can perform the broom ceremony. Thy be the man of God here.

LUCY
Broom? Thou suggest that thy jump over a broom for my marriage ceremony? Never! . . .

Never! Never! Do you hear me, Reverend Ashley, sir? You bigot! You pompous village lout! You small, wee worm of a christian tyrant! . . .

Well thy be not a slave no more, even though thy be held as a prisoner here, and made to do slave's work to pay my way out of bondage, and to save the head of my lovely husband. But thy be no slave. Thy be married under the universe of the heathen heavens, under the laws of savages, more civilized than thee, Reverend Ashley, sir, and under the eyes of God; aye, married as an Indian Princess, and I shall never return willingly to slavery.[21]

How interesting that this theme of "blood mixing" so infuriated the critic Burt Supree that he called the play a "muddled historical fantasy—ultraserious, lazily flip, half visionary wishful thinking and polemic, half snippety comedy that pretty thoroughly obscures the impressive woman that Lucy Terry Prince must have been, judging from the bare facts of her long life."[22] Supree complained that Bullins buried Lucy's accomplishments as freedom fighter and legal defender, as well as her steadfastness and persistence, in a fantasy of her being carried into the forest by the Indians and being lectured by their shaman on how the red man's blood will mix with the black man's blood, thereby legitimizing blacks as the spiritual heirs of the Native Americans on this continent. Supree even resented Lucy's marrying her man in the forest in a mystical Native American ceremony. Supree viewed this as Bullins turning "Indians" into "exotics. They got rhythm, and they talk funny ('We Indian braves are heap brave.' 'We kill white eyes at sunrise! Ya!')." Supree saw the play as but "a flagrantly careless use of undigested historical material." He concluded that although much of history needed rewriting in order to do justice to ignored or minimized minority contributions, the way to do this is not with Bullins's introductions of "new fictions and false impressions, new foolishness, new distortion. [Bullins] owes it to the black youngsters, whose traditions and spirit he specially wants to affirm, to treat them with more respect, to more thought and less hoke."

What perhaps most disturbed Supree was Bullins's clever revision of history in order to make allies out of African Americans and Native Americans, who, in some cases, had been arch enemies. However, in several instances—the ex-slaves and the Seminoles in Apalachicola, Florida, for example—the two peoples did, indeed, form unions. In Florida, the progeny of such unions became known as the Black Seminoles. They defended their freedom at Fort Negro for over fifty years. This stronghold was brought down in 1816 by an authorized attack of government forces and Creeks. Despite such alliances, Lucy Terry was afraid of Native Americans. The principal reason was that on August 28, 1746, when she was only sixteen, sixty Native Americans attacked two white families in the southwest corner of Deerfield, Massachusetts, a section called "the Bars"—so named because the settlers felled trees and milled them into lumber, which was used to corral stock. Terry was so stirred by the sight that she wrote the ballad, "Bars Fight":

August 'twas, the twenty-fifth,
Seventeen hundred forty-six,
The Indians did in ambush lay,

Some very valiant men to slay,
The names of whom I'll not leave out:
Samuel Allen like a hero fout,
And though he was so brave and bold,
His face no more shall we behold;[23]

The irony is in Bullins's use of the entire fearful ballad as the triumphant climax of the play, wherein Terry's dramatic recitation of this fright-
ful picture so touches the townspeople that they vote to let her be
purchased by her husband. The ballad, then, is no longer a strong warning
to African Americans to stay clear of the "savages," which was the official
government policy. Taken out of its historical context, the ballad in the
play encourages an alliance between Native and African Americans, something that the government historically feared most—so much so that almost every U.S.-Native American treaty required the latter to return
runaway slaves. Because such stipulations were often ignored, a strong
solidarity existed between these peoples, who did indeed intermarry, producing such heroes as chief of the Crow nation James Beckwourth, the
Black Seminole chief Garcia, and the Revolutionary War hero Crispus Attucks. That Bullins remade Lucy Terry into an advocate of such alliances
might be more than a "flagrantly careless use of undigested historical material," as Supree suggested. The play might be an engaging way of showing young people how life might have been had not the "genuine heroine"
Lucy Terry been on the wrong side of "the Indian question."

Equally as important as the message of *I Am Lucy Terry* is Bullins's
successful marriage of straight plots, characters, and themes to comic sub-
plots, characters, and spectacles—the source of Jules Irving's problem.
This marriage changed completely the formula for music drama and musical comedy—a change sought by W. E. B. Du Bois. After seeing Bob Cole
and J. Rosamond Johnson's *The Red Moon* (1909), the one Broadway musical comedy that Du Bois did not despise, Du Bois requested that Cole
write protest musicals.[24] Cole's decision to decline the request—because
of the difficulties of changing totally the formula common to minstrelsy,
vaudeville, and musical comedy—points to the historic importance of Bullins's ability to match in a quite natural way, the straight and the comic.
The process with subplots might be best illustrated in *I Am Lucy Terry*
and *Storyville*. The *Terry* subplot tells the humorous story of Jinny, Lucy's
guardian and the village peacemaker. As narrator, commentator, and
comic, Jinny spares no one from hearing the truth—as fortune reveals it.
When she and Lucy first meet Abijah, for example, Jinny sets him straight:

JINNY (*startled*)
Gawd! Where did thou springest out of, black man?

ABIJAH

I'm an Indian fighter, African lady. And I'm here to protect this village
. . . especially you women.

JINNY

Protect we women, mon? By the look of thee, thou'll see nothing to
protect but little Lucy's petticoat here. Take your eyes from the child,
you brazen bush bum! She be merely a lass!

ABIJAH

Aye, mam, but a comely one.

This nosy and bossy African woman controls everything, even her master,
whom she forces to face the truth about his drinking. After defending
Lucy and Abijah's marriage, Jinny bears a child for the Native American
shaman's son, Cato. (Legend has it that Jinny's baby's cousin was the revolutionary war hero Crispus Attucks.)

Just as Bullins uses this comic subplot to relieve the tension in the
straight story, he devises a straight subplot to give substance to the love
troubles between Tigre and Butch in the musical comedy *Storyville*. This
subplot tells the story of Tigre's struggle to leave the red-light district in
order to give her son Punchie a better life. Although Tigre works all night
as a cabaret singer, she is very strict with her son. The reason is that she
wants him to be a "great classical musician"—not a jazz musician like her
father, who died "dearly from gin, TB and a broken heart"; and certainly
not like Punchie's father, a musician who, after leaving his family to go on
the road, dies broke in San Francisco. Punchie would rather not be a
classical musician, however. He enjoys playing around in Congo Square,
where he steals and returns Butch's trumpet. He and Butch become
friends, so much so that when Butch and Tigre break up, Punchie helps
get them back together, thereby creating a family. These subplots work
because they help to realize fully the serious—or the comic—messages,
which were neither attached to the end—as in Flournoy E. Miller, Aubrey
Lyles, Noble Sissle, and Eubie Blake's *Shuffle Along*—nor poured into
barely related songs and dances, as in Cole and Johnson's *The Red Moon*.
By unfolding the contrapuntual subplot throughout the play, Bullins adds
depth and lightness.

This airiness is sustained through spectacle, magic, dance, and song/
music. Bullins uses these devices for more than the usual startling of the
audience in order to make memorable some important moment in the
play.[25] All are devices for structure, production, and wonder. Magic helps
to develop structure, for example, by revealing background information
or hidden motive. In *High John*, everybody wants to know Massa's real
reason for setting up the fight between High John and "a black bully boy."
Mama Ju Ju goes to work:

MASSA

So it's a bet. You'll fight at Town Hall 'fo the month's out.
(*MASSA turns to go.*)

MAMA

[*Unseen and unheard by MASSA because SHE is within a golden halo.*]
John . . . John let me hex him a lil'. Please.
(*JOHN tries to restrain her, but SHE steps out of the halo.*)

MAMA (continued)

I's got to find out . . .
(*MASSA turns and catches sight of MAMA.*)

MASSA

Now what?

MAMA

(*Magic.*)
Curambodallah!!!
(*MASSA is struck stiff, like a zombie.*)

JOHN

Mama Ju Ju, you are oversteppin' yo . . .

MAMA

Please, let me ask him one question, John. Please. . . .

JOHN

(*Shrugs.*)
Yo gots it.

MAMA

Good. . . . Craven spirit of the bad massa. . . . Tell us why you want John to fight the baddest nigger in Mississippi an' maybe de world?

MASSA

(*Trance-like.*)
I can't wait for John to git killed. Thurty thousand dollahs is too lil' to pay to be rid of him. Also, I gits the pleasure of seein' John murder-lized . . . and (*giggle giggle*) . . . what a treat fo' mah ole racist heart would that be. . . .
(*JOHN snaps his fingers. MASSA awakes fully, but is completely oblivious to them. HE absentmindedly wanders off.*)[26]

In addition to its usefulness in exposition, magic has production value. Whether sparked by a waving hand, "space mace," blinding light, or "goofer dust," magic causes scene and light changes. In *Wheatley*, for

159

example, Lord Africa's magical gesture shows Phillis standing at the prow of the ship, looking ahead into the unknown. In *High John*, Mama Ju Ju's waving hand takes the lights down on one scene and up on another. This practical use of magic reinforces its wondrous power to make people disappear, whether in High John's making Mama Ju Ju and the Young Girl invisible to Massa by surrounding them with a colored halo, or Mama Ju Ju's vaporizing the government hit man looking for High John:

SACKMAN

High John has to be stopped. Our gent, Uncle Tom, has reported that High John is about to bring hope back to the people, and this must be stopped at all costs. . . .
(*SACKMAN pulls out his gun.*)

SACKMAN (continued)

. . . With my .357 magnum, I'll terminate High John as soon as you tell me his whereabouts, and you will tell me, or I'll . . .
(*HE points gun at MAMA JU JU and the YOUNG GIRL. MAMA JU JU makes a magical gesture and a colored cloud of steam jets out of her sleeve and throws SACKMAN back until he disappears.*)

MAMA JU JU

Oh, my goodness. A government hit man is got a contract fo' High John. We's gotta git down to the plantation to warn him.

YOUNG GIRL

Mama Ju Ju. How? What? Can you tell me what you did to Mr. Sackman?

MAMA JU JU

Ah, honey, that was just a lil of mah Space Mace.

Although Bullins uses spectacle and magic for typical purposes, his employment of song and dance is not only for the typical use of defining character, expressing personal emotion, developing plot, alternating mood, and underscoring an issue. In addition, he makes song and dance into devices for foreshadowing, bridging and summarizing, and lightening. The foreshadowing song works so well because of Bullins's signature subtlety. In *Terry*, for example, Lucy's opening chant of a magic Native American incantation ("Xune qasa sune . . . hun hun hun! / Xune qasa sune . . . hun hun hun!) foreshadows her later marriage and her commitment being shaped by the Native Americans. What make songs for preparation, bridging, and summarizing so palatable is its catchiness and humor. Bullins sometimes couches very serious themes in light lyrics, like those in *Wheatley*:

The Flow Class

We're hot shots
because we got
a big shot
on our team

Yea team
Yea team
Yea team

We're the real McCoys
above the hoi polloi
and on the beam

Yea team
Yea team
Yea team

We have a celebrity
in our house
someone who is dainty
as a mouse
she doesn't scream and shout

Yea team
Yea team
Yea team

Our investment paid off
our ship came in
we got a superslave
and we don't feel any sin

Yea team
Yea team
Yea team

We got to win
We got to win.

There is little difference between the songs in the straight music play and those in the musical comedies *Storyville* and *Sepia Star*. For example, in the former, the nightclub singer Hot Licks sings the song:

We're the Razzy Dazzy Jazzy Spasm Band
And we play this jazz for kicks
If you like to hear us play
Playin' every day,
music you know
As you're steppin' down the street
Tippy tap your feet

Come join the show
Yeah!

Feel that spasm
Feel that spasm
Jerk and jazz em
With the Old Time Spasm Band.

In *Sepia Star*, Star and Ramon get their break by performing

Sepia Star
My chocolata will go so far
I dig on you cause you taste of honey
Taste of money, Sepia Star

Sepia Star
For my chocolata I'll play guitar
You and me, baby, we'll go so far
Far from the ghetto, El Barrio

. . . .

Suckin sweet
Suckin sweet
Suckin sweet

Chocolata, Suckin sweet chocolata baby
Chocolata, Suckin sweet, chocolata baby
Chocolata, Suckin sweet chocolata baby
Suckin sweet, Tasty treat
Finer than wine.

Such catchy lyrics were nothing new to Mildred Kayden, Bullins's co-author, who had written *Pequod*, based on *Moby Dick*; she had set to music *Vanity Fair*, the *New York Times* columns of Russell Baker and excerpts from the plays of Eugene Ionesco; and she had scored such films as *The Pumpkin Coach*, *Leaven for the Cities*, and *The Procession*.[27] Many of her tunes in both *Storyville* and *Sepia Star*, therefore, are quite good. This same was not said about Bullins's book, which was considered "soft and predictable."[28] This might have been predicted since *Storyville* was his first book. Additionally, Bullins was not all that interested in the project. He was doing almost no writing in 1976 when Kayden, according to him, "physically dragged me through this 'Storyville' play, but my heart's not in it."[29] The result was a book that was close to six hours long, which some-one at the University of California at San Diego eventually cut for the premiere. Kayden felt that the cuts substantially altered the concept of the production and made the plot too one-dimensional.[30] Given his lackadaisi-cal attitude about the play in the first place, it is surprising that Bullins was so devastated by the alterations to his work:

I just got a phone call from Mildred Kayden. She says that the dress rehearsal for *Storyville* was a disaster. The U. of Cal. folk screwed it up, almost deliberately. I'm depressed. Roger Stevens from the Kennedy Center in D.C. was going out to see it. Mildred had to call him and lots of other people who could have picked up the show to back off. What a drag. All that work, sweat and blood, and some California ego-tripping academics and TV talents fuck the whole thing up. Almost maliciously. But make the best out the worse, I try and say. Maybe the *L. A. Times* reviewer will see something in it, and we can get some mileage on that. There's not much good theater out there, so they don't know quality out there when it runs up behind them and bites them in the tokus. This is really a lesson to me. A real lesson. But what have I learned?[31]

Bullins had more fun with *Sepia Star*, even poking fun at himself:

> VOICE [*to* STAR]
> Please do a short tap routine for us.
>> (*"Sweet Georgia Brown" comes on, and* STAR *taps to it. The music abruptly cuts off.*)
>
> VOICE
> Thank you . . .
>
> STAR
> Is that all? Don't you want me to read . . . Shakespeare? . . . Bullins?

Even funnier is the scene where a dreaming Star, recovering from her terrible accident, asks her boyfriend for help:

> (*JASON, dressed as the* ANGEL, *enters [the hospital room] unnoticed by* NURSES.)
>
> STAR
> You're Jason, my angel? But I always thought you were Jason, my sometimes boy friend.
>
> JASON
> Well, not now, Star, baby. I'm Jason, your boy friend, when you're awake. But now, in your death dreams, I'm your own, personal angel, Angel.
>
> STAR
> But I don't want to be an angel. And I don't like death dreams. . . . Oh, Jason, honey, take off that corny costume and do something, man. Wake me up! Huh? Make love to me or somethin'.

JASON

I can't, baby.

STAR

You . . . my Jason, the one who grinds so fine, can't make love? Well
. . . I'm not in the real world now.

JASON

That's right, Star. You're not . . . Besides, my wings would get in the
way.

Bullins got equal pleasure from writing the second type of plays in
the Musical Subclass, the five Social Type musicals. Their plots tell bal-
anced stories of innocent protagonists struggling against issue-antago-
nists. Bullins collaborated with Idris Ackamoor, a musician and performer,
and Rhodessa Jones and Danny Duncan to create three of these experimental, multi-disciplinary performance pieces: *American Griot* (1991),
first produced at La MaMa E.T.C., with direction by Ackamoor; *Raining
Down Stars* (1992), which opened at Theater Artaud in San Francisco
with Ackamoor as director; and *Emergency Report* (1993), first directed by
Ackamoor at the Lorraine Hansberry Theater in San Francisco. The historic importance of these pieces lies in Bullins's response to Locke's 1926
question about how best to "liberate" the African American "gifts of song
and dance and pantomime" from the "shambles of minstrelsy."[32] Bullins's
answer was to write the protest musicals that Bob Cole had refused to try
in 1909. Bullins solved the contradictions in clarifying versus simplifying
an issue by making his plots tell symmetrical stories. In *American Griot*,
for example, the social issues of ignored African American contributions
to America are filtered through the trying story of a jazz musician's family:
His mother is fired from her teaching position because she takes part in a
political protest. This causes one of Chicago's longest strikes, and helps a
young man to grow up. During the telling of this story, the audience is
introduced to the development of jazz, from its African connections to its
European influences. The musician, importantly, grows, so much so that
he wants to dispel myths:

> Like all black jazz musicans don't have a whole lot of women. They
> good, strong family men, and wouldn't be caught in anything wrong
> or embarrassing, like band bitches, unless abroad. . . .
>   The image of the junkie/high/out-of-control jazz musician has
> coated the lense of reality. Lester, Lady Day, Bird and so on and so
> forth are fact, but not the whole truth. This doesn't represent *all* of the
> musicians. No, some just stuck to booze and cigarettes. And some are
> working on purity, and naturalness, and spirituality, and space. . . .

164

A more enlightened young musician reveals that he works on his body. He encourages all to "Stop the drugs . . . No more booze . . . Off of tobacco . . . Get in shape. Become fit for the new world."

Raining Down Stars (1992), which Bullins wrote with Rhodessa Jones and Idris Ackamoor, explores "the cultural diversity that is found within the African American bloodline. Racial purity became a concept we attempted to dismantle, dissect, and recast; especially in light of the cultural and racial mixture that is America."[33] The piece shows that when he wishes, Bullins can be among the funniest playwrights, both in concept and language. His images in *Stars* are so outrageous and piercing that the audience often does not know if it is laughing at itself. For example, in Scene 1, written by Bullins, there is an encounter between a mad female scientist and a Changeling. The scientist salivates over having created a computerized kinky hair analyzer, called "Hair/Comb/Space/Time/Race/Continuum/Analyzer," a device that enables her to map a family tree for the past ten thousand years. The Changeling, who is unable to talk intelligibly to anybody but the scientist, thinks that her father should get credit for the invention because he is the one who financed the project. The scientist will not hear or it—especially since the father got his money from drugs. Furthermore, she smells the Nobel Prize. Scientist and Changeling fight. Scientist wins, having beaten Changeling into submission with a straightening comb. Scene 2, "Welcome to the Era of POPS!" written by Rhodessa Jones, tells of a time when anyone can have spare parts in order to look like someone of another race. The parts are called POPS, for PRESS ON PRODUCTS, which include Melanin for skin, Attack Black (for whites wishing to turn black for affirmative action purposes), Sound Brown, Press on Lips, and, for blacks, Press on Noses.

In *Emergency Report* (1993), teenagers Omar and Ameera are killed by drive-by shooters. A chorus of ghostly figures (the Oakvalley Death Crew) resurrects the two. They hear that the chorus is assigned to guide and guard all gang-age newly dead victims of gangs. The young couple learns that it is lucky to have been picked up by the Oakvalley Death Crew because the Hell's Point Mob (HPM), a rival spirit-gang, kidnaps the newly dead in order to make them into slaves. While leading Omar and Ameera to holy places, the Oakvalley Death Crew runs into Hell's Point Mob, which demands that the couple be turned over to them. A gang war among the spirits breaks out, allowing the couple to escape and to make a promised visit to the living to make them realize that they must work to strengthen the good within them in order to wipe out evil.

Collaborating on this piece were Rhodessa Jones and Danny Duncan. As with most collaborations, Bullins's synopsis differs considerably from that of the produced play, which one reviewer characterized as follows:

Emergency Report blends drive-by shooting with gospel uplift, hip-hop dance numbers and a nightmare fantasy about a promising black scholarship student who gets shot for stepping on another kid's high-price sneakers. . . . More a communal achievement than a telling social critique, *Report* has its moments of theatrical acuity. In one scene, masked actors representing a television, boom box and videocam taunt a young boy in his bedroom with their insistent messages of doom. A smooth trio of stylish back-up singers sway to the beat of a chillingly offhand chorus about the "ultimate reality—Baby, you're dead."[34]

Bullins himself thought even less of the play: "My *Emergency Report* was picked to death by my collaborators. They acted happy. They messed up my book. And even had the kids improvising long, amateurish scenes. I walked away from the project. And some of the staff and I felt we had been 'stiffed.' But I have an interesting script. Maybe I'll turn it into a novel."[35]

Bullins wrote his Social Type musical, *Sinning in Sun City* (1987), with the South African playwright Salaelo Maredi. First directed by Maredi at Buriel Clay Memorial Theatre in San Francisco, this musical comedy indicts America's contributions to apartheid in South Africa. The plot centers on two American entertainers (Jeffrey, an African American man, and Sharlene, a white woman), who perform in Bophuthatswana, the South Africa-created country-of-political-convenience popularly known as Sun City. The performers' producer-host, Victor, who is infatuated with white women, takes the Americans to his village, where he is considered a traitor to the political aspirations of his people. Victor's brother, Monnanyana, verbally attacks all of them. This helps Jeffrey and Sharlene fully understand the implications of their performing in Sun City. Sharlene apologizes for her "sin" of having broken the performer-boycott of Sun City. Jeffrey breaks their three-million dollar contract. They spurn all of Victor's bribes before they leave for the United States.

What distinguishes the play is the authors' presentation of a hard-hitting political message within a frothy form designed for high entertainment. The difficulty in such a project is in delighting and entertaining an audience while clarifying such a serious subject as apartheid, which requires people to ponder the significance of their own actions or beliefs. The authors' problem is how both to clarify and delight. Bullins and Maredi solve the problem by making people laugh at the norm, a reversal of the tradition of making fun of the abnormal. Interestingly, although the authors make fun of the typical, their humor derives from atypical and cross-cultural comments and actions: Victor, for example, calls his ancestral home "The Ponderosa"; Joyce and Sharlene slap hands and say "Right on"; and

166

VICTOR

I just wanted to extend my cordial invitation to you all to join my family and me in the celebration of my parents' fifty-fourth anniversary.

JEFFREY

Where, Victor? Around here in Sun City?

VICTOR

No, man. Out in the village.

JOYCE

It's about seven miles.

JEFFREY looks at SHARLENE.

JEFFREY

Village, heh? Are we going to do that voodoo stuff, brotherman?

SHARLENE

Well, I don't think . . .

VICTOR

Oh, no! My parents are civilized, brotherman. We live in the modern world, babee, with a toilet almost inside the house.[36]

Equally as important as the wit and slapstick are the songs, which explain and develop the plot while advocating an issue. The issues include the customary submission of one's body for a job and money, the sale of one's principles, and the inhumanity of the very idea of a Sun City:

How insensitive one can be
To sing, dance,
Wine and dine in a brothel
Where young women are robbed
Of their virginity and become
Child bearing machines

   . . . .

Go on, you vampires,
Sing, dance
Wine and dine in Bophutha-Tswana
The brothel home
The mass grave
Take no notice of the dead.
They're only black
They're only black corpses
So, sing and dance . . . it's
Art for Art sake.

Although this rebuke characterizes the intent of *Sinning in Sun City*, the play ends positively, welcoming all who have "sinned" to

> Come back, brother
> Come back to the people
> They need you.
> Don't be caught up in this
> Commercial world
>
> .   .   .   .
>
> Freedom shall come
> Not through Sun City
> Riches we shall have
> Not through Sun City
> Presidents we shall be
> Not through Sun City
>
> .   .   .   .
>
> Sinning in Sun City
> Sinning in Sun City
> Sinning in Sun City
> Sinning in Sun City

Like *Sinning in Sun City*, *Home Boy* (1976), the final Social Type play in the Musical subclass, focuses on land—this time that belonging to African Americans. The musical argues that African Americans should stay on their land (or in their space) and make careful plans for their future. Two buddies (Jody, 20, and Dude, 16) pass through the rites of growing up, each fantasizing about having the riches offered by distant places. Consequently, they pay little attention to their present lives, causing each to be in less than desirable situations five years later, prompting further dreaming but little actual planning. A decade later, therefore, they are strung out on drugs in one of the dream-places. They fancy going home "to change things" for their people. They now realize, though, that they must first change themselves.

Bullins tells this simple tale in a most complicated way, using six actors to play the two boys at the three stages (or "Time States") in their lives: 1950, 1955, the 1965. Additionally, there are three "Eternal Women of Timelessness" and four "Ageless/Always Presences." The play winds back and forth sixteen times, the episodes connected either by a slight subplot or a song-and-dance routine. As if this is not enough for the audience to follow, the songs, unfortunately, simply repeat the sentiments already expressed in the play's dialogue. In the second episode, for example, Dude, a visitor from Philadelphia, tells Jody, a native of Maryland's Eastern Shore (Bullins's vacation spot as a child) about real city life:

168

DUDE

All the city got is cold concrete streets, and buildings reaching along the sides like a window-paned canyon . . . and the wind blows through like a rolling power saw. . . . There's nothin' to find but blues north . . . and broken futures . . . and welfare for the weak and witless . . . if they be lucky. . . . Stay in your land, brotherman . . . your fathers would have wanted it.

This fine prose poetry dialogue introduces the theme song, sung by the boys' girlfriends, May Lee and Emma:

Stay in your
land
brotherman
there's
only your
nation
for you
Stay in your
land
brotherman
your hope
for the
future
is before
you
Stay on your
land
brotherman
whether
it's
Philly
PA.
or Georgia.
Stay on your
land
brotherman
where you
at
is
where you
is
Stay in your
land

brotherman
your women
and children
are the
hope
and they
adore you.

Although the playful lyrics are catchy, this typical repetition of an already-expressed idea slows the development of the book—but not so much so to prevent the critic Edith Oliver from calling the performance "lively and satisfying."[37] She especially liked Aaron Bell's music and the dance by Judith Dearing. In fact, the show, which was first produced at the Perry Street Theater in New York with Patricia Golden as director, was nominated for an AUDELCO Award as the best Musical Production of 1976–77. One reason for winning the award, oddly enough, might have been the fact that the play's repetitiveness worked well to emphasize Bullins's serious social statements about the Korean war, family disintegration, substance abuse, economic discrimination, union busting, and sexual abuse, as well as wistful dreaming instead of planning:

JODY 1

And I'm goin' to get me a car . . . a big hawg . . . long as a city block. Yeah . . . I'm gonna git me a 'chine. Long . . . and shiney . . . with glass and rubber . . . and real leather on the seats. My car . . . my car is gonna have windows that roll down by electricity . . . huh, I'll just have to sit back and push little buttons. And I'm gonna have a bar in my car . . . a bar . . . and serve drinks as I cruise down the highway of happiness with the air conditioner on. It'll ride better than Dynaflow . . . better than anything really 'cept 'n airplane . . . yeah . . . a jet airplane.

Bullins's Romantic Type musicals, the third category in the Musicals Subclass, are the revues *House Party* (1973), first produced at the American Place Theatre and directed by Roscoe Orman, and also known as *Women I Have Known* (1976), which premiered at the American Place Theatre. Both revues ignore the traditional love-story formula of having two lovers pulled apart by fate. Bullins makes egos and social conditions the lovers' troubles. In *House Party*, for example, twenty-five people complain about everything from being seduced and abandoned to being misunderstood. Bullins takes these characters—as well as the dialogue—from his *Street Sounds* (1970), which consists of forty-seven monologues. For *House Party*, he intersperses one monologue with another, converting previous monologues into dialogue. Lover Man, for example, recites his "lines" to Seduced & Abandoned, whose monologue is so well cut that she appears to respond. The same happens with Black Writer and Girl Friend. All monologues remain intact, but are put to different uses. Scrap Book Keeper, for example, becomes master of ceremonies. Other monologues, like Wild Chile, remain intact.

For the second Romantic revue, *Women I Have Known* (1974), Bullins uses only those female *Street Sounds* monologues that deal with sexual experiences and with man troubles. There are, again, Seduced & Abandoned—followed by the same chorus from *House Party*: Fun Lovin', The Quitter, The Loved One, The Groover, Wild Chile, Virgin and so on. These Romantic revues, significantly, show that producer/director Bullins has no qualms about putting the knife and suture to playwright Bullins when there is some money to be made.[38]

The fourth type of the Musical Subclass, Personality, usually celebrates the lives of leaders and entertainers—often by using their music. Bullins chose the jazz trumpeter Louis (Satchmo) Armstrong and the rhythm and blues artists Ike and Tina Turner. The unproduced and unpublished play *Satchmo* (1981) examines the relationship between Armstrong and his mentor, Joe "King" Oliver. The book for this musical is among Bullins's least successful efforts. The principal reason is that the plot has no overriding conflict. It simply details the two men's encounters, from their first meeting at the Funky Butt Hall in New Orleans to Armstrong's first Carnegie Hall performance, which he dedicated to Oliver. Sandwiched in between are scenes that show Armstrong organizing his first band in a New Orleans waif's home, where he gets his nickname Satchelmouth—changed by Oliver to Satchmo; playing his first gig with Oliver and the development of their father-son relationship; Oliver's departure for Chicago; Armstrong starting his own band and marrying his first wife, Daisy, a woman whom he later divorces because she cannot give up "entertaining" the sailors; Oliver sending for Armstrong to join him in Chicago; and Armstrong becoming such a big hit in Chicago that he eclipses Oliver. These incidents are related through flashbacks after Armstrong discovers Oliver, who is down on his luck, working as a peanut hawker at a Savannah, Georgia, train station. There is too little humor, however, and too much exposition along with almost no sustained tension between the principals, thereby making the Armstrong-Oliver scenes boring.

Although Bullins uses the same flashback device in the other Personality Type play, there is much more dramatic tension in *I Think It's Gonna Work Out Fine: A Rock and Roll Fable* (1989)—written with Idris Ackamoor, Rhodessa Jones, and Brian Freeman. First directed by Ackamoor at the The South of Market Climate Theater in San Francisco, the revue is a dramatization loosely based on the well-known triumphs and tribulations of the singer Tina Turner. The two-act musical opens with the world-famous Rita secretly returning to a run-down Dew Drop Palace to help her former husband Prince Golden get back on his feet. She says: "I went up, and you went down. It makes me sick every time I read about your latest escapade. . . . Prince, how did you get so low?" This sparks Prince's retort that when he first met Rita, she was the definition of "low," which introduces the flashback covering their meeting: She, an admiring fan of this well-known musician—and "hot-tempered street hustler,"[39] is from a very religious family. It is hush-hush, therefore, that she is even at the club—not to mention that she auditions for him with "Elijah Rock." He teaches her the ropes, and he meets her "bible-beating" family, which leaves little doubt that it wants nothing to do with him. Rita's decision to run away appears to have been a good one—until after they become big names with two children, when he turns so brutal and abusive because of her star quality that she decides finally to leave him:

RITA (washing feet)

Moma said, "That man is gonna make you wring your hands and cry. You gonna rue the day you didn't listen to me." Daddy said, "Swamp seed, you make your bed hard, you gonna have to lie in it." Wrennetta say, "I'm glad daddy didn't live to see this; you sacrificing yourself to a man who ain't worth the bullets it would take to kill him." Well, I'm rueing. I'm sacrificing. And I'm lying in a bed that don't get no harder than this. (RITA knocks on bed.) Are you'all happy? I'm not. (Innocently) He's so good and kind. And with just a little love and support, he'll change. (RITA shakes HER head sadly) Yet, here I am singing all the time, everywhere and never hearing my own voice. (Introspectively) "Use your thinkin' thoughts, gal. Time to get gone. Find yourself a new home. Gotta grab a piece of the sky." (SHE turns upstage.) Prince Jr! Tyrone! Get dressed. We're leaving. (SHE turns back to audience.) I don't know where. I'm just walking.[40]

Rita sings "Breaking Up Is So Hard to Do." Time returns to the present by means of the entrance of Prince wearing clothes from the opening scene. Rita gives him money on the condition that he not contact her or the children within five years, that he donate 50 percent of his royalties to the R. Love Center for Battered Women, and that he attend a support group for those who abuse their spouses. He agrees. She leaves. Then Prince's other self lets the absent Rita know that he believes that she is shortsighted:

See, Rita. That's part of your problem. You could never see the future. After this club takes off, I'm gonna invest in a radio station. How you gonna have a say in the music if you don't have a piece of the action?

Black musicians, we have to be the movers and shakers. Own things. Reclaim things. For future generations. You thought you were slick, breaking up the act. Running off with those white boys. But this rock and roll thing can get old quick. A follow-up to a million seller does not always materialize. And admiration can change to patronization overnight. That's why you have to control your stuff. Rhythm and blues wasn't taken away from us. Shit we gave it away.

This incident grants to Prince a maturity that was never evident in the character's real-life model, Ike Turner. The fact that this important message, which makes the play a substantial statement on racism in the music industry,[41] is delivered by Prince, who still makes the papers with stories about "drugs . . . the police . . . cancelled gigs," would seem to discredit somewhat the critic Beth Coleman's notion that Rita is a driving force who lived to tell about it.[42] Having the self-destructive Prince deliver an indictment of an exploitative entertainment industry to his own victim seems to have compromised Bullins's otherwise "sharply defined" characters,[43] along with his "direct and divine" theme.[44] This slight flaw does not hurt the play, however, which, as the critic Stephen Holden pointed out, is "an unusually clear-eyed, unsentimental book" that contains "crackling" dialogue.[45] *I Think It's Gonna Work Out Fine* must be considered "a tight and funny"[46] "archetypal American story of social mobility, race, and black-on-black violence."[47]

Not even this fine work, however, can match *The Work Gets Done* (1980), Bullins's only play of the Sacred Type, the final type in the Musicals Subclass. This type aims to inspire audiences with stories about people who find love and peace. *The Work Gets Done* tells the story of a husband and wife—called simply Man and Woman—who meet again after a long separation caused by his "sleeping around." They trade insults, compliments, memories, and frustrations. They talk out their differences, viewed by Man as no more than the differences between any man and woman: Man is made to wander; Woman to be the faithful conscience. Seeing no repentance on his part, Woman starts to leave, only to be stopped by a Female Figure—dressed in a veil and a dancer's body-suit. She teaches Woman to play again. Man criticizes her for being out of shape, which causes her outburst:

WOMAN

Negativity . . . in the air . . . slip . . . (*mumbles*) . . . slip . . . (*clears mind*) . . . slipping . . . Oh, Great Spirit, save me from negativity, and forgive my transgressions . . . spare me from foul thoughts . . . point me toward the true the strong and . . .

MAN

Now you want to make me feel guilty. But I'm not going to.

173

A Male Figure, wearing a different color suit, enters to teach Man to
lighten up. The Male Figure and the Female Figure inspire Man to overcome his depression/block. The figures not only break up Man and Woman's fights, but they also encourage Man to show Woman more love. When
Man and Woman truly reconcile their differences, the figure turn into
children. The individuals become a family.

What makes this piece so powerful is its style and language. The absurdist nature of the latter alerts the spectator to expect the rapid flow not
only of ideas but also of events:

WOMAN

You! . . . Is that you?

MAN

Well, it's me all right. . . . But, you do know me, don't ya?

WOMAN

Oh, my yes. Oh, most certainly. You're you.

MAN

Yes . . . I'm me. . . . And you?

WOMAN

Oh, I'm just me. You know me, don't you? Have I changed that much?

MAN

Changed? Now that you mention it, well, there is a difference . . . of
sorts . . . in you. But. But! There is a similarity also.

WOMAN

Really! Do I know you? And you me? In fact, have we ever met?

MAN

I don't think so . . . but . . . there's something faintly . . . faintly . . .

WOMAN

Familiar. Yes.

MAN

Yes, perhaps I did know you. When we both were younger.[48]

Only when the spectators accept the absurdist premise does Bullins
interrupt their enjoyment of this repartee to interject the business at hand,
delivered by Man in a discursive style and rejected by Woman as mere
"pretension":

MAN

You know, I feel great. I've accepted middle age. And I'm loving life
and not giving much of damn about people who—

174

WOMAN

Who cares?

MAN

Well, I do, of course.

WOMAN

But nobody else gives anything for your trite reveries about your navel
. . . or penis, or whatever.

MAN

Look, if taxes, inflation and debt hasn't destroyed me, I'm not allowing you to get to me.

WOMAN

Really!

MAN

I love life. And if it ended this very second, I would be satisfied that
I, at least, did part of the work I was sent here to do.

WOMAN

(Ridicule)
Work? You were sent here to do? Like what? Layin' on the couch with
a bottle of gut-buster, lookin' at the Superjock Show? . . . And you
were sent here by who?
(HE ignores her and gives a speech to the AUDIENCE.)

MAN

The other political, artistic and cultural social figures of the by-gone
decades have disappeared, except in memory, diminished because of
their lack of substance, their reliance on hollow rhetoric and ideological cant and bugga boo.

WOMAN *(cutting in)*

Say, man, I want to talk to you.

MAN

I've lasted because I've kept my artistic vision, whatever the circumstances, however grim. *(Points to WOMAN.)* And I've sentenced myself
to the task of teaching a difficult, hard-earned skill; plus, living with
flair, to this monstrous vibration of these times, the not becoming too
filled by my own bullcorn.

This is not really the work that needs to get done, however. Man's—
and Woman's—most important work is to become a family. Bullins makes
this heavy theme through such light devices as childhood songs, games,

175

and actions. Female Figure, for example, stops Woman from leaving Man again simply by singing:

Teddy Bear, Teddy Bear, turn around
Teddy Bear, Teddy Bear, touch the ground
Teddy Bear, Teddy Bear, shine your shoes
Teddy Bear, Teddy Bear, read the news
Teddy Bear, Teddy Bear, how old are you

To help Woman gain her composure, Female Figure and Woman jump rope as they count from one to thirty-five. When Woman becomes so angry with Man that she cries inconsolably, Female Figure gives Man a flower, which he caresses and then places in Woman's hair. She stops crying. Man sings:

Flowers
Flowers in your
hair
you bear them
a halo
in your hair

.   .   .   .   .   .

your eyes
brown bark
your skin
dark
velvet violet/like
skin

Flowers
Flowers in your
eyes
you reflect me
a lover
in the garden
of you.

This little musical piece shows how grave themes might be presented in light forms without heavy-handed preaching and wailing. Although a formidable task that has eluded many dramatists, Bullins considerably improves this mixture in the Forms Subclass, which, through four types, fills fun structures with quite substantive thought. The first type is the Happening, *The Play of the Play* (1973). In this performance piece, the audience is locked inside a room with wide, bare walls, except for some panels and murals that complement the lighting. When the lights go down, the audience sees colors and images (spots, light shows, slides, film projections, televised images, and so forth). Every sound in the audience and in the "acting" space is broadcast throughout the room by means of unseen microphones placed in the audience and under the floor. Music with a heavy beat, played by unseen musicians, encourages the audience to dance. Heard over the music is poetry, along with compelling speeches or "anything else" that can be conveyed through lights, images, sounds, movements, and colors.[49]

Although this happening might appear to be just a rip-off of paying customers, *The Play of the Play*, significantly, was ranked as the "purposefully composed form of theatre in which diverse alogical elements, including nonmatrixed performing, are organized in a compartmented structure."[50] The first of five qualities that make *Play of the Play* a Happening, according to the critic Michael Kirby, is the panels and murals. These in most happenings are abstract or surreal. Therefore, in order that the observer would not look for any meaning beyond the paintings' "own special qualities and physical characteristics," *Play* might exhibit Bernie Casey's surrealistic "Schizophrenic Moon Folly" (1968), Eugenia V. Dunn's "Brush Fire over Arkansas" (1964), Donald O. Greene's expressionistic "Antelers" (1965), or Samella S. Lewis's "Banyon" (1965).

The second mark of a Happening is that it consists of nine events (participants, paintings, colored lights, colored images, broadcast sounds, along with music, dance, poetry, and speech), none of which are in any way connected—either causally or associationally. Each is a "hermetic scene." Such sealed episodes, like the paintings, are chosen only for the sake of the experience, the third criterion of a Happening. For example, the compelling speeches, heard after the poetry and music, might be orated as the audience enters the space. Even the speeches carry no "rational public meaning or duty beyond stirring the listener on an unconscious and alogical level." They are chosen, instead, only for the joy of sound and for the sound's sake. The choice of the scene only for the sake of the experience offered by that incident means that *Play* as a whole follows no irreplaceable order or logic. The structure of *Play*, therefore, consists of "compartmented scenes," which differ from other kinds of scenes in that the demarcations might be a single grunt or dance or flashing image. Because each scene is sealed and unconnected, the structure consists not of exposition, development, climax, and conclusion but of what is observed—the fourth element of a Happening found in *Play*. The final signal is the nonmatrixed performances, which means that any audience member who dances, talks, screams, or simply sits is performing. Because this "performing" is without a context or imaginary time and place, however, the activities are "nonmatrixed performances."[51] Although the fact that Bullins even tried his hand at Happening shows how adventuresome he is as a writer, the truth is that this Happening, insofar as obeying laws of structure is concerned, is not too far removed from anything else that Bullins had written.

The second type in the Forms Subclass, Prose Poetry, more so than any of the other types, consciously infuses the dialogue with what Locke terms accents of rhythm in prose, verse, and music, including color and tone of imagery, idiom and timbre of emotion and symbolism. Bullins wrote two of these types: *Street Sounds* (1973), first produced by La Mama's GPA Nucleus, Hugh Gittens, director; and *Salaam, Huey Newton, Salaam* (1993), which premiered at the Ensemble Studio Theatre in New York, with Woodie King Jr. directing. As previously indicated, *Street Sounds*, a performance piece, is composed of forty-seven monologues about African American life. The characters are the typical array of African American urban dwellers: self-styled black heroes, self-hating blacks, junkies, flunkies, intellectuals, revolutionaries, groovers, losers, rappers, soul sisters and brothers, as well as a snooty black critic and a pompous black lady poet.[52] There are moments of rage, but more often Bullins's weapon is wry humor: the seduced virgin who suddenly turns bossy; the black man who apologizes for his white wife; the chatty bowler who marries for a place to stay; the wistful thief who dreams, "I wish I had me a typewriter, I'd sell it and get me something to get high on."[53]

Typical of most critical reactions to *Street Sounds* is the view of the *New York Times* critic Mel Gussow that Bullins's dramatization of these "real people with real problems" makes for "refreshingly original, specific, and very effective theatre." Gussow added, importantly, that Bullins's tone manages to be both cooly ironic and lovingly sympathetic—sometimes seemingly mean but always caring.[54] There lies the same problem that fooled Jules Irving in *Duplex: Street Sounds* is a primrose path. Behind what appears to be a refreshingly loving picture of some corner people in the African American community is a blistering indictment of the people. Every monologue—viewed not only from the character's perspective but also from the author's—elucidates and opposes an endemic and devastating flaw in human nature and/or organization. Bullins analyzes roughly twenty-one conditions, covering almost every human blemish. He begins with the well-covered crisis of the absent father. The take on the problem by the character Seduced & Abandoned, however, is so intensely personal that the predicament is almost disguised:

> By why? . . . Why? . . . I love you. . . . But why do this to me? Why? Why? . . . Do I deserve this? Is this right? I ain't much to look at. We both always knew that. I know I'm awkward and clumsy . . . but you said you love me. I'm black with a flat, wide nose and big lips. You said you admired me because of my mind . . . ha ha . . . You married me because of my ability to understand you, you said. I didn't want a

child. I only wanted to be with you and for us to go on together. Oh, baby . . . oh, baby . . . please please please . . . don't do this to me . . . Oh, baby . . . I'm not just askin' for me . . . My ego ain't that much, honey, really. Remember . . I've even worked since we been together so that you could keep doin' the things you need to do. So I'm not just askin' for me . . . Not really for me, honey. It's for you . . . for you yourself. How can you be the man you always said you wanted to be if you do this . . . if you abandon me and our baby . . . oh, baby. . . .

Oh, man, I don't like to cry . . . don't make me . . . don't make me, baby. Why? Why . . . you make me want to die at such an early age, man?

Bullins's views of black male chauvinism and egomania are equally as engaging but deadly ("My work will grow through the years in importance, naturally, and command great sums after my death, no doubt"). Bullins shows a special contempt for confidence-breaking (The Rememberer and The Loser), for making excuses to do nothing (Trapped), and especially for economic exploitation of the black community:

Yeah . . . and this is your Jivin' Jones' hippy dippy SOUL hour . . . Yeah! Jivin' Jones . . . the hip one. . . . Jivin' Jones . . . brought to you by the Primitive Products Co . . . created by your friendly neighborhood Jew . . . Abe Goldblatt . . . Mr. Abe give you a full line of Afro hair products . . . Afro Keep, Afro Cool, Afro Out and Afro Keen. For all you groovy, *together* Black folks. Swingin'. Yeah . . . the Jivin' Jones hip SOUL hour. Remember . . . Afro Primitive Products . . . 'cause Mr. Abe says "BLACK MEANS BUY!" . . . Hit it! The Jivin' Jones SOUL hour. Yeah! Niggers got more records than books . . . yeah, dance your lives away . . . yeah . . . Jivin' Jones will tell you, listen Black people . . . while you jive your lives away.

Bullins rebukes families for thwarting a member's ambitions (Black Writer) when they do not coincide with what the group wants. He reprimands all kinds of get-over artists, from the obvious street hustlers (Corner Brother, The Thief, Confused and Lazy, the Dope Seller) to the white-collar ones (New Negro Publisher, Black Student, the Harlem Politician). Their flaws are almost as lamentable as the intellectual impotence of the wordsmiths (Black Revolutionary Artist, The Theorist, and The Rapper), or the mindless idealism of The Bowler and the Workin' Man, or the specious friendliness in Bewildered, or the pseudo feminism of The Quitter, which was the prototype for the characters in *Leavings* almost a decade later. Of special interest is Bullins's indictment—a decade before President Ronald Reagan took office—of what became the Reagan Administration's

179

money-saving policy of emptying psychiatric hospitals. This is seen in the tragic case of Traffic Man, who directs at a busy intersection:

> You think I'm crazy, don't ya? . . . Don't ya? . . . Well, I may be . . . and I may be not. . . . Hee ha ha . . . got cha fooled, ain't I? Just 'cause you see me blowin' this tin police whistle and swingin' this fake head-whuppin' stick and directin' traffic with my play badge on, wearin' my dirty sneakers and greasy officer's cap . . . don't make me out to be crazy . . . understand? . . . I'm just takin' care of . . . uhmmm . . . that's why I'm blowin' this whistle in the middle of the street fo'. And tellin' this here traffic where to go. It's my job. Mine! Well, nobody had to give it to me . . . but somebody did. Long time ago. And I'm the only one who knows who that was. So if you'll excuse me . . . I'll get back to work. The traffic's backin' up on the uptown side of the street. Now looka here . . . I know what you think' an' all . . . an' it's confused thinkin' I'm a professional man . . . just doin' my job. Don't be thinkin' I'm crazy. Crazy folks locked up where they should be. They ain't out here doin' services to mankind. You can understand that, can't you? . . . Good. Now I got to get back to work . . . fo' my boss calls me up.

Bullins studies the various kinds of race hatred in *Street Sounds*. There is the classic white police brutality:

> Yeah . . . beat him . . . beat his ass . . . beat his ass, I say . . . yeah . . . give it to him . . . crack his damn ribs. Break the bastard's head! Use your club more . . . yeah . . . like that . . . like that. Don't forget your hose . . . yeah . . . that's right . . . Ooooooo. Jesus! . . . the blood. Christ! . . . you're give'n that boy just what he deserves . . . the Black Panther . . . the black nigger . . . the Black protestor . . . the Black student . . . the Black bastard. . . .

This hatred pales in comparison to the devastating self-hatred caused by one's own race—as seen in Slightly Confused: A black man who is married to a white woman goes with his white friend's black wife, but would never think of marrying her because he hates her "for talking black and sleeping white." Then there is the Pan-African hatred of Young West Indian Revolutionary Poet, who believes that Continental Africans are stupid for looking down on Africans in the diaspora because "we were not born in Africa." African Americans are not that much better, Poet believes, because they reject most other African peoples for being "foreigners." West Indians, too, do not think too much of African Americans because they "were born in America," which means that they are lazy and expect handouts. The poet demands—rather confusedly—that "we unite in revolution as one people."

The race haters are only a rung up the ladder from the plain self-haters (The Reconciled, The Virgin, and Fried Brains) and three steps above these selfish individualists (Non-Ideological Nigger, Woman Poet, The Loved One, The Explainer, and The Recluse). The race haters are also fifteen risers above the sexual predators (Lover Man, Fun Lovin', The Doubter, The Groover, and Wild Chile) and nineteen treads below those mired in urban decay (Errand Boy, The Oldtimer, and Harlem Mother). The most noteworthy monologue, however, belongs to Black Critic, whom Bullins uses to voice the early criticism so often hurled at himself.

> This type of expression just has got to stop! What you do is not art, is not playwriting or theater or anything worthwhile. . . . Look at what you are doing to yourself and the negative image of the race you create. We've had it hard enough. We don't need to be showing *them* that side of us. It's a disgrace, that's what it is. I wasn't raised that way. Nobody I knew was. We were refined, man. And here you are, at this late date, creating profanity, filth and obscenity and displaying it to the masses, the Black people you so hypocritically harp about forever into the future, as art and culture. You should be ashamed of yourself, you cynical pimp! You hustler, you. You nigger con man. The idea; those awful despairing figures you deal with are grotesque the totally uncalled for and unrealistic. The work lacks range and its author fails to demonstrate a measurable degree of responsibility to the depiction of the unlettered masses. The very rudiments of the fine art of dramaturgy are not adhered to. It's a disgrace! Why should he be allowed to continue doing this filth and denigrating the people? Can we allow this not-so-disguised pornography to continue to infect the community? The people should not stand for it! . . . As a theater craftsman, it's as if he never heard of the word craft, not to mention art, as I've said previously, above. This so-called artist cannot continue doing just as he pleases with our Black Art. He's immoral. He takes all and gives nothing. Those dirty things he does and says up on stage can't even be mentioned by responsible Black people and critics, like me. Black people, we are the ones to lose in this situation. Sure is a heavy game. I wanna thank you. Just doin' mah thang. Salaam, ahki. Kill the night blackness and groove.

Such hardhitting—and Du Boisian—blows had come from those of Bullins's critics who never understood the difference between his images and messages, or, for that matter, the messages of the images—as seen, for example, in the second—and more subtle-type of Prose Poem play: *Salaam, Huey Newton, Salaam* (1993). The source of the material is the poet Marvin X's "Autobiography of a North American African," then a work in progress. The slight plot dramatizes Marvin X's last encounter with the

Black Panther Party leader Huey P. Newton before Newton's murder on 22 August 1989. As Marvin, Huey, and Young Brother smoke crack, the former two reminisce about people and events of the sixties. They depart. Marvin reports that Huey is killed.

This short one-act play is distinguished by its utterly simple structure, timely theme, and poetic imagery. The structure, an adaptation of Greek tragedy, contains an opening that reveals not only background but also outcome. Bullins uses the character Marvin X as the *prologos* chorus, discovered in the *Orchestra* (or playing area) of a street corner beside the powerful symbol of the fallen Cypress Expressway. This chorus, significantly, also establishes "the ethical framework of the events and sets up a standard against which the action might be judged."[55]

Immediately after taking a hit from the crack pipe, the choric Marvin announces the theme: Get help for your addictions. Bullins then has the chorus narrate the consequences of not obeying the theme. He does this not through the action of the play but through the display of the chorus himself. The spectators learn, for example, that the chorus, too, has had a tragic life: he was once a "strong," learned, and economically comfortable entrepreneur. He discovered his tragic flaw, a love of crack, only in his fortieth year. Crack made him lose all: songs of praise to Allah, as well as to his "beautiful parents," to "beautiful brothers and sisters," to "beautiful, intelligent women," and to his "most beautiful children." Bullins considers this loss so important that he gives it music:

MARVIN chants.

I lost my wife behind the pipe
I lost my children
behind the pipe
I lost my money
behind the pipe
I lost my house
behind the pipe
I lost my mind
behind the pipe
I lost my life
behind the pipe[56]

This *prologos* dirge not only telegraphs and telescopes the downfall of the title tragic hero, but it also personalizes the full action of the play. This particularization creates spectator-empathy, which is, of course, a prerequisite of tragedy. This compassion cannot be generated by the body of the play because the episodes move so swiftly. The audience's sympathy is guaranteed by a tale whose horror depends, in great part, on a comparison of the tragic hero's conditions before and after The Addiction.

182

The *stasima* (or middle episodes) precede the introduction of the chorus's foil, Young Brother, and of the title character:

MARVIN

We walked toward the basketball court. . . . A brother passed us looking like the bum of the week . . .

A FIGURE enters, passing MARVIN and YOUNG BROTHER.

MARVIN (cont'd)

. . . Now I don't recall if I was looking a hell of a lot better . . . maybe a little better, since I was in a drug program at Glide Church in San Francisco. Reverend Cecil Williams was doing everything he could to help me regain my sanity. . . . *(Calls to figure)* Say, brother . . . don't I know you?

The FIGURE half turns and looks at MARVIN and YOUNG BROTHER.

MARVIN *(narrates)*

But the bum needed a shave and a hair cut. Something told me this bum was my old friend . . . so I called him. Hey, Huey!

The FIGURE walks toward MARVIN.

HUEY NEWTON

Hey, Jackmon . . . what's happening?

HUEY and MARVIN embrace. Then MARVIN, hands upon each of HUEY's shoulders, looks at him closely.

MARVIN (proudly)

Dr. Huey P. Newton

With this close of the *prologos* and beginning of the *stasima*, Bullins inverts the Greek tragic structure. Instead of introducing the tragic hero during his rising fortunes (or in his glory), the spectator sees first the tragic result of his downfall, displayed not on the *ekkyclema* but in living (dis) color. Continuing the reversal, Bullins fills the *stasima* with episodes extolling the former glory of both the tragic hero and the tragic chorus: Huey brags that Marvin taught him; Marvin praises Huey for introducing him to the African America Great Books; Marvin honors Huey as one of "the craziest Black men in the hells of North America"; Huey boasts of surviving death row three times; and Marvin honors Huey for having "changed the course of history for Black people." To assist the spectator in further appreciating Huey's fall, Bullins continually contrasts these proud achievements with Newton's present disgrace—matched, no doubt, by his alleged abuses of power, as well as of women.[57] With rhetoric as empty as that of the Rapper's in *Street Sounds*, Bullins shows Newton's infamy:

HUEY *(serious)*

Too many people lost their lives behind Eldridge [Cleaver]. There's too much blood on the path between us, man. Too much blood. So

183

even though I might want to get together with him . . . out of respect to the loved ones of those comrades who went down, I cannot deal with him. I will not deal with him.

MARVIN

Why not, Huey? . . . Hell, Arabs kill each other in Lebanon and Jordan, but the next day they're in the mosque praying together. King Hussein of Jordan massacred Palestinians, but Yassar Arrafat is still talking with him. Why can't Black men come together? . . .

You know our community needs signs and symbols of unity. You see what condition our youths are in. (*Points to* YOUNG BROTHER) Look at this fool sitting over there.

HUEY

Yeah, I know they disrespect us, Jackmon.

MARVIN

You're the general, get on your post, soldier.

The sadness of this talk is that it becomes but the doxology for a funeral. Bullins makes the spectator see this in Young Brother. Trying to belong, he sings the ironic refrain: "Yeah, Huey, I really respect you." Even Huey understands the praise to be disrespectful: Young Brother doesn't know or care about the historic importance of this celebrated presence, causing him to challenge Huey to "throw down." Young brother is not even impressed that Huey has three times escaped dying on death row. When chastised by Marvin—told, in fact, that Huey is "one of the craziest nigguhs in the world . . . and one of the most violent"—. Young Brother shrugs it off: "Man, I don't care. I'm a man just like he is. He can end up in a box like anybody else." Bullins uses his *epilogos* (or closing episode) in ways that marry the tragic and comedic forms. Although the choric Marvin laments the murder of Huey, the born-again revolutionary Marvin closes the play on a happy note: "I have no doubt that I will fully recover from crack. Each day I get stronger and stronger. I shall return to the battlefield." This returns the action full circle to the *prologos*. It occasions a call to arms—as in expressionism—to fight crack, a theme heightened by the play's elegiac and rich language, which is sprinkled with the common vernacular, figurative speech, image-filled narrative, stylized construction, the rhythmic prose:

MARVIN

For those of us still addicted to crack cocaine, we should feel blessed that we're still alive and have the chance to save our souls, for the sake of ourselves, our families and our community. . . . I have no doubt that I will fully recover from crack. Each day I get stronger and stronger. I shall return to the battlefield. I have no choice except to fight or die. For sure, the Black Nation is at war with America. America is using chemical and germ warfare against us—crack, AIDS—along with an infinite supply of guns for our self-destruction.

The main weapon we have is our spirit. We must reclaim our spirit, which is the spirit of God. We are in Him and He is in us. When we forget this, we fall victim to the great lie that all is lost. Yeah, it's raining now, but look, see the sun coming through the clouds. See the rainbow?

Rise my people. Rise from the projects, rise from the hills, rise and reclaim our souls. A warrior has fallen. But we must continue until victory. But the greatest battle is to win our souls. And for that reminder, I thank you, Huey. Salaam, Huey, salaam.

The play generated considerable nonpublic controversy. In a follow-up letter to a telephone call in which Marvin X reportedly screamed repeatedly at Bullins's agent Helen Merrill, Marvin X made a serious accusation[58]: "I'm really tired of going through changes regarding my material, which Ed Bullins stole from me. I never gave him permission to use any of my material in any way, shape, or form, and I'm thoroughly disgusted with this entire matter of stolen material and now stolen royalties. I would like you to inform Mr. Bullins to stop fucking with my material or anything derived from my material."[59] Bullins dismissed the letter:

> Though it would seem otherwise, Marvin and I are still friendly. We run into each other every few months and have a good, friendly chat, usually on BART [Bay Area Rapid Transit] or a bus. He told me a couple of weeks ago that his ex-girlfriend got his [royalty] check. . . . She's mad at him for beating her up, so she messes him around whenever she can. I think his angry letter is for the white folks so he can get leverage of different kinds. It's mostly show biz. And [Marvin] brought the work to me, for me to get it out in any way that I could. So I wrote the play from it. He gets a third of the income. I get the other third and Huey's wife is supposed to get the other third. Marvin won't give me the wife's address, so my agent is holding her part so far. Isn't the world strange?"[60]

Significantly, Bullins's title page of the manuscript for *Salaam* credits Marvin X as the play's author. Bullins indicates there that he only "dramatized" the material, which he acknowledges is taken from Marvin X's autobiography. Bullins has said that when he was given the autobiography, the section on Huey Newton was prose, "except for a few pages of dialogue."[61] He added that Marvin also gave him the play entitled *The Devil and Marvin X*, which Bullins said that he never finished reading because of its "rambling negativity." The new version of this play—sent to the author by Marvin X—contains a thirteen-page scene (Act III, Scene 5) that almost identically matches Bullins's *Salaam, Huey Newton, Salaam*—as revealed by a comparison of Bullins's previously cited final monologue with the following Marvin X monologue:

MARVIN X

For those of us still addicted and those recovering from crack, we should feel blessed that we're still alive and have the chance to save our souls, for the sake of ourselves, our families and our communities. As for myself, I am confident that I shall recover from crack, *in sha Allah* (be it the will of Allah). Each day I get stronger and stronger, and if I slip, I'll just keep on gettin up, keep on gettin up. As Mao used to say, "Fight, fail, fight again, fail, fight again, until victory." An African proverb teaches us "To stumble is not to fall but to go forward faster."

I look forward to rejoining my people in our struggle for freedom, justice and equality, although I recognize the greatest *jihad* or battle is to win one's soul from *Saitan* or the devil, who whispers into the hearts of men.

Arise, arise, my people, arise from the projects, from the alleys, doorways, streets and crack houses with no lights, no food, no hope. Arise and reclaim our souls. All is not lost. Yes, it's raining now, but look, see the sun coming through the clouds—see the rainbow. *As-salaam Alaikum wa rahmatulahi wa barakatuhu* (Peace be unto you and mercy of Allah and His blessings.)[62]

Bullins claims that Marvin X must have copied his dialogue because the original version of *The Devil and Marvin X* does not have a scene between Marvin X and Huey.[63] Marvin X disputes the claim, however, saying that since he never read Bullins's play, he could not have possibly copied Bullins's dialogue.[64] The result is hard feelings between two very old and close friends: Marvin X has said that although he respects Bullins's talent, he will not "ever forgive the theft." This misunderstanding might have been avoided had the play been credited to Marvin X *and* Ed Bullins: Bullins added so many of his own distinctive elaborations that whatever the genre of the source, the finished product definitely qualifies him to be considered its co-author. The question might arise, however, why the critics failed to give Marvin X total credit, as Bullins had done on the manuscript and as the publisher of *The Best Short Plays of 1990* had done in a letter of agreement to reprint *Huey Newton*. The answer is that for some reason, somebody crossed out "By Marvin X. Dramatized by Ed Bullins" on the agreement. In Bullins's handwriting on the agreement there appears "by Ed Bullins. Material taken from a work-in-progress by Marvin X."[65] Bullins evidently requested that Helen Merrill make the same change on a later production contract, because the agency wrote thanking him for "letting us know that you applied for the copyright to *Salaam, Huey Newton, Salaam*, and about the billing 'by Ed Bullins, taken from the autobiography of Marvin X, a work in progress.' We'll change your Applause agreements accordingly. Helen has also alerted Ensemble Studio Theatre, since they'll be doing the play in June."[66] Subsequently, not a single press release or flyer about *Salaam, Huey Newton, Salaam* mentioned Marvin X. Not even Ethel Pitts Walker's thoroughly researched introduction to the play in her *New/Lost Plays by Ed Bullins* (1993) acknowledges Marvin X as author or co-author. The fact that Bullins is credited as sole author is perhaps just cause for Marvin X's feeling that somehow he has been shafted—especially after Howard Stein of Columbia University chose *Huey Newton* for one of the *Best Short Plays of 1990*.[67]

Film for the Stage is the third type in the Forms Subclass of the Flow Class of Drama. The first play of this type to be discussed is *Dr. Geechee and the Blood Junkies: A Modern Hoodoo Horror Yarn* (1986). First produced at City College of San Francisco, and directed by John H. Doyle and Bullins, the play tells how Tanya Elliot avenges the death of her boyfriend, Greg Settles, a fast-rising man on the New York City political scene.[68] After discovering that he has been murdered and turned into a blood junkie by his "friend," Reggie, a drug lord who uses a designer drug to accomplish the blood-junkie feat, Tanya goes to Louisiana to seek the help of the Hoodoo artists Dr. Geechee and Mama Rhea. Armed with their knowledge, she returns home, where she, with the aid of a reporter, destroys Reggie and kills the blood-junkie Gregory, whose soul can now rest. The historical importance of the play lies in its being the only produced horror play and the only film for the stage in African American theatre.

Bullins has said that it took him close to fifteen years to finish a version of *Dr. Geechee* because his concerns were to address a burning issue and to pay tribute to the B-movie form. He was "a mild horror-film buff" who grew up on the various "Frankensteins, wolfmen, Draculas, mummies, zombies, Things—from out of space and from black lagoons—Exorcists, numerous Jaws, Nights of Living death on into dawn, and a thousand more."[69] This interest caused him to try integrating film and drama. He first wrote *Go Go* (1969), a film script that he called "a staged documentary" of Mi Mi Harris's company of go-go dancers. The story is set at a night club in the Williams bridge section of the Bronx, as well as at various other locations found in the lives of the dancers. Not much happens: The dancers talk to an interviewer about themselves. Importantly, Bullins co-wrote the script with the filmmaker Bill Lathan, who taught Bullins the vocabulary and technique of film. Bullins used this knowledge, typically, with video and film clips in *Goin' A Buffalo* and *We Righteous Bombers*. These filmed actions give background and motivation for staged actions, a use he similarly made of video in *Dr. Geechee*:

> TANYA sips her drink. The STEWARDESS exits.
>
> TANYA puts her drink down and closes her eyes. Music plays.
>
> LIGHTS UP on GREG SETTLE's coffin in the cargo section of the plane.
>
> A TV screen lights up above TANYA's seat. A montage of scenes between TANYA and GREG flashes across the screen: their shopping/their dancing/their riding in GREG's jaguar/their making love/their nightclubbing/their attending a basketball game/their making love/their relaxing before a fireplace/their jogging/their swimming/their sailing frisbees/their making love. . . .
>
> In the cargo section, GREG's coffin opens, and the corpse sits up. Strange music plays.[70]

This restricted use of video signals Bullins's plan not to integrate film and theatre but to create a type of theatre in the form of film. The question, then, is how does Bullins make *Dr. Geechee* into this new genre called "film for the stage"? He does so by three means, the first of which is to treat the lighting design as if it were the camera lens. He shows this with the very novel beginning, which teases the audience with Greg's overdose and Tanya's discovery:

> TANYA looks and dresses like a top fashion model. SHE kicks off her shoes, wiggles her toes in relaxation, slips off her spring coat, and reveals an impressive figure.
>
> SOUND of running water catches her attention. SHE calls out:
>
> TANYA
>
> Greg! . . . Greg?
>> SHE shrugs, moves toward bathroom side of stage. Spotlight tracks her.
>
>> LIGHT on GREG's body. TANYA sees it. SOUND effects. MUSIC. LIGHTING effects. Anguish.
>
> TANYA
>
> GREG! OH NO! GOD! EEEEEEEeeeeeee!!!
>> TANYA freezes. LIGHT off the CORPSE.
>> A neon sign FLASHES on. It gives the TITLES:
>> Dr. GEECHEE AND THE BLOOD JUNKIES

The Flow Class

By Ed Bullins

Directed by (??????????)

Music by (???????)

Etc., etc. . . .

At the end of the play, lights again announce the credits, adding: "Look for the sequel to *Dr. Geechee and the Blood Junkies*, *The Children of Dr. Geechee*, soon at your neighborhood theaters." Then comes the tag, "Drugs is Death!" A skull with bones is the final view.

Lights serve several other functions: Spotlights give closeups (hands springing from the ground and holding Tanya), middle-range shots (Tanya's dream-self leaving her body), and long-range shots (a shower of red roses). In addition to typically starting and closing scenes, lights also slow down the action, create shadowy effects, make unnatural illuminations, and reveal hideous facial details. Coupled with the lighting are the amplified sounds of keys entering doors, telephone receivers being picked up and hung up, water running and splashing, and hearts racing and stopping. Even more important than the sound and lighting effects are such spectacles as Greg's coffin sinking slowly out of sight, a Blood Junkie crashing through a wall and disappearing into the dawn, Tanya being caught in a force field, as well as the stunning feats of a Blood Junkie drinking from the wound in Doorman's neck and of Greg becoming a snake. With the possible exceptions of Bert Williams and George Walker's *Abyssinia* (1906) and Loften Mitchell's *A Land beyond the River* (1957), few other African American plays have ever utilized sound, lighting, and spectacle as well as *Dr. Geechee*.

Bullins almost pulls off this bold experiment. The trouble, in fact, is not in the cinematic but in the dramatic element. Bullins has the protagonist Tanya, after her initial encounter with the antagonist Reggie, wander off to Louisiana without the antagonist in hot pursuit. The audience is introduced, instead, to Tanya's fears of—and Bullins's fascination with—the powers of hoodoo. Because two thirds of the play is set in Louisiana, the play, then, is without dramatic tension for so long that by the time Tanya returns to face Reggie, Bullins has all but lost his audience.

Bullins has no such troubles in the final type of the Forms Subclass, Musical Structures. This type shows how structure and theme in a play might be made to conform to the structure of a musical composition. Bullins almost totally abandons known dramatic structure in *The Fabulous Miss Marie* (1974) and *The Duplex* (1971), both of which premiered at the New Lafayette with Robert Macbeth directing. Bullins makes his structure and theme resemble those of a jazz composition (*Miss Marie*) and of the sonata and the symphony (*Duplex*). In *Miss Marie* there is almost no plot. Ten old friends have a Christmas party, where they watch a pornographic movie. Through parallel and collapsed time each character tells of troubles, triumphs, and habits that are not so different from those in the movie. The play, like a jazz number, has a head, a body, and an end. While stating the melody and theme, the head introduces each of the ten musicians making up the combo: The leader is Miss Marie Horton, a mid-forties clubwoman who drinks Ambassador scotch, loves young men, and collects friends. She meddles, all the while not missing a beat in either her front-line or rhythm sections.

Miss Marie's arranger and bassist is her husband Bill, whom she never lets solo, although the story of him and his white woman gets told. The tambourine player/songstress is her niece, Wanda, whom Miss Marie dismisses as dumb. Wanda pays Miss Marie back by having affairs with her husband Bill and her secret love Marco Polo Henderson. On drums is the young Art Garrison, Miss Marie's main rhythm "piece." Art's young cousin, Steven Benson, sits in as sometime guitarist, although he has his eyes on drumming Miss Marie. Leading Miss Marie's front-line section is her "cut-buddy," Ruth. She plays her soprano sax so well that she cannot believe that she seduced her best friend's husband Bud, the tenor sax player and schoolteacher. Ruth's best friend is alto sax player and Marie's homegirl Toni, who is so jealous of Miss Marie that she had an affair with the drummer Art. On trumpet is the "revolutionary" Gafney, whose shrill notes are counterpoint in the band, causing most members to ignore him. Playing bells is Marie's invisible lap dog, Whitie.

The body of the composition—composed of a series of highly improvised solos, duets, and trios—elaborates the theme, which is that mankind's search for self-completion is an infinite cut-throat game. This notion, found in all cultures, is well explained both in the novel, *The Palm-Wine Drinkard*, by the Nigerian writer Amos Tutuola, and in Plato's *Symposium*: Aristophanes says that Man was once a strong being—globular in shape—"with rounded back and sides, four arms and four legs, and two faces, both the same, on a cylindrical neck, and one headed with one face on one side and one the other, and four ears, and two lots of privates, and all the other parts to match." Angry at these powerful beings for trying "to scale the heights of heaven and set upon the gods," Zeus "cut them all in half." This bisection "left each half with a desperate yearning for the other, and they ran together and flung their arms around each other's necks, and asked for nothing better than to be rolled into one"[71]:

MARIE

(*On phone*) Yeah, girl . . . we still partyin' . . . yeah, this is some Christmas. Yeah . . . really, Bea. We started at Shadow's place two days ago, girl. I really wanted to wait to at least Christmas Eve, honey . . . but those niggers couldn't wait to swill some liquor and call themselves having a good time . . . Sure she's with him! Yeah! . . . Ruth's still with that nigger, child . . . Ahuhnnn . . it should have been somethin' . . . Ahuhnnn . . . would be still over to Shadow's, but you know how he is . . . wouldn't give Ruth a moment, girl . . . ha ha . . . that man is the biggest cockhound in town . . . Gawd! . . . Didn't give anybody a chance . . . ha ha . . . bad enough for Ruthie it was her old man who forever had a sweaty . . . and I mean *sweaty*! . . . wet palm on her booty . . . but we other girls had to suffer the consequences . . . NO! . . . Nawh, whore . . . don't put that off on me . . . he ain't my type . . . none of ours . . . ha ha . . . not even Ruth's . . . Heee ha ha ha . . . I want to thank, chick . . . him and Bill . . . ha ha ha . . . Toni calls them the Gold Dust Twins, honey . . . Yeah! . . . Bill's still fucken that funky ole white bitch, girl. Yeah . . . sho is corny . . . He swears to me that it's all a product of my imagination . . . yes, he does . . . but he don't know I know he's got that litle old red baby by her . . . I hear tell it looks like a wrinkled-up pink baboon . . . yeah . . . Ha! . . . Iris tell me that

(*Whiny voice*)

"Maybe you should have a baby for Bill." . . . WHOOP! . . . hee ha ha ha . . . ain't that the limit, Bea? . . . The only thing Bill Horton's getting from me is a hard time if he don't bring some money in here, and I mean some money . . . Ha! . . . The Gold Dust Twins.[72]

Such continual searches, as elaborated in the body of the composition, turn people truly fabulous, that is, into empty vessels who spend inordinate hours, friends, and funds in what the critic John Lahr correctly labeled "ritual squandering."[73] This applies not only to Miss Marie, whose very definition is fear of growing plain, but also to that "pretty yellow nigger" Marco Polo Henderson, who frets about the day when "all the little Black mamas who like to run their hands over curly hair" might have only fuzz to rub. In solo after solo, the partygoers reveal similar terrors. The characters serve structural functions as well, setting, bridging, and updating actions. Each singer, additionally, helps to develop Miss Marie's character by telling stories that connect the soloist to Miss Marie: Miss Marie's friend Toni believes that she knows Miss Marie better than anybody else, although Miss Marie's best friend, Ruth, swears that nobody could ever really know Miss Marie; her lover, Art, blabbers that she enjoys bedding down with young men when Bill is away—or drunk; and from the niece Wanda, no less, comes the scandal that even Miss Marie's mama was once a wild chile—having had Miss Marie out of wedlock and not knowing who the father was. The solos function, furthermore, to keep time and order. Because Bullins's time is parallel and his episodes associational, both time and event could be difficult to follow. Solos solve the problem.

In Miss Marie's third solo, for example, she lets spectators know that here is a three-day party. After the head (or beginning), signaled by a light change, Miss Marie again alerts the spectator that the end of day one has come by telling her lover, Art: "You've slept so long . . . baby. And you've missed the movie and my guests have gone an' everything."

The duets and trios aid in setting the pace and tension: alternately loud and hard and quiet and introspective. In the former, opposites play out contrapuntal arguments. In Marie and Bill's three duets, for example, they battle heatedly over both of their initial sexual infidelities. In the first duet, Bill gives Marie fits when he catches a man sneaking out the back door. In the second, Marie methodically sprays Bill with hot grits not so much for having a white "side whore" but for taking "Miss Thang" and that yella baby down to the "Sportsman Inn," Marie and Bill's watering hole. Bill's purpose was to prove to his friends that it's his hot mama Miss Marie—and not he—who is infertile, the result of a teenage abortion she had in order to spare her grandmother a world of shame. This frantic pace is slowed considerably in Marie and Bill's third duet, which showed Bill crying on his wife's shoulders because he has lost his job for having taken his white lover to work. This duet, significantly, reveals that Marie and Bill have a "good understanding": Marie "spends time" with her white boss, whom she persuades to reinstate Bill into his job—as much, of course, for her own take-and-spend sake as for his pride.

The end of this jazz composition restates the melody and the theme. Miss Marie's horror that she has indeed gone to seed sprouts when she discovers that her "steady," Art, has been laying it to her best friend, Toni. Marie grabs a new shoot on the youth-tree, however, with the news that her old man has his job back, and that the hot young Steve has buckets of love to help her soothe whatever needs soothing.

The critics raved about *Miss Marie*—about its strong characterization, structure, dialogue, audience reaction, and overall excellence. The characters were judged "vibrantly alive and engrossing,"[74] as well as "funny and unfailingly interesting."[75] Critics loved the way the characters take turns in stepping outside of the activity and addressing the audience directly, telling about themselves and each other."[76] *Miss Marie* was deemed "a good choice as a company project" because it "offered young actors an assortment of diverse roles, almost all of them with at least one strong speech."[77] Interestingly, Bullins was not massacred this time for his structure, which, while "not tight or slick,"[78] was accepted for what it is. One critic even considered the play Bullins's "most composed"—probably because she felt that the play keeps up a good beat, thanks to the Miles Davis music that was played by a band on stage in the initial production.[79] The dialogue itself was said to have the riff-like feel of jazz.[80] The language was characterized as a "ghetto argot raised to [the level of] poetry,"[81] with such a convivial air that it talked right to the audience—which talked back.[82] The overall performance was considered so "convincing and totally satisfying"[83] that it, as in most of Bullins's other plays, was deemed "theatrical poetry [that] unraveled like magic carpets."[84] Mel Gussow of the *New York Times* called *Miss Marie* "a salutary reminder of the breadth of Mr. Bullins's vision."[85] Some believed that there was oblivious commercial potential" in the play that could make it into a profitable film.[86] All agreed that *Miss Marie* had, as one critic put it, the "stunning quality and artistic purity" that made it "approach the status of a masterwork."[87] Bullins received the 1970–71 Obie for the distinguished playwriting found in *The Fabulous Miss Marie* and *In New England Winter*.

Such consensual high praise was not given to *The Duplex* (1971), the final play in the the Musical Structures Type of the Forms Subclass. In this work, Bullins crams twelve of his usual backstreet characters into and around a duplex. These Bullins people do the usual things, play cards, drink rotgut, and smoke reefer, as well as lie and fornicate. The story centers on the typical triangle, this time among a landlady (Velma Best), her husband (O. D.), and her tenant (Steve, who is also Miss Marie's new man). So hackneyed is the plot that it invites yawning: O. D. runs around with so many women and abuses Velma so badly that she "turns to" and falls in love with Steve. Although he simply hustles her for a while, he eventually falls in love with her, so much so that he confronts O. D., who all but kills him. In the end, Velma foresakes Steve for her drunken husband.

What saves this tired plot is that Bullins pours it into the combined sonata and symphony forms. He divides the play into four "movements," the first of which—called exposition or statement in the sonata and allegro or quick movement in the symphony—consists of four phrases (or scenes). Typically, the first phrase briefly introduces the characters, as well as the primary and secondary themes: the main theme is that one flirts with death when one gets caught messing with other people's spouses; the secondary, that each person is parked at death's door. The second phrase gives the background of Steve and Velma. "Night rider" Steve is a struggling student with big plans. Velma is a southern woman with no plans but to hold onto someone, even if he is not worth the bullets needed to kill him, as Wrenetta says about the Ike Turner character in *I Think It's Gonna Work Out Fine*. The third phrase introduces the friends and neighbors: Mamma, the old neighborhood drunk who is being tended by "old-timey" Pops, her man for the time being; pretty boy Marco Polo Henderson, who makes it with the "silly little bitch" Wanda, the niece of leg-kickin' Marie Horton, who, while longing for Marco, fights off old farting Montgomery "Saltsprings" Henderson, Marco's father, in order to get to Tootsie "Mad Dawg" Franklin, who sidesteps her in order to grab Velma's friend, fat-booty Sister Sukie. Bullins uses this family-chorus to comment on the action and to offer dire warnings, thereby further developing and complicating the action, as well as the themes. The fourth phrase shows how awfully complicated—and confused—each of the principals is. Velma, for example, pays back her husband O. D. for cheating on her by having sex with Steve. She refuses, however, to let him love her in the bedroom because it is her "marriage bed." Instead, they have sex on the floor.

The second movement—called development in the sonata—consists of five phrases. Although usually played *andante* (of moderate speed) or *adagio* (rather slow), this movement is altered by Bullins in each of its five phrases. The first, powerfully *allegro* (or lively), introduces the almost-human O. D.:

> O. D. BEST and CROOK *stand in front of the door to the* BEST *apartment.*
>
> O. D. *kicks the door in, breaking off its lock, and enters the bedroom.*

VELMA (Bolts up in bed)

O. D.! Man, what's wrong with you!
> *(Upstairs . . .* STEVE *swings his legs to the floor and sits upon his couch, listening.)*

O. D., ANSWER ME! WHY'D YOU BREAK IN THE DOOR? YOU GOTTA KEY!
> *(O. D. begins pulling out drawers, pulling their contents out, and lifts objects from the dresser, looking for something.* CROOK *saunters in, smirking.) . . .*
>
> *(*STEVE *has begun to dress.)*

VELMA

No, O. D., don't do that!
> *(O. D. has found her purse in the closet and is looking through it. She jumps from the bed and pushes him; he puts his big hand in her face and shoves her back across the bed.)*

STEVIE! STEVIE!
> *(Money is taken from the purse and the purse is thrown at her head as she ducks.)*

O. D. (Saunters out to CROOK)

C'mon, man. Let's make it!
> *(*HE *leads the way into the hallway.)*

VELMA (Cries)

You sonna bitch! You dirty black sonna bitch! Don't take my money and give it to that whore!

> (*STEVE* comes running down the stairs; seeing the two men, he stops
> halfway.)

CROOK (*Faces STEVE, to O. D.*)
Who's dis little sucker? A marine . . . or sumpten? . . .

O. D. (*Stares up at STEVE: sneers*)
C'mon, Crook . . . it's only the guy from upstairs.[88]

The other four phrases return to the assigned function of a second
movement, that of showing the main and secondary themes in such a
variety of keys and rhythms that they often become difficult to recognize.
Bullins organizes and weaves the themes through a non-stop party, where
the chorus leader Marco tells tales that complement the theme: The first
story is about how Tootsie "Mad Dawg" Franklin knocked his wife's lover's
"front teeth all over the lobby." Another story tells how Tootsie gave all of
his money to his unfaithful wife Lola because he loves her. The movement,
interestingly, is distinguished not by Bullins's varied repetition of the
theme but by his incredibly poignant contradictions. He shows Velma's
strong defense of and deep love for her abusive husband. And Steve takes
Velma to a gay bar because he knows that her homophobic husband "is
scared silly of fags and won't be seen on the same side of the street with
one." O. D., incidentally, believes that Steve is gay because he sees him
standing in front of the gay bar. What O. D. does not realize is that Steve
was waiting for Velma.

Instead of using his third movement for the usual SCHERZO (a light
and prankish composition) or a waltz, minuet, or other dance, Bullins
makes the five phrases of this movement develop further the Velma-Steve
(poor) connection and the Velma-O. D. (dis)connection—both of which
are placed in perspective by the misconnections of each of the women
dwellers. It is during this movement that Bullins reveals that the characters themselves are duplexes: Steve recognizes that he is madly in love
with a woman who in no way could possibly fit into his future plans.
Although warned to stay away from Velma, he resolves to get her, knowing
full well that O. D. will never let him have her. In a most eloquent aria
(or monologue), which shows Bullins at his very best, Steve searches for
answers:

> Nobody knows the love and beauty I find holding my woman in my
> arms. . . . My woman . . . a poor little scared black girl that's even
> dumber than I'm supposed to be. Nobody knows that I don't care if
> she has kids . . . children who will hate me forever if I get her like I
> plan. Nor will anybody know that she'll never know me . . . really
> know me . . . this black man . . . with this mind . . . they'll never
> understand the thoughts that flash through my head and scorch the
> back of my eyes . . . these eyes that see her being beaten and raped

. . . these eyes that see the flames of the hell that we all live in . . . live our black lives in here . . . in our cool dark little lives . . . getting ready to become something we ain't now or will never be . . . really.

The two phrases making up the fourth movement, another powerful allegro, recapitulate and restate the theme before the coda (ending). Bullins shows the results of Steve's refusal to accept his anagnorisis (or realization) that neither he, Velma, nor O. D. will ever complete the searches for their other halves, the continuation of the theme in *Miss Marie*. As usual, Bullins ends the play with a battle. There is something different, however, about this simultaneously prophetic and futile fight between Steve and O. D. When Steve walks calmly to O. D. and punches him squarely in the face with all his might, it causes O. D. almost to "kill" Steve—grabbing him like a rag doll and strangling him until he no longer breathes. This fulfills the prophecy announced by Tootsie in the first phrase of the first movement: "I wouldn't wanta be in yo shoes if that ugly gorilla ev'va ketch ya with his ole lady."

Of the three principal characters (Steve, O. D., and Velma), the most troubled—and troubling—is Velma. Bullins shows just how mixed-up she is in the short *Steve and Velma: An Epilogue to The Duplex* (1978). Although an epilogue, which means that the play continues the stories of the characters in *The Duplex*, *Steve and Velma* was not intended to be appended to *Duplex*.[89] Bullins directed that the two plays not appear on the same bill, which raises the question, "Why not?" Finding possible answers must begin with the plot: Marcos, still the chorus leader, reminds the audience about the end of *The Duplex*: O. D. has almost killed Steve. Then Marcos, along with the other duplex dwellers, lets the spectators know that Steve and Velma have run away together, and that they have not been heard from for three days. The point of attack in the play shows them back in Velma's bed after having run out of money. Because O. D. has taken her insurance policy and because Steve has not yet received his military severance pay, Velma blames Steve for messing up her life: "I'm broke and on the street without a home." When she sees O. D. outside the window, she runs Steve upstairs and grabs a pistol. O. D. has decided, however, to end the marriage and to send Velma back to her parents. In fact, her father is on the way to get her. Although O. D. promises to send money to their children, Velma begs him not to leave her: "O. D. . . . . O. D. . . . don't go to her . . . Don't go to that little bitch." When he insists on leaving, she shoots him in both legs. Thinking that O. D. has shot Velma, Steve rushes in to discover the crying Velma cradling O. D.'s head and kissing his face.

There might be three possible answers to the question of why this play should not be attached to *The Duplex*. The endings appear repetitive as if Bullins had pondered which to use. The only difference between them is that the shooting of O. D. in *Steve and Velma* replaces O. D.'s whipping Steve and cutting Velma in *Duplex*. This raises the second possibility, that the ending of *Steve and Velma* switched protagonists: Velma's aggression makes her no longer the suffering heroine, the victim of a drunken brute. She has become a selfish and scheming "bitch" who shoots O. D. in order not to end up either on the streets or back in her rural hometown, which she hates so much. It is as antagonist, then, that she frustrates O. D.'s plan, which an audience must surely conclude is a reasonable decision by a now rational and sober anti-hero. The final possibility why Bullins did not want *Steve and Velma* tagged to *Duplex* might be that *Steve and Velma* turns Velma into a hopeless psychotic. This is the last thing that Bullins needed—since women were already calling him a misogynist.

These possible reasons raise yet another question: Why did Bullins not simply rename the characters? The answer might be that *Steve and Velma* would have been simply too prosaic—even boring. What makes this epilogue exciting, then, is the very connection that its author did not want. Bullins created a hornet's nest. The separation of the plays is the only thing that kept him from being attacked again by the feminists, who, for some reason, never granted him the license they did to such playwrights as Sam Shepard. In Shepard's *A Lie of the Mind* (1985), for example, the protagonist beats his girlfriend so badly that she ends up in a hospital: "Despite Shepard's obvious misogynist proclivities, he remained the darling of the white left-liberal theatre establishment, especially in academia. Why a red-necked cracker like Shepard is excused for his brutality toward women, while Bullins is lambasted by the left wing for being anti-woman, bespeaks volumes about the hypocrisy and double standards of the white liberal establishment."[90] The critics let Bullins have it again, this time by ignoring *Steve and Velma*. This is quite different from the critical reaction to *The Duplex*. In reviews of the Lincoln Center production, critics almost apologized for loving it: Clive Barnes said that he was "mildly embarrassed."[91] Most reviewers agreed with *Village Voice* critic John Lahr that the music, which was called "tuneless" by the *New York Newsday* critic George Oppenheimer,[92] did not add to the power or the statement of the piece.[93] *Newsweek* critic Jack Kroll asserted that the music pulled the play loose from its trajectory, and that the director Gilbert Moses should have let the play speak entirely for itself.[94]

Audiences were deeply affected by the play. One woman, "who had been laughing raucously at comedy and drama alike, broke up entirely and yelled 'I can't stand it.' "[95] In the New Lafayette production, a spectator felt so totally at home that he decided to walk into the play and live there for a while. He sat on stage for several minutes—completely under the spell of the action, until he was politely escorted backstage by one of the characters in the play.[96]

The Bullins-Jules Irving fight over the Lincoln Center production of *The Duplex* was caused, Bullins recently admitted, by his own inexperience with dealing with unions and professional houses.[97] Bullins's home, the New Lafayette Theatre, had not been run by hard-and-fast union rules. When Bullins took his play to Jules Irving, Bullins believed that, although he had signed an agreement, he could make any changes that he wanted. The trouble started over the music. The composer Pat Patrick, who for a long time had played with the Sun Ra Myth-Science Arkestra, had written the music for the premiere of *Duplex* at the New Lafayette in 1970. Although Bullins preferred the Patrick score, he, for some reason, verbally agreed to let the director Gilbert Moses write new music to his lyrics for the Lincoln Center production.[98] Bullins had every reason to trust Moses' judgment because Moses, a co-founder of the Free Southern Theatre (1963–82), had directed highly respected productions of Amiri Baraka's *Slaveship* and *Ain't Supposed to Die a Natural Death* by Melvin Van Peebles. When Bullins heard Moses's score for *Duplex*, however, he realized that he liked the Patrick blues score much better than Moses's rock music, which he felt would sensationalize the show in order for it to be accepted downtown.[99] Bullins told Irving about his objections, but the truth is that there was very little that Irving could have done to address Bullins's concern.

Irving could have addressed, however, Bullins's concern about the casting of Velma (the very fine actress and Bullins's good friend Mary Alice got the role). Although she had starred in Bullins's *Street Sounds* at Cafe La Mama, Bullins did not believe that she was right for this role: to Bullins, Velma is "a young, dark, shapely, and desirable love object. A whole woman. [Steve] wants her because she is not owned by her husband, and yet she wants to be wanted. In some productions, they have her cast as an elderly undesirable woman, while in actuality she is even younger than Stevie Benson, the man she loves." When Gilbert argued that such a young woman would not have had so many children, Bullins answered: "I know women in their early twenties with five or six kids. My first wife was like that."[100] Had Bullins wished, he could have sued Irving over the casting because their agreement stipulates that "the cast (and all replacements therein), the director and the sets and costumes (and any replacements thereof) shall be subject to the Author's approval."[101] Irving could have used this clause to effect the change. He stonewalled Bullins instead, which infuriated the playwright because he felt as if he were being handled like an "office boy." Of course, nobody wanted to sit down with him, because Irving had not endorsed a change in actress. Consequently, one man would send Bullins to the business manager, who would send him two doors down to someone else. Bullins complained that when they said,

"Come on, let's negotiate," they meant, "Let's sit down so you can see it our way." He compared this behavior to President Richard Nixon's conduct of the Vietnam War: "He goes around and bombs somebody and then says, 'Let's negotiate.' What kind of negotiation is that? That's not negotiating—that's war."

Bullins claims that Lincoln Center threw the whole bureaucracy of the organization at him. So, he took on the organization.[102] He believes that the resulting big fuss caused him to be blackballed: he was never again produced at a major New York City house.[103]; The producer/director Woodie King Jr. of the Henry Street Settlement's New Federal Theatre in New York City saved Bullins, as he has done so many other struggling African American playwrights, by producing more than 120 of their plays since 1975. Like others in the theatre, Bullins is happy that King's talents and contributions were honored in 1994, when Ron Himes's highly regarded St. Louis Black Repertory Company named its annual award The Woodie.[104]

Although Bullins subsequently faced tough times, he did not at the time lose faith in Gilbert Moses, who later won an Obie Award for directing Bullins's *The Taking of Miss Janie*. Perhaps Bullins could have salvaged his relations with Irving had Irving known just who he was dealing with in Bullins, who never let on during early "negotiations" that he was capable of invading and stopping a performance. That, however, is Bullins: Two weeks after I woke him early one morning to ask him if he had ever been made so angry that he had wanted to kill somebody, he called back to amend his earlier answer of "I don't get that angry." Bullins said that when he was fighting mad, he always kept his cool, but that he immediately and quietly began plotting his retaliation.[105] Ironically, Bullins's counterattack, in the case of *Duplex*, backfired. Instead of closing, the play was extended one week beyond its scheduled two-week run, (9–25 March 1972). Apparently in an effort not to be outdone by Bullins, Jules Irving launched an advertising campaign that cited Bullins as "a dynamic playwriting talent," "Today's Eugene O'Neill," and "simply the most exciting playwright in the nation." These ads ended with the big bold announcement: "Engagement Extended Thru April 1 By Public Demand!"

INNER LIFE VERSUS INNER LIFE CLASS
OF BLACK EXPERIENCE DRAMA

For a while during the late 1960s and early 1970s, almost every time that New Yorkers looked at the arts and leisure sections of their newspapers, there was Ed Bullins either glaring at them or smiling impishly, as if he knew every family secret. Yet, New Yorkers knew almost nothing about this man—beyond the sanitized press releases put out by the New Lafayette Theatre. This is exactly what Bullins wanted: he loved being a mystery. *New York Times* editor Seymour Peck decided to put a stop to this because New Yorkers felt that such a public figure as Bullins had no right to absolute privacy. Peck asked *Times* critic Clayton Riley to crack Bullins's shell.[1]

Peck chose Riley because of the respect that Bullins had for him, a native New York writer, educator, and freelance journalist. After graduating from Iona College and doing a stint in the army, he joined that early group of African American actors who studied at the Luther James Studio in 1960: Cicely Tyson, Godfrey Cambridge, Lou Gosset Jr., Robert Hooks, Lonne Elder, and Douglas Turner Ward. It was there that Riley met Robert Macbeth, whom Riley later helped to inspire to found the New Lafayette Theatre. Among Riley's writings is the famous introduction to *A Black Quartet: Four New Black Plays by Ben Caldwell, Ronald Milner, Ed Bullins, and LeRoi Jones,* where he calls Bullins a "remarkable artist" who "created, during the sixties, a roster of dramatic figures best described as street-nigger royalty."[2] Riley had taught, furthermore, at the Fordham University Graduate School of Education and at Sarah Lawrence College. In addition to *The New York Times*, his articles had appeared in *Ebony, The Liberator, The Chicago Sun-Times*, and *The New York Amsterdam News*. Therefore, when Riley invited Bullins home—with the understanding that they would talk about the reasons that he had "cancelled" *The Duplex* at the Lincoln Center—Bullins accepted.

When Bullins arrived in Riley's living room that Sunday afternoon in March of 1972, Riley had Sly and the Family Stone on the stereo. The conversation was easy, as Bullins admired Riley's huge record collection. Riley put on the Miles Davis Quartet, circa 1958, he poured a glass of red wine, and asked Bullins a safe question about north Philadelphia. Bullins sipped his wine, gave the standard line, and added a few new twists about the world he now inhabited. "Never changing his Sphinx-like expression,"[3] Bullins spoke pleasantly, calmly, "but with a measured caution, almost never revealing very much about himself, the private person, beyond his new and growing public reputation as a dramatist."[4] Riley gently probed; Bullins countered: "I just don't discuss personal aspects of my life. The theatergoers access to me shouldn't be a personal thing. If they see me in my plays, okay. If they see my people in my work, all right. But that's as far as I go. My private life, my life with my family is my own."[5]

Riley was not through, though. He let Bullins talk on and on about Jules Irving before he slipped in a comment about how much like Bullins is the character Steve "Nightrider" Benson in *Duplex*. Bullins was curt: "Steve is a character created for the stage. Period." Bullins returned to his well-rehearsed script of his public self. After five hours, Riley put on the stereo the newest recording of The Temptations. After several minutes of silence between the two men, Riley decided on one last try: "Do you want to talk at all about your family?"

"No."

Bullins finished his wine, and left Riley with The Temptations. Riley had no recourse but to tell his readers only that he knew that Bullins was married, that his wife worked with him at the *Black Theater Magazine*, and that he had been introduced to a son who greatly resembled the father.[6] Why was Bullins so secretive about his private life? Was it because he had not yet had time enough to answer truthfully such questions as, Who am I, really? From what have I come? and What is my life about, and what should it be? He certainly probed his private life by raising these questions in the eleven plays making up the Inner Life versus Inner Life Class of drama. Of this class, Alain Locke theorized that:

> The artistic problem of the Young Negro has not been so much that of acquiring the outer mastery of form and technique as that of achieving an inner mastery of mood and spirit. That accomplished, there has come the happy release from self-consciousness, rhetoric,

bombast, and the hampering habit of setting artistic values with primary regard for moral effect—all of those pathetic over-compensations of a group inferiority which our social dilemma inflicted upon several unhappy generations.[7]

In each of the five subclasses of Bullins's Inner Life versus Inner Life plays, which time has shown to be in part highly autobiographical, he strains for even hints of answers that, at the time, he was not at all sure even existed. In the Truth Subclass play *Goin' a Buffalo* (1974), for example, Bullins contends that truth is unknowable because people intentionally ignore hints that contradict preconceived notions. First produced at the New Lafayette with Robert Macbeth directing, the play tells the story of the twenty-nine-year-old Curt. A recently released inmate and grand-thief con artist, Curt invites a fellow ex-inmate, Art, to live with him and his beautiful call-girl wife, Pandora. Curt solicits Art's help in selling some stolen dope so that his family, along with some friends, can leave Los Angeles and move to Buffalo in order to set up a crime organization. Because Art wants Pandora for himself, he telephones the police when Curt leaves to drop off the narcotics. The police catch Curt. Art takes Pandora to Buffalo.

Bullins was concerned in the play about what blinds Curt to the truth about Art. The first answer is gratitude: Curt feels indebted to Art because Art saved his life in prison:

CURT

Yeah, if it wasn't for Art here, I wouldn't be sittin' here.

RICH (*bored*)

Yeah?

CURT

This is the kid who banged Scooter aside the jaw during the riot last summer in the joint.

RICH (*sounding more enthused*)

Yeah . . . you were doin' a stretch down at county jail when that happened, weren't you?

CURT

Yeah, man. I was there bigger den shit. Yeah, that paddy mathafukker, Scooter, was coming down on me with an ice pick, man . . . we had all been rumblin' up and down the cell block and I slipped on somethin' wet . . . I think it was Cory's blood 'cause Miles and his boys had stomped the mathafukker so good . . . And I went to look up, and all I could see was that grey-eyed mathafukkin' Scooter comin' at me with that ice pick of his . . . He reached down and grabbed my shirt

front and drew back his arm and WHAMMO . . . (indicating ART) . . .
just like a bat out 'ta hell my boy here had scored on the sucker's jaw.

ART (pleased)
Well . . . I couldn't let that white sonna bitch do you in, man.[8]

This feeling of indebtedness causes Curt to ignore Art's own warnings
that he is a cold taker—not a giver; that he has a "weakness" for other
men's women, as seen in his having shot a man in order to take his wife;
and that he does not get involved in other people's games, choosing, instead, to exploit other people's troubles and dreams. He is surprisingly
chivalrous:

PANDORA (ridicule)
You and your friends, Curt . . . I thought . . .

CURT (heated)
Shut up, bitch . . . you talk too much!

PANDORA (rising anger)
Why shouldn't I when you bring some square-ass little . . .
        (CURT slaps her; she jumps to her feet and spins to claw him, but
        CURT lunges forward and slaps her again, causing her to trip back-
        wards across the edge of the coffee table. From the floor, removing
        one of her shoes)
Goddamn you, Curt . . .
        (She begins to crawl on her knees, and CURT moves the table
        after her. ART steps between them and pushes CURT backward on
        the couch. Surprise is upon CURT's face. . . .

CURT
WHAT THE FUCK'S GOIN ON, MAN?

ART (low)
Don't hit her anymore, Curt.

CURT (incredulous)
What? Man, are you payin' this woman's bills . . . have you got any
papers on her? . . .

ART
I'm sorry for buttin' into your business between you and your old
lady, but somethin' just happens to me, man, when I see a guy hit a
girl.

Such foreshadowing, which highlights Bullins's theme that irrational
faith or loyalty destroys truth, damages the play in this case by making
the plot too predictable. One can guess so early that Art is going to take

204

Pandora that interest is lost even in how he is going to do it. The options are narrowed so early that the play is clearly a young writer's first full-length work. Written in 1965, *Goin' a Buffalo* is a showcase for Bullins's testing such devices as flashbacks, interior dialogues, swift light changes, character freezes, reality switches, and what became his signature "Big Fights." It is understandable, therefore, that the critic Mel Gussow would believe the play not to be Bullins's "most sustained effort" because of a "burdensome symbolism": Pandora has a box containing marijuana and a gun.[9]

In the play, interestingly enough, Bullins calls upon his navy experiences. He could have told Clayton Riley about the time that he had gone absent without leave in order to avoid going to the brig again—he had spent a lot of time there for a variety of tough-guy infractions. This time navy steward Bullins told a drunk white officer, who had given Bullins an order, to clean up his own puke. Bullins then ran from Newport to Providence, Rhode Island, where he hid out for almost nine months. Like Curt, he was captured when a jealous Art "dropped a dime." Bullins would not have wanted New Yorkers to know about his own early experience with failing to recognize truth because of trust.

This failure evidently hit Bullins so hard that he wrote again about the Rhode Island treachery in *In New England Winter* (1969), the single play in the second subclass, Order. Arguing the case for respecting rank and tradition within a group, this double-plot play tells of Steve Benson, who, while in Los Angeles, remembers being in New England. In L.A. he plans and practices the robbery of a bank with his half-brother Cliff and two other friends. Steven needs the money in order to return to his woman, Liz, in New England. The robbery never takes place because Steve kills one of the robbers for attempting to reveal that while Cliff was in prison, Steve fathered a child by Cliff's wife—a secret that Cliff already knows. What Cliff does not know makes up the second plot, Steve's memory of the reason that he is not with Liz: a New England man, bent on having Liz for himself, turns in Steve, a navy deserter, to the shore patrol.

What must amaze about this drama is the fact that the young Bullins was able to pull off such a sophisticated structure. This was only his fourth full-length work. Yet, he deftly handles the extreme difficulties of dramatizing parallel past and present time, as well as real and surreal situations revealed through street and poetic dialogue. What glues these elements together is the startling notion that when order is sinned against—even among thieves—there must be the blood sacrifice of an innocent victim for the purpose of propitiation or homage. Bullins attacks this full plate of armor by adapting the tenet of the early absurdism of the French dramatist Alfred Jarry (1873–1907), which defines life as monstrous, irrational, inane, and ugly. Bullins also modifies the principles of such late absurdists as the Irish playwright Samuel Beckett (1906–90), which show life to be meaningless and random.[10] Bullins juxtaposes these kinds of absurdism in his principal characters. Steve, typical of the characters in early absurdism, must have clarity:

STEVE

Madness, madness, madness . . . God, I can't take this . . . I can't live this out. It can't be *this* way. This isn't it . . . there must be order . . . perfection . . . there must be form . . . there must be reason and absolutes . . . There can't be only madness and reaching out and never touching the sides . . . everyone can be felt, can't they? There has to be something for me besides this emptiness . . . this living death . . . this white coldness.[11]

On the other hand, Cliff, like the free spirits in late absurdism, believes that order simply stunts growth:

STEVE

Is somethin' wrong with you or somethin'?

CLIFF

Yeah . . . there's somethin' wrong with me. I feel. Mostly I feel good. I have emotions. Mostly I'm so emotional that I have to drink myself to sleep after I become exhausted by a woman. And I don't give a damn who knows I feel or have the emotions of a man. . . .

STEVE

I got to get myself ready to meet the future, Cliff. Don't you see?

CLIFF

The future is with us right now, brother. We drown in our future each breath we take. Its phoney promises leak into our brains and turns them to shit!

STEVE

Come off it, Cliff. It's because of not planning that our futures are always so bleak.

Notwithstanding these defining differences, there exists within the brotherhood of robbers the order of Steve as brain trust, Cliff and Bummie as enforcers, and Chuckie as driver. Similarly, there festers in New England the homegrown and transplanted order of Liz, her married sister, Carrie, Carrie's husband, Oscar, and Liz's childhood friend, Crook. By falling in love with Liz, Steve transgressed against the New England order, causing him barely to escape getting his throat cut for innocently—he claims—falling asleep with Carrie on the sofa. Nevertheless, he paid dearly:

CARRIE

Steve! Crook's gone to get the police and the shore patrol . . . Oscar knows it and told me before he went to sleep. They're comin' for you, Steve! They'll arrest you for desertion . . . they'll get you and I'll never see you again.

STEVE *(dressing hurriedly)*

Oh, God! Oh, goddamn!
  (OSCAR enters.)

STEVE

Carrie . . . something's wrong with Liz. Take care of her, please.

CARRIE

Hurry, Steve. Hurry! Don't let them get you.
  (Outside, sound of cars' doors slamming. OSCAR comes up behind CARRIE and punches her, knocking her on the bed.)
No, Oscar. No! Please don't!
  (OSCAR begins choking her, but STEVE breaks a chair across his back, flooring him.) . . .

  (STEVE runs out the door and down the stairs.) . . .

  (Sound of a brief, violent struggle on stairs below. Silence.)

That the enforcer Bummie pays with his life for having sinned against the robber order in Los Angeles shows how Bullins skillfully invokes the traditional shedding of blood by slitting the animal's throat. Nine times Bullins foreshadows Bummie's sacrifice by showing knives as common as the kitchen variety and as exotic as a bone-handled switchblade. Bullins talks about blood offerings, ranging from simply cut throats to carved up fatted calves. Then, suddenly, he springs the dramatic and unholy crucifixion:

STEVE

You're talkin' too much, Bummie.

BUMMIE

No . . . not enough! You know what I'm talkin' about. Don't you?

STEVE

Yeah . . . I know.
  (STEVE picks up the knife from the table and plunges it into BUMMIE's throat.)

CLIFF

Steve!
  (BUMMIE writhes upon the floor, gagging on his blood.)

The very idea of having to appease a robber-god in such a fashion matches the equally odd notion that the low-class people's Eucharist contains poetic liturgies. Nevertheless, Bullins gives some of his finest prose poetry to the drunks and crooks and fools. The Prologue surprises by infusing a narrative with images that do not rightly belong: Bullins uses the expected image of sweating bodies at noon, but he makes "brood hang close" upon these bodies. Fueling these ill-fitting images are *wrong* verbs: A car *burps* reliably in its infirmity. Even the typical personification takes unforeseen turns, making "Indian summer" ride with bandits and grow into a "spent brave," a "savage to the last." The imagery is carved meticulously: groped nudity, chanted Whitman, read Superman and Mickey Spillane, along with "gluttonous eating from a lone pot," and— unforgettably—"drinking muscatel from a mayonnaise jar." This gorgeous imagining is matched only by the sounds, from crazy Liz's ordinary similies ("cold as snow, brown as a coconut") to her sublime "Oh, we must love quick . . . quick and hot and hard . . . for they might come for him . . . they might come to steal him away. Steal his blackness . . . steal his spirit and soul . . . steal his manhood and make him not mine . . . nor his son's to be."

The pleasure of the sound of Bullins's dialogue delights almost as much as the polyrhythms, whether pumping the highly stylized or the ordinary. The sounds and the rhythms work, interestingly enough, although they come from crude minds:

CLIFF

You still think about Liz, don't you? . . .

STEVE

You know . . . I think about her all the time. (*Reminiscing.*) It's snowing up there now. Snowing . . . Big white white flakes. Snow. Silent like death must be.

CLIFF

Our death will be roaring hot.

STEVE

The dying will . . . not the death . . .

CLIFF

Red and orange and blue . . .

STEVE

Death must be still and black and deep.

CLIFF

. . . with white heat reaching all around us.

STEVE

Deathly cold.

CLIFF

Hell is a safe place for black boys.

STEVE

And Christians.

CLIFF

But private.

What amazes is how well Bullins uses rhythm even in the alley-talk of the scoundrel Oscar:

> Yeah, I've cut fourteen cats and I'm goin' cut some more. I'm a young man . . . this state ain't got no capital punishment. Even if I kill somebody, the most I'll get is seven to fourteen years. Be eligible for parole in seven and be out. I'd be a young cat . . . and I'd have my reputation . . . my rep. I'd really have a rep. Just like Philly Billy . . . or One-eyed Sim.

It is no wonder that *In New England Winter,* which premiered at the New Lafayette with Robert Macbeth directing, won the Obie Award in 1971, or that the critics called it everything from "a fine, strong piece of writing" to "triumphant."[12] Bullins saw it as a "stylized nightmare that depicted the bottom of a tortured subconscious . . . whatever that might be, but Liz and Steve would know."[13] And so did we all, thanks to what Clayton Riley called Bullins's "lyrical" writing.

In the third subclass of the Inner Life versus Inner Life Class, Logic, Bullins poses the question, Why do people use reasoning to mask true identities, feelings, and/or desires? He pursues various answers in the two plays making up the Logic Subclass. In *The Pig Pen* (1972), the plot of which is continued in *The Taking of Miss Janie,* Bullins theorizes that some logicians have hidden political motives. In the play, which was first produced at the American Place Theatre with Dick Williams directing, Len Stover (an "intellectual/artistic/pseudo-bohemian type" with an Afro, glasses, Levi's, and a Jewish wife) preaches black nationalism to his interracial disciples. They gather regularly at Len's house on the outskirts of Los Angeles in order to break bread and to rest from their posturing by smoking reefer, drinking wine, reading poetry, and playing music, as well as having sex with Len's wife, Sharon: Len believes in "sharing." At one early-morning high communion in February of 1965, an unseen police officer dances through, blowing his unheard whistle. Like the cock that crowed during St. Peter's sleepy watch for Christ, the officer three times sounds his joyful noise. When one of Len's white followers returns from gathering more wine, he brings the news that Malcolm X has been murdered. Sharon shouts her joy. The shepherd Len tolerates his wife's shouts of "Oh good," causing the scales to fall from the surprised eyes of two apostles, the poet Ray and the beauty Margie, who hurry away. The others return to partying.

Bullins would strongly object to the recasting of his plot in terms of religion. He went out of his way, in fact, to squeeze into the play the evils most despised alike by black nationalists and Christians: preaching black and sleeping white, wife-swapping, and free sex. The play appears on a first or second reading to be but a typical Bullins loose-party piece—this time with live music. The readers' own logic, stemming from the face of things, suckered them into dismissing all but the quick-fix theme to be truthful, which appeared to have been stitched hastily to the end. There is more to this deceptive little portrait, however. This highly sophisticated play subtly and searingly indicts some black nationalist "leaders" who repeatedly sabotaged the black nationalism movement. As in the play, these podium stompers hid behind people's logic, which led most to assume that the bringer of the Word was also a doer. There was no room for doubters:

ERNIE

So you turn me on to some books, Len . . . and you broke some things down for me, man. But so what. . . .

LEN

You say so what, brother? . . . You say so what. . . . But where would you be now if I hadn't given you Garvey? Where would you be if you hadn't read Du Bois, Richard Wright, James Baldwin, Ralph Ellison, LeRoi Jones, Elijah Muhammad and Malcolm X from my library? . . .

ERNIE

. . . I would have found them on my own.

LEN

Inevitably . . . but the fact is that you found them here earlier than you would have in the public library . . . and certainly Black Arts, Culture and History aren't given you at our college . . . not in 1965.

ERNIE

Well . . . man . . . I don't have all the answers like you do.[14]

Ernie's sarcasm is the quiet evidence that Len pimps his wife, along with the literary and political leaders, in order to undermine any serious carrying out of the Word. Although a white actor portrayed the title character Pig Pen in the original production, Len, himself, in nationalist regalia, is really the pig. Len's whistling Du Bois, Richard Wright, and the

Honorable Elijah Muhammad is really Pig Pen's nickel-plated police whis-
tle-blowing. Pig Pen's dancing with the worshipper-women is, as seen in
the end, Len's victory dance with himself. The poet Ray and the beauty
Margie have only themselves to blame. Len was not totally deceptive: He
let slip such warnings as "Blaming whites for your own inadequacies . . .
is just another form of whining"; "Before you go parroting the current
'ism,' you should do more investigating and reading"; and, after the news
of Malcolm's death, "We must take into account the different life patterns
and allow for conflict."

An important aspect of this play is its structure. Although Bullins had
previously connected episodes by association rather than cause-and-effect
linear patterns, there is in this play the distinctive collapsing of "fast forward" or imagined linear time. This means that the audience sees the future before the characters do, which translates into present and future
time being played simultaneously. For example, the initial entrances of all
characters—other than the leads—are unseen by the other characters:

> (*Margie* enters from outside. . . . In one hand *She* carries a small,
> transistorized radio; with the other she pops her fingers as *She*
> skips and dances to the music.
>
> *Ray* and *Sharon* are not aware that *She* is in the room.
>
> While dancing, *Margie* dips her fingers into the pans and comes
> out with bits of bacon and pieces of scrambled egg.)

RAY

Could I have some more coffee, Sharon?

MARGIE

    (*Holds imaginary cup*)
Me too, Sharon.

SHARON

Of course, Ray.
    (*She pours*)

RAY

Thanks. . . .

> (*Margie* scowls *She* walks down the hall toward the bedroom.
> Then slowly walks down and disappears around the corner.)

Not until the future time (or imagination) catches up with the present
do others acknowledge Margie's presence, her coming out of the bedroom
with Len. Interestingly, all time runs into itself: Although the day turns
into evening, then night, the action in the house continues with what
Bullins called "apparent flashforwards." Bullins throws out rapid—and

easily missed—word clues about time: Opening time is three o'clock in the morning, then "Looks like noon," "You mean this afternoon," and "a stoned night." Much of this so puzzled the critics that Edith Oliver, a Bullins admirer, confessed that she did not "know exactly what Mr. Bullins is driving at this time, but I have total confidence that he does."[15] Other reviewers were not so honest, hypothesizing the play to be everything from a "warning to black and white youth"[16] to "an indictment of white intellectualism in favor of black militance."[17] Clayton Riley was most taken by the character Pig Pen, whom he called a "comic strip refugee" and a fantasy rendering of the police establishment."[18] Riley found the character to be a "disturbing symbol," however:

> The police are what they are, whatever they are to whoever encounters them regularly. [The police are] . . . dangerous in their ignorance and compromised to the point past paranoia by the low esteem that historically has attended their work. Not cartoon, however. And not fantasies. Not dreams that go away in the dawn, that stop being because we wake.
>
> One can respect the choice Bullins has made in shaping the image of the man only to the extent one regards the relationship existing between police and residents of the Black community as defined past logic or common sense. The play, then, pushed along by tentative, convoluted interaction between the guests at Lennie's, shifts into a remarkable fifth gear when the constable shows.[19]

In considering the question why people use reasoning to mask true identities, feelings, and/or desires, Bullins pursues totally different possibilities in the second play of the Logic Subclass, *Daddy* (1977), which opened at the Henry Street Settlement's New Federal Theater under Woodie King's "firm and sensitive direction."[20] This is one of Bullins's few elaborate plots: After almost twenty years of hard work, jazz musician Michael Brown finally has a series of hits. Instead of bringing happiness, the songs uncover the past and the buried present. His success causes Candy, Michael's secretly pregnant live-in lover, to unleash her fear of losing him to the women who chase him. Her anxiety is fueled by Michael's vow never to marry again. The hit songs prompt Michael's abandoned two sons and daughters to leave their black Newark ghetto to find their father, who, after only having recently arrived from California, lives in a yet-unfurnished Central Park West apartment in Manhattan. Their worlds clash. The children pull their father to the past, presided over by Michael's alcoholic ex-wife Jackie, who has eight other children, only one of whom by her man-of-the-moment Carter. Michael gets her permission for the boys to live with him. They do not like it—notwithstanding his putting them in an expensive private school. Things boil over when the older boy overdoses, followed by the news that Carter has physically abused the younger daughter. Michael resolves to kill Carter. When the armed men meet for the showdown, Carter asks that it be delayed. He helps Michael to understand the troubles of having "fathered" Michael's family. Michael decides that Carter is more important in the children's lives than Michael himself has been. He reorders his priorities not only about Carter but also about his own role and life. He marries Candy, and he welcomes his children to visit—on their own terms.

Daddy argues that people too often use reasoning to mask their true selves for three reasons, the first of which is that they value the material over the metaphysical. Michael's family broke apart primarily because of his efforts to satisfy his ex-wife's hunger for things:

JACKIE

Nigger . . . are you crazy? Are ya, huh? Whoever heard of a nigger writin' a jazzy . . . Oh, 'scuse me . . . a Jazz Symphony? There's no such thing, fool!

MICHAEL

But Duke Ellington and John Lewis . . .

JACKIE

I don't care what Duke what's-his-name or what John thing-a-mah-jig says . . . you just want to get out and meet some girls . . . like you did when you was in the service. Here you are wastin' all your time goin' to night school and practicin' the piano like a little sissy, when you could get yourself another job drivin' a cab or somethin'. We got two kids now . . . and another in the oven. That little ass piece of check the government send you ain't shit! Yeah . . . you got one job but need another one to take care of me and these here kids. Besides . . . I want a fur coat . . . Sheet . . . and I saw a fine 23″ TV down in the window of Bamberger's that I'm gonna get. Sure we got a roof over our head and enough to eat. But that ain't enough, is it? Man, I waited for you when you was in the service and now I'm due to get some good things out of this life. And you my husband . . . and you gonna get them for me . . . and if you don't, nigger . . . I'm puttin' you in court. So don't come 'round here with no more of that goddamn music. I want money, honey, not no music or song or dance or any of that weak-ass do-do.[21]

People hide themselves, secondly, because they spend inordinate amounts of time *preparing* to be rather than *being*. The principal reason for hiding, however, is guilt. Carter believes that Jackie drinks so much because of her guilt about having driven Michael away. Bennie, Michael's manager, feels that Michael stays broke trying to give too much to his children because of guilt. Bullins argues that guilt might be avoided by staying clear of esteem-crushing welfare, by stopping abortions, by being self-reliant, and by learning to resolve conflict by means other than violence.

CARTER

I know you've come to kill me, Mike . . . You don't need to say anything. I know you got that gun in your pocket. And you've been waiting for everyone to clear out so we can have our little "talk." . . . Well, you'll have to wait for a little while until I finish these here dishes, put out the trash and take off my apron before I go outside with you. . . .

When Jackie gets started on her evil days and wants to fight, Nikie picks an argument with me, and before you know it, I'm punchin' Jackie around. This last time we was fightin', Jackie kept screaming that she still loved you and always would . . . and I'd never be half the man you was. She only said it to make me mad, I know; it's Jackie's way. But I hit her til my fists hurt. Then Nikie tried to get me with the butcher knife . . . and I hit her too . . . I didn't mean to do it. It just happened that way.
(MICHAEL *stands.* CARTER *reaches under His apron.*)

MICHAEL
Okay . . . okay . . . I've got the message . . .

CARTER (*half-turns*)
I only got this little bit more to do, Mike.

MICHAEL
Yeah . . . Carter . . . but I'm leaving. . . .

This ain't my scene. You got it, brother. . . . Ha ha . . . that's funny . . . *daddy* . . . *daddy* . . . they call me. But the day-in-day-out thankless hassle of being *daddy* when the chips are down doesn't seem to be my thing, Carter. For my next kids . . . perhaps I'll be some kind of father. But it's funny. Nobody around here knows who the real daddy is . . . and it's you, Carter. And I bless you for it.

In terms of dialogue and structure, *Daddy* is among Bullins's most sophisticated plays. The dialogue ranks among his best prose poetry: "I hardly exist as an economic being. I've been forced to survive like . . . some junkie jagged out beside the garbage cans in the deep negro night"; or "For all I need, really, is a bit of weed and a suck on a bottle of grape to make things better for me. And all I need is the warmth and wetness of a willing woman"; or "I didn't want to be that faithful fool. . . . A wife who birthed the bastards, who sat out the nights before her man came in to beat her and make her pregnant again and give her what he had left of wornout adventures."

The structure, like that in *In New England Winter,* must accommodate scenes from the past and the present. Bullins accomplishes the time transitions not only with the uses of lights and slides but also sound, movement, and dialogue. There are amplified and magnified voices, slow-motion movements, eerie lights, and deep and weird shadows. Bullins uses parallel time in ways he never before tried. For example, in an effort to move in and out of the time, space, and reality of Jackie's and Michael's minds, Bullins introduces Little Mike in the past—in a scene in which the child is sent to the store. When Little Mike returns from the store in the present, he is a man. For one of a very few times, Bullins ends his acts on highly dramatic or suspenseful notes: Act I finishes with Candy crying her heart out in Michael's arms. At the end of Act II, the overdosed Mike is discovered. Act III has Michael carrying Candy across the threshold—heightened by Jackie's lie that she is so glad that he has left.

The reviews of the Henry Street production of the play show, significantly, that Bullins by 1977 had developed both entrenched admirers and detractors among the New York theatre critics. Leading the friendly camp was the *The New Yorker* critic Edith Oliver, who found it hard not to love a Bullins play. *Daddy* has a "richness and depth and complexity," she wrote, that make it one of Bullins's "most accomplished plays so far."[22] Oliver, in fact, had come almost too close to the New Lafayette Theatre company to make an unbiased judgment of its works. Theatre personnel regularly attended to her every need, including taking her home after performances. On the other hand, Terry Curtis Fox of *The Village Voice*—perhaps influenced by her editor, Bullins's nemesis, Erika Munk—joined other *Voice* critics in attacking every Bullins play, calling *Daddy* "a fraud. A complicated fraud to be certain, but a fraud nonetheless":

> The play hoists the black flag of rebellion only to sail straight for the shores of social order. An attempt to vitiate criticism of Bullins's previous attitude toward women, *Daddy* emerges as a special plea for the only person Bullins respects, the black artist with a prick.
>
> Because this is Bullins trying to play fair to females, Michael admits Jackie was not at fault for his going away, although he gets to absolve his own guilt at the same time. And Candy gets what she wants: to get both married and knocked up. . . .
>
> Bullins defends wife-beating on the part of not one but two men. (Jackie hurts some, but she does so like the fucking that comes after.) . . .
>
> The social problem in *Daddy*—Michael Brown's desertion of his kids—is a smoke screen. It exists, all right, but it is peripheral to the

real content of the play. . . . Bullins may know deserting fathers exist, but the problems kids face, like those of women, are merely road-blocks thrown up in the artist-hero's way.[23]

The Village Voice asserted as well that even the issues raised by Bullins's plays are sexually and socially conservative, their aesthetics borrowed from nineteenth-century melodrama, and their style and structure copied from American dramatists Clifford Odets and Arthur Miller. Balancing this extreme view, along with that of the Bullinsphile Oliver, is the centrist criticism of the *Soho Weekly News* reviewer William Harris, who wrote that *Daddy,* although not faultless, is, indeed, "rich, imaginative, and moving."[24] Harris correctly argued that the play is about guilt, a "waste-product" of the newly emerging black middle class, a group torn by their conflicting desires to affirm their blackness, while satiating their materialism and achieving status in the white-oriented social structure.[25] Bullins could have told Clayton Riley that *Daddy* represented for him an emancipation from his own guilt over having been an absent father for his many children left behind in the several places where he had lived.

Bullins's freedom from guilt had begun seven years before *Daddy* was first produced, while he was writing the five pieces making up the fourth subclass, New Spirituality, which dramatizes the attempt to purify one's self from the corrupting influences of other people's values, beliefs, and practices. Ironically, as Bullins and the New Lafayette company were undergoing this uplifting search for true self during the period 1969–1971, the New Lafayette theatre itself was dying because Harlemites had stopped attending the plays. The people simply did not like the fact that Robert Macbeth had replaced Bullins's representations of their lives with mimes, rituals, and mystic dramas. Macbeth ordered the change from Western-based dramas after he let himself be cornered during the heated symposium with the armed Marxists, black cultural nationalists, and revolutionary black nationalists. As was previously recounted, some of them threatened to burn down Macbeth's theatre because of what they considered the anti-revolutionary beliefs and images in Bullins's *We Righteous Bombers* (1969). Although Amiri Baraka defused the confrontation, notwithstanding the fact that he and Macbeth did not agree on much, the cease-fire had come at a high price.

During the symposium at the New Lafayette Theater, Baraka drove home the point that *Bombers* had failed the African American community as much in its form as in its ideas. In fact, its Western form caused the biggest problem with the play. Baraka's ally, the critic Larry Neal, grabbed the baton: He said that the play was a problem because "you can't express the total meaning of what the author is saying because he's using a form that is dead. "You know, that West kind of intellectual formalization."[26] In order to deflect these heavy blows, Macbeth promised that he would soon stop producing plays with the "ragged' Western form because they did not "serve our purposes." The very next theatre season, 1969–70, he almost totally abandoned these plays. He produced, instead, Bullins's first rituals, the lost *A Ritual to Bind Together and Strengthen Black People So That They Can Survive the Long Struggle to Come* (1969), and *To raise the dead and foretell the future* (1970). Written in poetry, *To raise the dead* contains six sections. The first, "Spirit Cleansing," calls upon the "Spirits of our people" to

Take evil from our hearts
Take the evil from our hearts
Spirits of our people come
Burn the evil from our souls
Burn the evil from our souls
Enter into our inner secret places
and cleanse us
cleanse us
Oh cleanse us

. . . .

Spirits cut though the shell of [Om]
our ignorance
Cut through the skin of
not knowing ourselves
& release
& release
& release
us
to join our souls [27]

The second section, "The Welcoming," invites spectators "to the place where death is found":

Come
Come enter
You are welcome

We are going
We are going to another place than here
We are going to the place of death

hold on to . . . hold on to each other . . . hold on to us . . . we are going we are going . . . we are going . . . don't fight against the journey give up and journey with us come and release yourself up to the journey THE JOURNEY OF LIFE IS THE LONGEST the journey of death is only part of the supreme journey come come come . . . we are going we are going.

Part Three, "Processional," fills the spectator with images of the death-journey:

Our bones
bleached
white
in the
suns
of this
waste land

Clack clack
our bone clap

Our flesh
red
but the
tight press
of history
drains
blood
from our
eyes

drip drip
the blood
drops

Our skin
black
strained
over our
black shapes

. . . . .

we come
from
the wilderness

tramp tramp
stamp stamp
vamp vamp
clip clop
hip hop
oyee
oyee
oyee
oyee

The longest segment, "The We Sutra," contains six stations. At the first, the travelers celebrate having weathered the journey:

We are the Black and deprived
We are the Black Ones who have survived
We are the Survived
We have made the long journey
the middle crossing
We have lived
We have lived

.   .   .   .

And now we rise

.   .   .   .   .   .

We move into life
we move into spirit
we push
we push
we push ahead.

At the second level, the weary ones review the journey, acknowledging:

Africa
Africa
our home
Africa
we come from
the belly and breast
of we who were
stolen
we who were wiped from
the slavers' decks
and dumped here

This recognition of ancestry serves all other missions, which call all to awaken, unify, and rise:

We are dead and must rise ourselves
must rise as One
as One
as one people
the Black nation
We are the African nation
of the West
We are the African nation
of the West

We are the African nation
in this dead place

  .   .   .   .

We rise from the grave

  .   .   .   .

We rise as a smashing Black fist
as a smashing Black energy
as a screaming strength of Black will
aaaaaaaaaaaaaaaaaaiiiiiiiiiiiiiiiiiieeeeeeeeeeeeeeeee
aaaaaaaaaaaaaaaaaaiiiiiiiiiiiiiiiiiieeeeeeeeeeeeeeeee
aaaaaaaaaaaaaaaaaaiiiiiiiiiiiiiiiiiieeeeeeeeeeeeeeeee

To raise the dead and fortell the future shows that Bullins had finally improved his writing of poetry. The prose poetry in some monologues indicates that he knew the rudiments of poeticizing, but, as he admitted, when he sat down to write a poem, what came out was often too obvious and banal:

I'm tired
Undernourished
Slow
Bored
I'm not writing
Writing
It's what I do
or should
Writing
I'm getting fatter

A bad marriage is one of the
worse things in the world.
It saps the spiritual core of your
being.
It cripples you in many ways,
for years, and in some ways,
forever.[28]

This first draft of an unpublished work might be forgiven, but the published poems—"Creation Spell," for example—are not much better:

Into your palm I place the ashes
Into your palm are the ashes of your brothers
burnt in the Alabama night
Into your palm that holds your babies
into your palm that feeds your infants
into your palm that holds the work tools

I place the ashes of your brother
I place the ashes of your father
here are the ashes of your husbands
Take the ashes of your nation
and create the cement to build again
Create the spirits to move again
Take this soul dust and begin again[29]

The improvement and the added sophistication are nowhere more apparent than in the coda of *To raise the dead:*

We who left the big place left the place of gold and traveled
out against our will against our knowledge of where we were
traveling over the big water to a cold place of death
and savagery of white things and work of work of work
without pay
or praise into the generations here not of toil of hunger
of beatings of lynchings of begging of whipping of rape of
defilement of slavery of slaver we who
were killed and tortured who were branded and beaten we who
fell as a drunkard on the Boston common in the blood shed
for him we who walked from one end of the land to the other
preaching against slavery against inhumanity against the most
foul system devised in the universe
we know and come together

Although *To raise the dead* is fine to read, it proved peculiar to see for the Harlemites, many of whom had come to the New Lafayette theatre principally to laugh at recognizable people and situations. Even more bizarre and alienating were the Macbeth-directed mystic dramas, *The Devil Catchers* (1970) and *The Psychic Pretenders* (1971). The former, which Bullins subtitled a "philosophic prophesy"—whatever that is—is set in the future, thousands of years after nuclear wars have nearly wiped out all known life. There exist supernatural beings, called the devils. African peoples are divided into two continually warring camps: catchers and guides (or defenders). Every thirty or so years, there arises a messianic visionary, this time Y/rag. He tries to stop the fratricide. He, like those before him, is sacrificed.

The plot of *The Psychic Pretenders* is somewhat similar. It is divided into "three motions"—instead of acts. In the first, "The Place of Quest," two men (Libo and Mijo) escape the evil Land of Fools. They are pursued by White Death. In their search for Truth, they stumble upon what appears to be a ritual murder. They rescue the victim, Telle, who is the wise black magic mother who will lead them, along with executioner Rago, from a "nigger zombie death." They become pilgrims, guided by a chorus

221

of Psychic Pretenders. In the second motion, "Place of Love," the pilgrims are transported through The Gate of Love and across the Bridge of Purgatory. There the warriors meet two sorcerers, Soro and Moto, who make them face up to their inordinate sexual desires. The now five people reach Heaven, the Place of Intuitive Knowledge. Their way to this land of the future, however, is blocked by Tihwo, whose only duty is to bring Truth. He disables the five warriors (two are put in comas, one becomes a sheep, and two become invisible). They recover and gain truth only when Telle kisses the feet of Tihwo. All enter heaven dancing and chanting, "The attainment of harmony is known as Heaven."

Devil Catchers and *Psychic Pretenders* create a myth of order to demand, again, that African Americans stop dividing themselves along lines of allegiance to another race, and that people stop blocking themselves from knowing truth. The principal components of the ritualistic pieces are their novel spectacle, language, humor, and theme. The spectacle, like that in *The Mystery of Phillis Wheatley* and *I Am Lucy Terry,* is in the magical setting and action. The setting in *Devil Catchers* is *Black. Void. Darkness deeper than before time. A prehistoric silence. Before time. Beyond the future. Emptiness. Silence. Pause. Black . . . then a vibration. A hint of sound. An imperceptible glow. Sound. Smell of scorched elements. . . . A rumble. Build. A growl of smothered energy. Faint light pulsates to sound. Colors . . . and then a shadow crosses the mystery: BOLOOOOOSSHH!* In order to bring two files of chanting actors into this setting, Bullins creates an opening scene of a kind seldom seen in African American theatre:

> *From the beginning, THEY [all characters] file in. Two columns, clothed in their magical costumes: on one side, THOSE IN THE WAY; on the other side, THE DEVIL GUIDES. The two SPIRITUAL SCIENTISTS march at the center of the procession. THEY chant and move in unison. The women carry candles and pewters of varied colored scented smoke. The men's swords and shields compliment their uniforms.*

THEY

    (In procession)
In a place beyond time
In a place before the future
In a place that is this place
that is all places
In a place where past is linked to the history of the future
Where the sun sets in a crimson horizon of dust
is the land of the Devil Catachers
is the place of the Devil Catchers.[30]

Equally as mysterious and spectacular is the setting of *Psychic Pretenders*:

> *Music. Light. Varied greens. Tones of yellows. Brightness. Splendid feathered creatures flit and float in the perfumed air.*
>
> *The hushed shove of entrance into a peculiar reality. Sounds: water splattering among rocks. A rodent's squeal. An eagle's shriek. The shape of the vulture near. Silence.*
>
> *A shadowy . . . then a dim* VEILED FORM *moves silently into sight. It stands and waits, looking off. . . .*
>
> *Then* ANOTHER VEILED SHAPE *moves in toward the first form with measured steps, tracing out a path. And upon the invisible path comes a* RED-HOODED FIGURE *that drags a* WOMAN, *bound and gagged, dressed in black, and he ties her to a stake, and ceremoniously begins to prepare her for execution*
>
> *Meanwhile, the* TWO VEILED PRESENCES *prepare the death place for the tied woman, then produce an awesome knife, which the* RED-HOODED MAN *receives, and moves away to witness the proceedings. With the* WOMAN-IN-BLACK *calmly watching,* HE *begins an evil ritual, and unsheathes the blood-letting knife.*

> RED-HOODED FIGURE
>
> (*Consecration*)
>
> Zo wan-we Sobadi sobo kalisso Maitre-Carrefour.[31]

The action in *Devil Catchers* challenges the imagination. Typical is the climactic war: *The two lines [of warriors] tense but do not waver at first.* THEY *stare each other down.* THEIR *psychic power forceful as body blows, immense in intensity. Flashes of light jump from . . . eyes and bounce off the polished armor of antagonists.* Then the two lines face off and strain their brains to bursting. Lights flash, rays of energy strike, thunder thunders . . . steady electric forces. There is a standoff. The spectacle in *Psychic Pretenders* is even more elaborate, with cracking skies, raised dead, flying black cloth, shadows escorting other shadows, talking heads looking for their bodies, and people holding their melting eyeballs.

Bullins was obviously having a good time:

> OYAM
>
> IT IS TIME FOR THE TEST . . . IT IS TIME TO SEE WHO IS THE BEST . . . PLAY MUSICIANS . . . DRAW NEAR SPECTATORS . . . WALK GHOSTS . . . DESCEND DEMONS AND BE OUR HOSTS . . . THE MOON HAS WAXED . . . THE LUNAR MONTH HAS WANED THREE HUNDRED AND SIXTY TIMES . . . AND NOW THE TIME FOR NIGGERS TO BATTLE AGAIN. . . .
>
> HEAR ME, OH TRIBE OF EVIL, NATION OF DEVIL LOVERS, BE READY FOR OUR RIGHTEOUS WRATH TO TAKE HOLD OF YOU

AND SHAKE YOU LIKE THE DREGS OF DISEASED WHORES
THAT YOU ARE!

NAHTAL

TALK ALL YOU WANT, OLD SPIRITUAL SHYSTER . . . WE KNOW YOUR GAME
. . . AND WE GONNA SEE YOU HOME LAME IF YOU MESS WITH US. . . . NOW
DON'T SHED NO BLOOD . . . THERE'S ENOUGH GRAVE FOR ALL OF US STUDS
. . . EXCUSE ME, SISTERS . . . NO OFFENSE INTENDED . . . . OLD OYAM AND
YOUR BOYS . . . IF YOU THINK SO BAD . . . JUMP CHUMPS AND YOU'LL BE
HAD.[32]

Even more comedy might be found in *The Psychic Pretenders:*

ROTO

No more of your nervous questioning, please. The witching hour flies
almost as swiftly as death.

SORO

It is said that the shadow of the devil precedes death . . .

ROTO

Enough . . . we must act.
    (Pause)

SORO

. . . . And its shadow is cast toward the West.

ROTO

Be still . . . serene sorcerer.
    (Pause)

SORO

Is everything in place?

ROTO

It appears so.

SORO

Did you bring the matches?

ROTO

I left that for you to do, my brother.

SORO

You did?

ROTO

Yes.

SORO

(Searches HIMSELF unhurriedly.)

You are certain, my brother?

ROTO

That vital detail could only be entrusted to you, brother Soro.

SORO

I see.

(SORO concentrates. A VEILED ONE appears and hands HIM matches.)

You are exact as you always are, brother Roto. The matches are in my hand.[33]

Bullins's ritualistic and mystical plays differ from those by other writers in that Bullins did not take them too seriously. Like Amiri Baraka's *A Black Mass* (1965), which was based on the Nation of Islam myth of the Creation, Bullins's plays warn African Americans not to let others divide them along lines inimical to blacks' interests. What makes Bullins's plays stand out, however, is their abundant humor and really imaginative spectacle. White critics generally liked these mumbo-jumbo pieces, finding them to be a "subtle combination of turbulence and regularity, energy and repose"—as well as "enjoyable works of art."[34]

Too many black people in Harlem, however, disagreed. They turned, instead, to the earthly and earthy plays that were being put on by a number of young people in Bullins's New Lafayette Theatre Workshop. Using money from the New Lafayette, these young people—led by the playwrights Richard Wesley, OyamO, and Marti Charles—rented a small walk-up space in order to put on their non-ritualistic plays. Although the New Lafayette was nearly empty, the young bloods at the Workshop had to turn people away. Word soon got back to Robert Macbeth, who, when he briefly visited, was astounded to see most of his former audience madly enjoying "the ragged Western forms." Macbeth withdrew the funding for the Workshop because, according to Bullins, "fringe elements attempted a coup against the theatre. Naturally, I led the charge against the rebels. Macbeth and I together closed down the workshop."[35] Nevertheless, the crowds never returned to the New Lafayette. It was soon after this that the New Lafayette company voted itself out of existence, an act Bullins must have strongly disagreed with but never would have admitted to Clayton Riley or anybody else.

Bullins was asked in 1994—twenty-two years after the Riley interview—why he had once been so secretive. He replied that he had always loved being a mystery.[36] He joked that he would never write an autobiography because he would have to tell too many lies. It is amazing, therefore, that he agreed in 1992 to write a thousand-word autobiographical essay for publication, "Two Days Shie. . . ," for the reference series *Contemporary Authors*.[37] Even more wondrous is the fact that the essay is quite revealing—for Bullins. He opens with a sufficiently chilling experience:

> When I was young, I was bitten by a dog. . . . The dog leaped from an overhanging porch, attempting to tear out my jugular, but my twisted jaw caused its fangs to slip off, and I lurched forward, away from sure death, and the beast's chain strangled and halted the animal, as I silently raced for home, with blood spilling down my chest, and my cousin screaming and crying somewhere behind me, from the terror of my escape.[38]

In some ways, this horror might be seen as a metaphor for the final subclass of Bullins's Inner Life plays, Certainty. He did not mean the three plays in this subclass to exemplify those elements that are not variable or that can be depended upon. He shows, instead, that a person can bank on almost nothing in public or private life. How Bullins publicly dealt with this fact made up the three autobiographical plays. By comparing them, written over the course of twenty-seven years, one gets a glimpse of how very much a young man, who had grown up in the public eye, had changed in his attitudes about some aspects of his private life. In *A Son, Come Home* (1968), for example, Bullins dramatizes a showdown between a mother and son, which revealed hostility toward his own mother, stepfather, and aunt. In this memory play, which Robert Macbeth first directed at the American Place Theatre, Bullins uses a separate boy and girl to "weave about the central characters, giving voice to helpless silences." A twenty-four-year-old man, Son, who, like Michael in *Daddy,* is rising in the music world, returns to Philadelphia to discover that his mother has just about completely withdrawn from worldly concerns. She lives in the austere hostel of a religious sect, reserving her only passion to call down retribution on the defeated man who fathered her son but never married her.[39] There is rejection everywhere, the most poignant of which is of Son by his aunt in California:

BOY *(on telephone)*
Aunt Sophie? . . . Aunt Sophie . . . It's me, Michael.

GIRL
Michael?

BOY
Yes . . . Michael . . .

GIRL
Oh . . . Michael . . . yes . . .

226

BOY

I'm in jail, Aunt Sophie . . . I got picked up for drunk driving.

GIRL

You did . . . how awful. . . .

BOY

Aunt Sophie . . . will you please come down and sign my bail. I've got the money . . . I just got paid yesterday . . . They're holding more than enough for me . . . but the law says that someone has to sign for it. . . . All you need to do is come down and sign . . . and I can get out.

GIRL

Ohhh . . . Michael . . . I'm sorry but I can't do nothin' like that. . . .

BOY

But, Aunt Sophie . . . if I don't get back to work, I'll lose my job and everything.

GIRL

I'm sorry, Michael . . . I can't stick my neck out . . . I have to go now . . . Is there anyone I can call?

BOY

No.

GIRL

I could call your mother. She wouldn't mind if I reversed the charges on her, would she? I don't like to run my bills up.[40]

Son (Bullins's surrogate) is hurt by his aunt's not trusting and loving him, the man, as she had the child. He probably found it hard to forgive her, a woman whom he called "slightly bizarre"—as might be deduced from his description of her death: She had "supposedly died after arguing with her daughter, Charlotte, . . . [who] went into the kitchen to fix some tea[. W]hile there[, she] heard a gasp from the bedroom; when she returned, Aunt Sarah's eyes were rolled up into the top of her head, with the whites showing."[41] Although the play shows similar tensions between Son's mother and father, it is the strongly ambivalent feelings between Son and Mother that power the play. Bullins's 1966 short story, "He Couldn't Say Sex," helps to understand better the cutting exchanges in the play. Highly autobiographical, the story tells of the longterm psychological damage done to an adolescent whose religious mother refuses to let him even say the "nasty filthy" word. "sex," which so defines his landscape: "The word drifted down midnight hallways of tenements, finding him awake in frigid beds envying the couples clawing in the stairwells. . . . He smelled it; he dreamt; he lived through its discovering paradoxes each moment." Repressing what he sees and feels causes him to raise deeper questions:

> "Why, Mother?" he once asked. "Why should I grow up stunted and phobic? Why should *don't* be my creed, because it's yours? Don't say God, you say. Don't be immoral. Don't; no, never question—well—What was my father like?"
>
> "There's nothing you would want to hear 'bout your father that I can tell you, boy," was her reply.
>
> And she remained mum. He wondered, "Why? Why? It's about *why* that I want to know. Damn the rest!—give me the mystery of why!"
>
> He made himself an exile searching for truth, the whole big deal about the mighty why.[42]

As the man moves through seaports throughout the world, the question multiplies his drives, having "raged through adolescence and young manhood in conquests," fearing all the while that he is inadequate. He wonders, "How many bastards did he need to make himself a man? How many sleepless nights in strange beds spent probing for a Self that didn't make him puke did he need?" Would it take two hundred lies and ejaculations, or four trips to the man with the needle, or nine bastards scattered in the mainstreams—"with unsuspecting fathers, he hopes"? This fear turns the man into "bug-house bait," makes him "jail-house prone," causes him to be a "slum-seeking, woman-hating, wife-deceiving, respectability-faking, cynic sneering, paranoic (passive aggressive)—*an all-American black boy*—guilt-ridden, but now vocal." Because he never finds the answers to his *why,* he strikes out:

> "Sex, Mother," he says (Does it make you cringe? Burn a candle for him).
>
> "Sex, Daddy. Was it good to you, Pops?" he mourns farewell (and whoever you were, do you still remember what it was like?)
>
> "Sex, God," he curses (go sex yourself), and that goes for the whole shot.
>
> "Sex, sex, sex, sex, America," he roars from his manure pile (with your millions of sexless wonders).

This fury, although tightly controlled in *A Son, Come Home,* is apparent even in Bullins's choice of a title. The comma highlights the fact that "home" is ironic, that it is what Son calls an "anachronism . . . a person or a thing that is chronologically out of place. This searing distrust between mother and son is generated, oddly enough, over the latter's wish to claim exclusive rights to his mother, which causes hard feelings between the stepfather and Son:

SON

You never hear from him?

MOTHER

Last I heard . . . Will had cancer. . . .

SON

Why didn't you tell me? . . . You could have written.

MOTHER

Why? . . .

SON

Because Will was like a father to me . . . the only one I've really known.

MOTHER

A father? And you chased him away as soon as you got big enough.

SON

Don't say that, Mother.

MOTHER

The quarrels you had with him . . . the mean tricks you used to play . . . the lies you told to your friends about Will . . . He wasn't much . . . when I thought I had a sense of humor, I us'ta call him just plain Will. But we was his family.

SON

Mother, listen.

MOTHER

And you drove him away . . . and he didn't lift a hand to stop you.

SON

Listen, Mother.

MOTHER

As soon as you were big enough, you did all that you could to get me and Will separated.

SON

Listen.

MOTHER

All right, Michael . . . I'm listening.
(*Pause*)

SON

Nothing.

Bullins probably never forgave himself for having run off this "sort-of stepfather." Interestingly, Bullins said that the older that he became, the more he thought like his "surrogate father."[43] In 1992, he began a posthumous reconciliation by publishing a warm short story about a time when his stepfather took Bullins and his mother to baseball games. This short story developed into *Boy x Man* (1995), which premiered at North Carolina Agricultural and Technical State University with Miller Lucky Jr. directing. This is a memory play about a man looking back fondly on his growing up. He strains to come to grips with not having ever really understood his mother, and for having failed to say thanks to a stepfather who had been as much of a father to him as any man could have been. The play raises questions that might be posed as follows: As Bullins portrayed himself and his family in the play, who is Bullins? From where has he come? And what is his life about, and what should it be about?

The answers, gained through detailed plot analyses, might be, firstly, that Bullins (the character Ernie in *Boy x Man*) believes that his love of music—to the extent of his substituting music structure for dramatic form—came from his early and continuing exposures to music. In the first episode, the Young Ernie searches for his earliest memories, linked, he recalls, to music: perhaps to W. C. Handy's "The St. Louis Blues," as well as nursery rhymes. He recalls seeing from the crib his mother (Brenda) and stepfather (Will) dancing to Handy. He recollects—while he is between three and fifteen years old—playing a childhood game:

BRENDA (*sing-song like*)

Mirror, mirror
on the wall
who's the most beautiful baby
boy of
them all

ERNIE (*3 years old*)

I am, Mommy
I am, Will

WILL (*partially in shadows*)

Mirror, mirror
on the wall
who's the most
loving one of
us all

ERNIE (*e years old*)

I love you, Mommy
I love you, Will

BRENDA

Baby E
Baby E
our pride
so little
and manly

ERNIE (*6 years old*)

I love you, Mommy
I love you, Will. . . .

ERNIE 9 *years old*)

Do you like me, Mommy?
Do you like me, Will?

BRENDA/WILL (*In unison*)

Do you like us, Boy E
Do you like us, Boy E. . . .

BRENDA (*cont'd*)

Mirror, mirror
on the wall
who's the
manliest of
them all

ERNIE (*cont'd*)

Leave me alone, mother!

WILL (*moving from shadows*)

Say, Sonny Boy, that's your mother you're talking to.

ERNIE (*15 yrs*)

I'm a man, Will. I'm a man.[44]

This *prologos* game becomes the *stasima*, which, as in Greek tragedy, is used throughout the play to separate episodes. More importantly, the *prologos* introduces the full action of the play. What appears, then, to be a slow and repetitive opening is really an effective development technique to help the audience understand an extremely complicated person. The roots of this complexity might center in Bullins's belief that he is psychic, the second answer to the question of who Bullins is. This notion probably came from another memory of a near-death experience as a child. In the play, Ernie recalls having pneumonia and being rushed to the hospital. While being swept on the "rusted wheels" of a hospital table through the corridors, he has an out-of-body experience—until he is placed within an oxygen tent, where his "flying self fell and crashed within

231

myself . . . and that was when I was born, as far as I'm concerned." Near-death comes to characterize most of young Ernie's life, from the time his mother Brenda barely escapes with her life from an ex-lover who tries to rape her to the time his Aunt Sophia is cut badly by her ex-boyfriend for having been with another man, prompting her move to California.

Who Bullins might be, then, is as much shaped by this standing at death's door as by, thirdly, his special view of his mother and stepfather. In the play, Brenda is a dancer who reads voraciously and aims highly: she dreams of being a star at the Apollo Theatre in Harlem. She has a violent temper, which Ernie believes that he has inherited, "especially when we was young." When her mother dies, Brenda abandons the mother's wish for Brenda to become a nurse. She primps and flirts her way into getting pregnant by a man who neglects to tell her that he is already married. She leaves him, and drops out of school during her senior year to support her baby by doing "day's work for white folks in the suburbs, by waiting tables in the summer at the sea shore, and dancing at one of the honky tonks in our area." It is while dancing that she meets Will, who falls in love with her and the baby, which prompts Brenda at first to tolerate him—notwithstanding the fact that her sisters consider him a "low class workin' negro." A competitive woman who loves partying, she ignores her sisters because Will is her "ticket" to a better life, as well as to making her Ernie into "a great Negro leader." After six years of common-law marriage, she concludes that Will is not ambitious enough for her.

Will's going off to World War II probably delays the inevitable separation. The war, then, temporarily turns a battle of wills into one of passion:

Lights on BRENDA. *SHE enters in silk dress.*
WILL *and* BRENDA *meet and kiss for a moment.*

BRENDA
When they told me, I didn't believe at first.

WILL
Yes, hon. I was the same. The radio kept saying something about Pearl . . . Pearl. I thought they were talking about a woman at first, before I knew what they were talking about. Pearl Harbor. . . .
THEY are aroused. And slowly THEY *undress each other.*

WILL
They attacked our country. Bombed our American flag. I think I'll go down and join up, so I can give Hitler a lick, and slap ole ToJo up side his slanty-eyed head.

BRENDA
Will?

232

WILL

Yes, baby?

BRENDA

Wait until they come for you. I don't want you joining nothing but the YMCA, The Elks and church.

WILL

But, Brenda. By serving our country, we negroes proves ourselves.

BRENDA

I'm a New Negro Woman. We New Negroes spell our name, negro, with a capital N. We don't have to prove ourselves.

WILL

But this is a man's world, Brenda. A white man's world. I have to prove myself, so that the white man will give me what's owed me.
The lights are low. The COUPLE is ready to make love.

BRENDA

The whiteman's never going to give you nothing. He never has, and he never will. . . .
The lights go to near black.

WILL

Come here, baby. You got a real man here.

BRENDA

I know, Will. . . . So make sure you stay. War or no war, I want you here with me and Ernest.

Will's leaving, ironically, makes her "negro rich," from her own salary plus the money she receives from Will's savings bonds and crap-game receipts. This materialist streak, interestingly, makes her even more ambitious for Ernie, whom she punishes for shining shoes, a job below her expectations, especially with the rowdy bunch of his low-life friends. Ernie seems perplexed by his mother's pushy love, which first manifests itself when she has him memorize and recite "The Night before Christmas," a feat that makes his cousins wonder if his "little monkey head" hurts. When he, after having spent almost two months with his cousins, copies their calling his mother "Aunt Brenda," she takes him home because "I'm not goin through this suffering and struggle over you, and you're not goin to know me?" Yet, Ernie believes this to be but an empty gesture to prove that he already knows: she loves him.

Will's return from war hastens Brenda's recognition that being with him "may be the worst mistake I've ever made":

233

BRENDA

Will [is stopping me from going to the top]! He won't do anything with his life but stay where he's at. He came out of the service with the G.I. Bill. He refuses to use it. He won't go to school. If he'd learn tailoring, we could become partners and. . . . He won't buy property. Because he won't get a divorce, he would be a fool to buy anything anyway. . . . When he gets home from work from his little job, he sits with a beer and listens to the radio, waiting to die.

This frustrates her ever-expanding plans to use the money from dancing in New York City "to go to school for fashion design and open my own show and invest my money in property." She never realizes these dreams, however, instead, she separates from Will, and becomes a "Holy Roller" who considers Will one of the devil's henchmen. She believes that anything outside of praying and Bible-beating is a sin. The irony of this is that Brenda earlier refused to go to church because she felt that if there were a god, He did not "seem to be on my team. That's for sure."

Bullins's portrayal of his stepfather, oddly enough, is as a hero. A warm and caring person, Will falls in love with the baby, and offers to keep him while Brenda returns to work dancing. He is unafraid to show his love for Brenda by catering to her every need, which is unusual for a hardworking black man. A chain smoker of Camel cigarettes, he caddies, washes and waxes cars, works as a handyman sometimes, and drives railroad spikes. He also drinks port wine and keeps condoms and bullets in a dresser drawer, which is frequently "rumbled through" by Young Ernie, who wonders where the pistol is. Like Brenda, Will reads a lot, preferring the novels of Henry Miller. He might hate himself: Although he looks a lot like Nat King Cole, he despises the singer because "he is too black and ugly." Will hates politicians and intellectuals as well, along with America's brutality. He shares with Ernie the pain of having grown up in the South: as a young man, he was kicked in the behind by a white man for "wrecklessly eyeballin' a white woman's picture" that advertised a film. He told his mom, who blessed him out for being there. He daydreamed about dropping a huge rock on the white man's head.

Will tries his hand at disciplining the Young Ernie for being two hours late in bringing lunch, for having stopped to play, and for not being responsible: "I saw you riding down the fairway looking out for me. Well, now you seen me. . . . So good-bye. Get your no-bringing-lunch butt back to your mama . . . Get your behind out of here, boy." When he is afraid that he has been too tough, he pleads his case to the audience, reminding it of his love for the boy and of his hope to make him into a man who can withstand situations like Will's own curious reward for his patriotism:

WILL

. . . When I was on the front . . .
SOUNDS of artillery firing is heard in background.

WILL *(cont'd)*

We fired! and we fired! And we fired! . . . For days it seemed. I was
corporal. Ya durn right! A black Corporal. Rifleman 1st Class. Marks-
man. Teacher of recruits. And qualifying experts. Kicked up to full
gunner after I got my Purple Heart. Me, a colored corporal . . . 'N
back then, colored guys weren't treated like nothin' in this man's army
except for policing the latrines. . . . But it was WW II. And they needed
real ones, like me, even though I didn't stay quiet. Not after I fired . . .
and fired . . . and killed and killed . . . and killed . . . and bled inside
until . . . until at the end . . . we were at the front. We liberated . . .
liberated we went in and opened up the *camps*. . . . And I found
out that *this* isn't the world. This is Hell. . . . And I'm a trained, working dead man . . . (*HE cries.*) Oh, God, they made me a dead thing.
. . . They made me look . . . look upon the Hell-on-earth that they
created for white things that looked like them. (*Whispers*) *They were
killing the Jewish people like slaughter house animals.* The Germans.
The Nazis. But I looked into the faces of all of the things—the Killer
Things and the Slaughtered Things—and I could not tell which were
which with their clothes off when they was dead. The good or bad
things. The good or bad devils. *And I was their little black demon, a
well-trained dead thing.* A G.I. issued killer. . . . But . . . but . . . I'll . . .
I'll not accept it. I'll not accept this devil's world. (*HE screams/backs
away.*) Oh, I'm scared for my everlasting soul. I'm scared! MAMA!
MAMA!
Aaaaaaaayyyyyyyeeeeeiiiiiiiii!!!!

Having been an artillery man at the Battle of the Bulge leaves him
with the belief that "the whole damn world will be gone in six months."
It was perhaps this feeling that explains his unwillingness to plan for moving ahead after the war, choosing instead to be a fanatic about Negro-
League baseball: the Kansas City Monarchs, the Homestead Braves, and
the Philadelphia All-Stars. He delights in taking along Brenda and Young
Ernie to see the likes of Boston Blackie Jones, Brown Bennie Blackwell,
and Slick Sonny Boy Scott. When Brenda decides that she has had her fill
of baseball and of him, he does not question her leaving:

ERNIE *(after a breath)*

Will . . . you and . . . mom

WILL

Yeah. What about it?

ERNIE

You and her were together since I was a baby. . . . Before I can remember. . . . What happened?

WILL

What happened? . . . Yeah, that's a good question. What happened. Well, I don't know.

ERNIE

I went into the service when I was seventeen. . . . A couple of years later you two are living in different places. And now you say you might see mom once a year or never. I don't understand.

WILL

I don't understand it either Ernie.

This signals Will's recognition and acceptance of the beginning of the end—just as, as he told Ernie, Jackie Robinson's acceptance into major league baseball spelled the end of the Negro League. The *stasima* again sounds, this time becoming the *epilogos* coda:

YOUNG ERNIE *(dressed in black)*

Mirror, mirror
in the Funeral Hall
Who's death face
have you saw
    Light on BRENDA *(in baby blue)*

BRENDA

Mirror, mirror
on the wall
who's the most
beautiful baby
boy of
them all

YOUNG ERNIE

Mirror, mirror
in the Funeral Hall
Who's death face
have you saw
    Lights change.

YOUNG ERNIE

Mirror, mirror
in the Funeral Hall
Who's death face

have you saw

ERNIE (*mature*)

Mother Dear
Daddy Will
I've lost
you now
I love you still

YOUNG ERNIE

I'll love you
'til
I'll love you
'Til . . . til
'til . . .

Interestingly, *Boy x Man*, like *A Son, Come Home*, consists of complicated technical devices: elaborate parallel time, along with innumerable split-second light changes, unreal lights, amplified sounds, freezes, thaws, mimes, shadows, off-stage voices, period songs, and dances. These move the action from Ernie's present to his memory of the past in ways that connect episodes by associations. Typical of recalling a painful past, the narrative jolts, making the audience work hard to follow continually changing episodes, never, therefore, latching on to a story line and developing sympathy for a character. This is what Bullins intended, however. Like the German playwright Bertolt Brecht, Bullins goes out of his way to alienate his spectators in order to make them think. For example, just as the audience surely must have been siding with and pulling for poor Brenda, Bullins threw in a wrench. Her wounded sister Sophia rushes into Brenda's house:

SOPHIA

Ohhh . . . it hurts like hell.

BRENDA

. . . I'm taking you down to the hospital as soon as I get my things on.
    SHE *goes to a closet and pulls out a raincoat.*

SOPHIA

Hurry up, Brenda. I'm feelin' weak.

BRENDA (*turns*)

You got my towel! Where did you get one of my new towels, Sophy? . . .

BRENDA (*upset*)

Yeee . . . Oh, my Lord! The whole top of your hand is just hanging on by a piece of skin.

YOUNG ERNIE (*off*)

What's wrong, moma? What's wrong?

BRENDA

Quiet, boy!

SOPHIA

They had knives. I don't know what happened. Suddenly, the cops were comin' through the door . . . and all of us ran. That's when I found out I was cut.

BRENDA

You have to get to the hospital, sister. You're dripping blood all over my kitchen linoleum.

This full development of Brenda and Will, mixing the favorable and the unpleasant, shows Bullins's extraordinary ability to detach himself—even with subjects as close as his parents. The separation, along with the plays' absurdism, its refusal to take sides or to pander to those wanting gratuitous action—these make *Boy x Man* a precious work, one of Bullins's most difficult and accomplished. As the reviewer Anne Barnhill of the *Greensboro News and Record* says, *Boy x Man* is a play "you won't want to miss."[45]

Equally as sophisticated, although considerably less complicated, is the third play in the Certainty Subclass, *Blacklist: A New Play of the Eighties* (1982), which Bullins began writing as his marriage to Trixie was breaking up in 1981. He finished it in Oakland, California, where he had moved in order to get away from the New York scene. The unproduced play, consequently, is a partly autobiographical look at how betrayals and bans almost destroy a playwright: Art Kane is promised by his director, Willie Clarke, and a Broadway producer, Dean Mack, that Art's most recent play, *Blacklist,* will be produced on Broadway. The play-within-the-play tells the story of how a father and son are blackballed years apart—the father for getting involved in trade union, civil rights, and anti-war activities, and the son for being everything from a black revolutionary to a women's liberation activist. Because of the play's subject matter and Art's own "radicalism," Mack's partner, Ben Kopeck, persuades Mack to cancel the deal. Art later discovers that Willie and Ben have stolen his idea and now plan to produce a Latin version of his play (*La Liste*). Piled on top of this is Art's troubles with his Caribbean wife, Kitty, whom he suspects of cheating on him because of her frequent absences from work: She attends voodoo ceremonies to try to deal with her feelings of being "smothered" by Art. He is pushed under a subway train by forces out to destroy all black radicals. Art survives, however, only to discover that Kitty has left him.

The play shows that by the early 1980s Bullins had broken with several of his past playwriting techniques. His subtitle, "A New Play of the Eighties," means just that, including the very novel beginning:

> *At rise: a lighted window. The silhouette of a mature, buxom WOMAN is seen. SHE sits at her vanity table, primps, and begins singing a classic aria. As soon as SHE's sung a couple of bars, it is apparent that SHE is a gifted, trained BLACK SINGER. HER mood is infectiously warm. HER song rises and rises until at its peak, when glasses and crystal chandeliers begin shattering, a huge explosion blows out window, lights and life*
>
> *Lights change. Different music plays as the smoke clears and sirens sound out in the urban darkness.*
>
> *Then a VOICE broadcasts over TV:*
>
> TV VOICE *(in semi-darkness)*
> ... And that's the latest wrap-up in the Lilayette Prince bombing. Ms. Prince, retired world-renowned soprano, one of the premiere black women of her or any generation to break down the lily-white barriers in the classical music world, was killed this evening by a bomb planted in her home and set to explode when Ms. Prince reached High C in her daily vocal exercises. Ms. Prince is remembered as an activist who marched in the '60's with Martin Luther King, Jr., shared podiums with Malcolm X and sang Freedom, anti-war and Women's Liberation songs before it was chic.[46]

No other Bullins play opens so dramatically—and engagingly. More importantly, he abandons his signature freezes and thaws in favor of innovative transitions, fewer and neater parallel times, and more aligned spectacles. For example, the transition from the television-announced explosive beginning to the protagonist is achieved through Art's reflected image on the television screen, which shows him sitting and watching the news of the explosion. No other Bullins transition is so inventive and smooth. There is even the fresh parallel-time device of having Art read silently a four-page letter threatening to blacklist and kill him, along with other sixties radicals, while his wife talks about her life in England before and after meeting him. Bullins, again, is at his poetic finest:

> KITTY
> I'm in the lush years of my life. Not raw, nor overripe. But lush. Full. Womanly. Ready. . . . But sometimes, I feel that I'm evaporating from

the insides out. It's a slow, certain feeling, and soon, if I don't find a remedy for this symptom, I'll become forever hollow and vacant. . . .

Art and I met at a cocktail party in Earl's Court in swinging London. Our eyes met . . . and sparks fused. I was the only black girl there. A contemporary London bird, I was. A black bird. Raised and schooled in the British Isles and all that rot. . . .

I hung with the lay-abouts and Rasta fringe, but I was quality, you know, and progressive and sexy and really fine. I was 19 and sought after by whole shit-loads of men. West Indian, African, Mid-Eastern, Asian . . . and European. But when I met Art, my black yank, as I called him, my very own G.I., which made him furious, I was eager to be his. And blimey, was he ever eager for me. We were married and instantly after our first intimate moment together. . . .

Over the years, in America, I was merely a wife and mother, and I grew older. And I haven't been happy since. And I can't return to where I came from. I never fitted in there. And I have little here. But I know that I am in the lush years of my life . . . and Art . . . he still needs me so much.

Topping even this unself-conscious prose poetry (unlike that in *In New England*) is spectacle that aims not simply to surprise and titillate, as is the case with the smoke and gore in *High John Da Conqueror* and *Dr. Geechee and the Blood Junkies*. In *Blacklist*, the spectacle speaks more directly to the theme:

ART

Yes, Kitty . . . I was following her. I promised myself that I'd be rational and logical, no matter what I found. I knew it wasn't right to follow her, as if she were a common . . . a common thief or something. But I was frightened and disturbed that I was losing her.
(*Lights change.*)

Religious music rises. The music is of a Caribbean Voodoo sect.

A match lights a candle. KITTY is seen lighting a candle. SHE is dressed entirely in white. SHE does a ritual of lighting the candles, killing a small, caged bird, drinking its blood, then chanting.

KITTY

(*Semi-trance*)
Obatala . . . Ogun . . . Shango, etc.
(*ART enters. HE sees KITTY, with blood smeared upon her mouth.*

Is this sight a metaphor for Bullins's state of mind in 1982, as he unwound from a tight decade of politics, theatre, and family stress? Did he wonder, as he had done in *Salaam, Huey Newton, Salaam,* what had gone wrong politically?

WILLIE

. . . Now you can't even buy a Broadway production, if you're black, even if you got the money, unless you're singin' an' shuffling, so I know this is what you want, Art.

ART

Maybe. But these are funny times, brother. I just saw on TV a woman former Black Arts Nationalist, someone we both know so well, who used to write poems and position papers about why she wouldn't talk to white people . . . well, she just took a maid's role in a Broadway play. Wow! Impossible a minute ago, now she explains she needs the money, and she's going to breathe depth and meaning into the part by tearing off her apron in her last scene when the white folks leave the room. Damn! She and Eldridge Cleaver.

WILLIE

You've always been an idealist, Art. That's why you blew so many of your opportunities and are sitting here right now. Artistically pure . . . but not so affluent.

ART

I guess you're right. . . .
When did the turn-about come, man? What happened? Was it Nixon? Was it the destruction of the Panthers and the militant left?

Having no answers, Bullins replays all of the negative comments made about him, from the suspicion that he is a communist to the accusation that he doesn't believe in anything except "that the establishment is lousy. You got an idiot anarchist here with this Art Kane Jerk," Ben says. "You can't tell what you'll get from him." Bullins saves much of his venom for insensitive producers and directors—often hinting at whom in real life he means by making the number and the sound of the syllables in the character's name match and rhyme with the name of the real person. For Bullins, there could not have been anything more despicable than the Broadway producer who wanted Bullins to write the book for a musical on the Atlanta child murders, or the African American producer/director/middleman who would buy into that or any other play so along as it bulged his pockets. Such twisted sensibilities are no match, however, for the very painful accusation that Bullins hates black women, an accusation that was used by the actors during his sit-in on the *Duplex* set a decade earlier. Bullins believes, in fact, that it was this public brawl that caused him to be blacklisted by New York City producers.

241

The greatest ache centers not so much in nasty public judgments but in the spillover of those hasty opinions in domestic squabbles:

KITTY
You think I'm like you. Like you. You think I'm like you. You stuff your snout into any tail that wags by, and you measure everyone else by your low-down doggish ways. . . .

ART
If you'll just tell me the truth, honey. I can forgive anything.

KITTY
You think I'm like you. You think I'd love to go to bed with a blond European, Monique's brother perhaps. But that's not my dream, Art. That not my dream. You're the one who makes love to faceless blonds, brunettes, naturals . . . while I . . . I . . . You're probably in love with Monique. You want to replace me with her. That's just like you. You hate black women, don't you.?

Bullins does not paint himself only as victim in *Blacklist*. He shows how much his wife had tried to help him overcome the low self-esteem he analyzed in the short story "He Couldn't Say Sex." Although a widely respected dramatist, Art is convinced that "I have little or no success at all, believe me":

KITTY
See there, you don't even know and understand what you have. You're such a foolish, piggish American. Don't you know you're a success, man? Really. You have what some others would almost die for. Your name is in books, all over the world. Your books are in libraries, are read in schools. You can teach all over the world, if you wish. Many, many people know your name and have never met you. You don't have to work a nine-to-five, but can do what you want, which is to write!

ART
But I'm not a success.

KITTY
But you are! You are! And I'm your wife, a little nothing who stands in your shadow, waiting for someone to notice me. . . . But one day the world will notice me. I'll be a success, too. . . .

Irregardless of your support or indifference, I shall . . .

ART
You know, I've told you again and again that there's no such word as "irregardless."

242

When Art/Bullins finds himself refereeing battles between his wife and his daughter, Cookie, over such things as hair rollers, it brings out what he feels is the worst in himself:

ART

To me, this was all so terrible. Hair rollers. Something that my Black Is Beautiful generation thought of as almost evil. Something which represented Western decadence, cultural imperialism and all that rhetoric, something which was supposed to be rejected out of revulsion. Well, the revolution was over for us. We had come to a turning point. Kitty wanted to go away; she felt she couldn't deal with Cookie any longer. And she resented me. So we compromised, and Cookie was sent to a good girl's boarding school. I was so sad. But I felt that in a couple of years, things would be settled between us, and our family could be back together. But I have learned some things because of all this. While I thought myself a rational man, something snapped inside me, and I became a wife beater. While I prided myself in being logical and fair, I remained that to all except my wife. And I love her so much, but became frightened when I realized that I didn't know her, so instead of a husband, I became her jailor. I tried to make our family, our home, our marriage an island fortress from the world. I tried to completely possess her then. I wanted her to have no friend but me; I wanted her to have no activity or concerns except me. I believe I went a bit insane.

Art's "a bit insane" grows into a full-blown paranoid belief that someone is out to kill him, possibly to push him under a subway train—with the public announcement that he, like the singer in the play, Lilayette Prince, has committed suicide. Art survives the ordeal only to come home to Kitty's Dear John letter, to her "It's hard for me to tell you that I don't love you any longer"—this undams the years in New York City:

HE begins crying. HIS sobs build until they wrack his body. HE sits on the couch, almost drawing up into a fetal position.

ART

Kitty . . . I need you so much. So much, baby.

Bullins said in 1994 that he didn't know why he stubbornly refused to answer a single question about his private life put to him by Clayton Riley in 1972 until the summer of 1994, when his family had a reunion in Philadelphia. He found out then that a great aunt had been a spiritualist specializing in hoodoo, and that the family regularly held seances. This was during the twenties, when northerners looked down on such "backward stuff." The Bullins family shut its collective mouth, therefore, and went on with its cryptic other-world business. Bullins believes that his habit of never talking about his family carried over from his mysterious childhood.[47] Added to this might be his own suspicion that most people would not understand the private Bullins, the quiet man who had suffered stoically rejections by his mother, father, stepfather, aunt, and wife. The public might not have ever accepted the fact that in 1965, the then thirty-year-old fledgling author of the then detested *The Electronic Nigger*—with its brash pronouncements—and *Clara's Ole Man*—with its scores of verbal and visual profanities—this young man had now grown comfortable with what he was even back then, an introspective and quite sensitive person who continually questioned why he was and how he/we might become something more.

This atypically quiet quest partly explains the puzzled critical responses to the Certainty subclass of Inner Life plays. Reviewers called *A Son, Come Home* everything from "a touching, often moving, bit of theater"[48] to a "formal, ritualistic, stylized, almost-dance,"[49] which was of "more biographical interest than intrinsic value."[50] The unproduced *Blacklist* lived up to its title. With presently only two exceptions, *Boy x Man* has received a similar frozen shoulder: After having read it, some of Bullins's friends said that the play "needed more action"—possibly because so many of them had been conditioned to prime their pumps when the name "Bullins" was heard. Bullins's longtime agent, Helen Merrill, might have been so afflicted: she told him that she did not like the play, which caused him to be depressed.[51] The fact that people do not like *this* Bullins, however, can in no way change the fact that this memory play, as well as *A Son* and *Blacklist,* shows Bullins to be among the very best writers in American theatre.

CONCLUSION

In 1994, Ed Bullins continued having dramatic near-death experiences similar to that of the vicious dog going for the child's throat: "Marva and I were in a spectacular hit-and-run accident that could have cost us our lives. The other car flipped over, later proving stolen. Its occupants crawled out of the smashed windows and disappeared on foot. We only have scratches and sprains, plus a sharpened perspective about life."[1] Could the series of such outlook-honing ordeals partly account for Bullins's lifelong contrariness, confirming his adopted notion that "the whole damn world will be gone in six months"? Could the out-of-body watch over squeaking wheels rushing through a hospital corridor seen in *Boy x Man* have helped him later to stay outside of bodies in order to catch a clearer view? Is that the reason that while others were scrounging and screaming in their plays for civil rights, he had characters in his Inner Life versus Outer Life plays quietly hanging up on racist publishers, or stashing fish to spoil in redlining banks, or filling theatres with white spectators in order to make them watch the dark? Some unknown force propelled this man. Contrariness alone would not cause him to redefine rape so that it became a double-victim crime, in which the immediate physical act is measured within the context of historical and mental assaults.

Not even Bullins's hoodoo origins can satisfactorily explain what would make a peripheral (at best) Black Panther declare in 1993 that "Amiri Baraka, Huey Newton, Bobby Seale and I were the only true Black American revolutionaries—we just didn't understand each other."[2] Yet, he might have been correct, since his Black Revolutionary plays, too, "stood him slightly off-center, giving his plays a clearly observed objectivity"[3]: nobody else dared to set revolutions in stately living rooms, or in the tunnels of state office buildings, or in pig's feet emporiums. No other author weakened his "dialect determinist" arguments to assassinate assimilated negroes with equally compelling justifications for letting them live. Who would even have hoped to incite blacks to kill whitey by showing disorganized, scheming, and martyr-complexed urban guerrillas, whose leader sends them to the front so that he can screw their women? Yet, could Bullins have been a gourmet rebel if he aimed his charge at the insurgents themselves, demanding real commitment by making podium poems that matched such activities as crowding whites into theatres and shooting them? Furthermore, would even Eldridge Cleaver have appointed a lieutenant to steal and use an American flag for a public piss-in? This stuff is so outrageous that one could easily have mixed up freedom-fighter Bullins with but another electronic nigger wired to a J. Edgar Hoover discord-sowing machine. No wonder the New York Panthers started to burn down his New Lafayette Theatre home-fort.

Bullins's contrariness might have been partly caused by his then youthful thirty years, crammed to the brim with street runs, seaport romps, brown babies, and ghetto studies. His dramatizations of these experiences in his Binding Relationships plays disturbed audiences even more than his Black Revolutionary plays had. He had the polished bald boldness to shove back out on stage professional wine-drinkers and step-sitters, repainting the faded clown images that so many had worked to erase from public consciousness. How much our "traditional enemies" (as W. E. B. Du Bois put it) must have loved Bullins splashing spotlights on corner people making out in the backseats of broken-down Buicks, on lying and philandering preachers packing their pockets and emptying their nuts, on white men snatching black men's wives, on drug pushers stealing black lives, and on senior citizens pissing in swimming pools from high diving boards. The bigots must have rejoiced when Bullins pulled off the manhole covers so that Animal in *Snickers* and Big Girl in *Clara's Ole Man* could crawl out.

So lasting was the damage done by these and other featured creatures that when Bullins hauled out (in the Flow Class plays) such phantoms as Lucy Terry, Phillis Wheatley, High John da Conqueror, Satchmo, and Dr. Geechee, along with the sepia starlets—these characters could not even begin to restore the ripped image—especially when they had to share the limelight with the likes of Prince, a strung-out Huey Newton, an unseemly O. D., and the psychotics Velma Best and Traffic Man. Bullins had so exhausted all pity that his personal pain, rendered in the Inner Life versus Inner Life plays, seems like just payback. Who cares that he got caught in Rhode Island by the Navy shore patrol, or that he wept for Malcolm, or that his aunt would not bail him out of jail even with his own money, or that his mother all but shut him out of her later life, or that he got black-balled in New York? Not even his new mumbo-jumbo magic minstrel rituals persuaded anybody that he was really born again. The fact that he never said a proper thank you to his stepfather Bill was cause enough for him to be abandoned to the worst New England winters.

Yet, America still owes this mean and short Bullins. America's debt extends simply from his having dodged various vicious dogs—tied to porches meant to ward off low-income people from coming to their hard-earned seat at the table. For too many it would not have mattered at all had the "near" in near-death been eliminated—if, indeed, the baby on the screeching stretcher had never made it to oxygen. Then the peace that Ed Bullins's Inner Life versus Outer Life plays brought to the sixties would have been asphyxiated. When he rationally forced white publishers and bankers and theatre producers to let down their guards and to snicker at themselves for being stuck in muddy ways, when he calmly tied to the most heinous political act of rape the most abhorrent personal act of race oppression—when Ed Bullins did these things alone, he raised higher the honor due him for his contrariness.

It was this waywardness that helped Bullins's Black Revolutionary plays make young black people pause from their practice to radically change the African American lot. He stuffed in their ears some aching questions: What ever happened to undercover revolutionaries who would never utter a sound about their deadly and nourishing activities? How best could conservative and radical African Americans be so integrated that they would commit to tolerating different paths to common goals? And what would it take to get romantic gun-toters to lay down their Uzis until they could come up with a feasible plan for urban guerilla warfare—to be fought by seasoned heads whose stomachs do not quiver at the smell of burning flesh? These are Bullins's bullets. Some plays even ricocheted off of his fellow artists. When he showed whites in an audience being slaughtered, for example, he was simply calling the bluff of desktop "revolutionary" playmakers who continually egged on young minds to their romantic death. Perhaps Bullins had been correct: by being one of the very few *real* revolutionaries—who had courted death in the North Philadelphia streets and in Navy brigs and in seaport-bar brawls—he had the right to ask youth to think again about armed insurrection.

Bullins's Binding Relationships plays—with all the cussing and fussing and fornicating—were equally misunderstood. Perhaps they were but sacred hymns to what Clayton Riley accurately described as "nigger street royalty." If the middle-class African American despised these spirited ladies and gentlemen for having brought back the nightmare of the six hundred Broadway black musical comedies of the early twentieth century, so what? Bullins had not been party to any unwritten agreement to ban such images from the African American stage in 1946. He probably did not even know about the trouble that the poets and dramatists Arna Bontemps and Countee Cullen had gotten into for staging backstreet life in *St. Louis Woman* (1946). Not that knowing would have stopped him from putting on stage some of the most unforgettable African American characters in American theatre history. People simply fell in love with the fabulous Miss Marie—and even, in a funny sort of way, with the lesbian Big Girl. The hapless Cliff Dawson was in every family's album, and so were the squeaking backseat springs of a broken down Ford or Chevy. Significantly, Bullins made sure that when the laughter had died, there lingered some shocking questions that would not go away: he asked in *In the Wine Time*, for example, Who is willing to sacrifice so that inner-city youth, too, can have their shot at life? And in *The Corner*, What pain and suffering must street-corner toughs endure in the rite of passage into manhood? And in *Clara's Ole Man*, What power must be ceded and which battle vigorously waged and won over the transgressions against—and the redemption of—the family?

Such deeply personal questions—even in the sunny Flow Class of plays—left too few breathers for too many comfortable people, whose only scape-goat was the fatted calf Bullins himself. He had no right, went the feeling of the time, to mess with our safely dead heroes, using the pioneering legends to demand that we enlarge our visions, challenging even our self-knowledge—having the gall to say, for example, that the Aunt Jemima Phillis Wheatley might be just the revolutionary model needed in African American life. And who was he to have waved that drugged-out blood junkie Huey Newton as a call to search harder for the other half of our complete selves?

Thank God, some would say, for Bullins's own many Inner Life versus Inner Life troubles, projected through Cliff Dawson, Curt, Steve Benson, Michael Brown, Ray Crawford, Son, Ernie, and Art Kane. Others might thank God that whatever his troubles, Bullins, at sixty in 1995, seems poised to ask himself the really hard question: "At first, I had doubts that I could teach four classes at [San Francisco] State and two at Contra Costa [College]. But I found I could. Now I'm asking myself, 'What am I doing this for?' "[4] Bullins might have turned this question into a larger one about why he had written all of his plays. But, in the words of Cliff Dawson in *In the Wine Time*, the answer would surely be that he had dramatized the lives of the loud-talking step-sitters and the dog-dodging toughs in order that they, too, would get a better "shot at the world."

Introduction

1. In marginal notes on a draft of this manuscript, Bullins wrote that he did not remember any of this: "This is complete paranoia. Maybe there is too much of ourselves in here. You are weird, Sam. You imagined all this pseudo-intrigue." Not true.

2. Bullins prefers calling his early short stories "impetuous" instead of "mediocre," and he favors "naive" for his "bad" poetry. His early works appeared in such publications as *Contact, Nexus, Ante, Wild Dog, Illuminations, Soulbook, Negro Digest,* and *S. F. Oracle.*

3. Darwin T. Turner, "Langston Hughes as Playwright," in *Langston Hughes/Black Genius: A Critical Evaluation,* ed. Therman B. O'Daniel (New York: William Morrow, 1971), 86.

4. See my *African American Theatre: A Historical and Critical Analysis* (New York: Cambridge University Press, 1994), 78–134.

5. See my *African American Theatre,* 15–37.

6. The Black Communications Project was adopted and executed by the Black Student Union of San Francisco State University in the spring of 1967. For details of the project, see LeRoi Jones, "Communications Project," *The Drama Review* 12 (summer 1968): 53–57.

7. Bullins' letter to author, 13 July 1992, Letters file, The Ed Bullins Sr. Collection, Greensboro, NC (hereafter TBC).

8. Ibid.

9. Ibid.

10. Bullins, letter to author, 20 May 1993.

11. Quoted in Jervis Anderson, "Profiles: Dramatist Ed Bullins," *New Yorker* 49 (16 June 1973), 40–78.

12. Bullins adapted the William Penn incident into the following notes for an unpublished short story, "Big Butts/Fat Butts":

> You know, the size of women's behinds has drastically changed the course of my life. Yeah. Not once, but lots and lots and lots of times. . . . In fact, if it wasn't for a big butt, I wouldn't have been led this way in life. . . . I remember when I was bopping around one day in a strange city, with nothing much to do except find out what I was going to do next, when a lady crossed my path. And she had one of the prettiest and juiciest little fat rears that my old eyes have been blessed to fall upon. She was going into a door. I looked at that fat wiggly thing disappearing through that door and became hypnotized. I tried to find out where I was. And over the door was a sign, "The Shadoobie Do School of Natural Beauty." That's how I got in hairdressing school. But that's another story, really. But I only stayed a couple of years. Funny I couldn't pass any of the courses. Must be my concentration was off. Sixty-two students, and the other guy was named Rudolph. He lisped . . . like thith: "Ahh . . . go on," he'd say to me. "How ya gonna dweth thumbody's hair when ya eyes fathened to their butts?" I would tell him: "Rudolph, my man, it's all relative to where you're comin' from. Now you're a hair freak. I'm an ass man. They ain't got no school of fat butt culture that I know of . . . so, I take what I can get." Two years . . . on the G.I. Bill. . . . Now you know why men fight wars. So they can return and get back behind the lines to fat butt country. (Bullins Journal, 6 February 1975, Journal File, TBC)

13. Bullins, letter to author, 27 June 1993, TBC.
14. Ibid.
15. Ibid.
16. Ibid.
17. Bullins, *How Do You Do,* in *Black Fire,* ed. LeRoi Jones and Larry Neal (New York: William Morrow, 1968), 595–96.
18. Black Arts/West was patterned after Baraka's Black Arts Repertory Theatre/ School in Harlem.
19. Marvin X. Jackmon, "Autobiography of a North American African" (unpublished manuscript, 1994), 100.
20. The writer Joe Goncalves said that he last saw Black Arts/West perform at North Beach, at the Committee:

> I'm still not sure how it got there, to that white place, but I personally never saw it perform after the North Beach productions, where the audience was obscenely white. The rationale for appearing there, the only rationale I ever heard was that B.A.W. [Black Arts/West] was 'teaching the white man his death,' a sort of Theatre of Morgue. Something was wounded at the Committee, but I don't think it was the white man. After that scene, B.A.W. became a Theatre of the Mind. It opened up a storefront in the Fillmore. I would drop in about once a month, and though there were no performances, the place was under constant improvement.

A new paint job, lights, sound systems and finally a stage. But outside of a few minor efforts, there was never a play, never a poetry reading, despite the poets coming through town, despite the poets in town. Instead there were plans: talk of publications and other projects, rehearsals. An audience theatre. Finally, Black Arts West became an "Information Center" of sorts for Islam. It looked like Black Arts West was headed in a good direction. . . .

One day I found the place closed. B.A.W. had disappeared. The storefront where B.A.W. never or seldom performed was suddenly a dress shop. (Goncalves, "The Mysterious Disappearance of Black Arts West," *Black Theatre* #2 (1969): 21–25).

21. Marvin X, 106–7.
22. Marvin X, 110–11.
23. Bullins, letter to author, 25 July 1992, TBC.
24. In a marginal note to the author, Bullins wrote that "This might have been a ruse on Cleaver's part. I attended a meeting with the youths with Marvin. They denied the allegations, and they were never proven."
25. Marvin X, 121.
26. Bullins, undated note to the author.
27. Peter Bailey, "Controversy over Play's Title Fails to Cloud Author's Acclaim," *The Electronic Nigger, Ebony* 23 (September 1968): 97–101.
28. Ed Bullins, "For Aunt Bea's Church Testimonial," 6 July 1991, in the "Bullins Autobiographical Sketches" file in TBC.
29. Bullins, "Two Days Shie . . . ," in *Contemporary Authors Autobiography Series* vol. 16, ed. Joyce Nakamura (Detroit: Gale Research, 1992), 59.
30. Bullins, "For Aunt Bea's Church Testimonial," 6 July 1991, in the "Bullins Autobiographical Sketches" file in TBC.
31. Ed Bullins, "Journal, 1974–1975," TBC, 1–2.
32. Bullins, "Two Days Shie . . . ," 66.
33. Joseph Epstein, "Compose Yourself," *The American Scholar* (autumn 1992): 487.
34. Cited in William A. Raidy, "In Art There Is Nothing You Cannot Do," *The Staten Island Sunday Advance* (13 July 1975): E-5.
35. Ibid.
36. Ibid.
37. In a note to the author, Bullins said that he and Sanchez "met in San Francisco, where we collaborated in the Black Theatre Communications Project at San Francisco State University, with the Black Students Union Outreach, and at Black Arts Program at the Black House." Bullins later published Sanchez.
38. Martin Gottfried, "The Master Introduces His Pupils," *The New York Post* (23 July 1977).
39. Martha M. Jones, review of *Black Terror, Black Creation* (spring 1972): 13.
40. Ed Bullins, *The Hungered One*, in *The Hungered One: Early Writings of Ed Bullins* (New York: Morrow, 1971), 49–54.

Chapter 1. Inner Life versus Outer Life Class of the Black Experience School of Drama

1. Ed Bullins, telephone interview with author 6 July 1994.
2. Barbara A. Sizemore, "Sexism and the Black Male," *The Black Scholar* 4 (March-April 1973): 2.
3. Marginal note to the author.
4. Erika Munk, "Bullins: I Had My Way with Her," *The Village Voice* (8 November 1976): 87.
5. Cited in Patricia O'Haire, "Bullins: A Philadelphia Story," *The New York Daily News* (7 June 1975): 25.
6. Alain Locke, "Youth Speaks," *Survey* (March 1925): 660.
7. *Malcolm: '71, or Publishing Blackness* (1975), in *The Black Scholar* (June 1975): 84–86.
8. Thomas Angotti, "A Critical Assessment of Current Approaches to Housing Finance," *The Black Scholar* 11 (November/December 1979): 2.
9. *The Man Who Dug Fish*, in *The Theme Is Blackness: "The Corner" and Other Plays*, ed. Ed Bullins (New York: William Morrow, 1973), 85–97.
10. Ed Bullins, *The Theme Is Blackness*, in *The Theme Is Blackness*, 84.
11. Ed Bullins, *Safety Check*, 1971, TBC.
12. *A Minor Scene*, in *The Theme Is Blackness*, 78–83.
13. Bullins pared this scene down in the play from that in his short story by the same title. In the story, Mother adds that "Your sweating brings out such gorgeous tones in your skin." She even touches him. See "The Helper" in *The Hungered One* (New York: William Morrow, 1971), 67–75.
14. *It Has No Choice*, in *The Theme Is Blackness*, 38.
15. Bullins, "Two Days Shie . . ."
16. "He Couldn't Say Sex," in *The Hungered One*, 26.
17. Cited in Lionel Mitchell, "Ed Bullins: Shadow and Flame," *The Village Voice* (29 October-4 November 1980): 87.
18. Ibid.
19. *Leavings*, 1971, TBC.
20. Thulani Davis, "Stick Figures in Black and White," *The Village Voice* (6 August 1980): 69.
21. Bullins, "An Open Statement," *The Village Voice* (13–19 August 1980): 76.
22. Thulani Davis, "Reply to Bullins's 'Open Statement' " *The Village Voice* (13–19 August 1980): 76.
23. Davis, "Stick Figures in Black and White," 70.
24. Flyer advertising *Leavings*, TBC.
25. In *Judge Tom Strikes Back* (1992), the principal character, who resembles Justice Clarence Thomas, prepares for his appearance before the Senate Judiciary Committee, which is holding hearings on his nomination to the U.S. Supreme Court. He tries to get himself a morning "piece" from his wife, who humiliates him in order to turn him on. The president calls, giving the judge's wife the script for the hearing: it stresses the judge's pulling himself up by his jock strap, coming "up from the outhouse," beating up on his "welfare-receiving mother and sister," praising his "toilet-cleaning grand

dad," and being "a C-average colored genius scholar." After rehearsing before a video camera, the judge is visited by FBI agents Cale and Poopie, who toughen him up with racial insults. At the hearing, which is a game show, Ann Hall accuses the judge of sexual harassment. He covers his ears. Like a child, he repeats that he will not listen. He is confirmed—notwithstanding an earthquake, along with sirens, riots, gun shots, and screams. Judge Tom brags, and he warns the audience that he will repay them for the hurt he has suffered.

Instead of being a satire, this draft of the script reads like a farce for the very reasons that Davis states: Tom is not believable. Much of the action is slapstick, covering everything from stereotypes—JUDGE involuntarily scratches his head—to falls: TOM dives toward his wife to have oral sex with her, but he falls over the bed. Much of the action emphasizes the white woman's domination of the African American man. The JUDGE, for example, crawls on hands and knees toward his wife as she sits on side of bed. SHE puts her foot atop his head, and pushes his face into the floor, gently and like a lady. Bullins even pokes fun at the judge's physical fitness enthusiasm: "HE does a rigorous, and slightly ludicrous, set of calisthenics—part classic stereotype martial arts, part Charles Atlas parody. His routine ends with music accompanied by pseudo-aerobic-like movements." Bullins's purpose, of course, is to strike at African Americans who permit themselves to be exploited by white politicians and their operatives. See *Judge Thomas Strikes Back*, 1992, TBC.

26. Referring to the book, *The Innocence of Joan Little* by James Reston Jr., which Roger Wilkins reviewed, Jo Anne Little wrote to Ed Bullins that she was "very concerned about the disposition that James Reston takes in the book on [her]. Not only is it inaccurate, but can be considered judgmental and biased. [It is] based on facts that he does not know. [Nor does he know] the character in which he is writing about. And the book was written without any prior consideration of any kind from me." Bullins added the note: "Jo Anne Little has not seen the book that James Reston has written about her, nor had she been contacted that the book was being written about her. She states that her first parole in 1975 [was] denied because of a fight with another woman inmate, a 160-pound prisoner who attacked her ninety pounds. She told N.C. authorities that she was protecting herself. Parole was denied her." See Jo Anne Little, letter to Ed Bullins, 12 December 1977, *Jo Anne!!!* file, TBC. The description in the text is from Roger Wilkins, review of *The Innocence of Joan Little*, by James Reston Jr., *The New York Times* 17 December 1977.

27. Erika Munk, "Bullins: I Had My Way with Her," *The Village Voice* (8 November 1976): 87.

28. All quotations from *Jo Anne!!!*, manuscript in TBC.

29. Munk, "Bullins: I Had My Way with Her," *The Village Voice* (8 November 1976): 88.

30. Interestingly, during the trial Bullins jotted down only five sentences: "I've done 4 years for these pigs—But I've learned a lot from them," which was

probably said by Little. Somebody said, "If they murder Steve Biko, they'll do it to me." Although this sound as if it might have been Little, Bullins thought not because she was not "conscious enough to know the Steve Biko reference" (marginal note to author). Then Bullins wrote, "I want my life to mean something"—with the name Vernell Muhommad (Smith) by the quote. "Turned in by lover because of jealousy" has the name George Mc-Crae by it. Finally, there was "Flemming—arresting officer."

On the plane back home, Bullins wrote the lyrics for a song, which did not appear in the play:

Jo Anne . . .
Jo Anne . . .
The Ballad of
Jo Anne . . .

She was sittin'
in her cell
One black
Dreadful night
And a creature
Walked in
And demanded a bite
Of her womanhood
And she said, "No!"
You'll get nothin'
Here without a
helluva fight

Jo Anne . . .
Jo Anne . . .
The Ballad of
Jo Anne . . .

The creature
Put an icepick
To her throat
It said, "Give
It all up, gal,
Or it's all
You wrote." (*Jo Anne!!!* file, TBC)

31. Don Nelsen, "review of *Jo Anne.*" *The New York Daily News* (5 February 1976): 76.

32. Bullins, letter to the editor, *The New York Amsterdam News* (13 December 1975): D-2.

33. Mike Steele, "Playwright Tries to Expand Work beyond Black Theatre Audience," *The Minneapolis Star* (28 October 1977): 19.

34. Bernard Weiner, "A Dramatic, Surrealistic Interpretation of a Trial," *The San Francisco Chronicle* (26 May 1981): 42.

35. *Jo Anne!!!*

36. Munk, "Bullins: I Had My Way with Her."
37. Barbara Lewis, "A Woman Scorned," *The Villager* (25 October 1976).
38. When Bullins began writing *The Taking of Miss Janie,* he toyed with concepts in his journal. In huge letters blocked within a disconnected rectangle, he printed the word, "Control." See Bullins Journal, 29 December 1974, TBC.
39. The intellectual Monty, according to the critic Martin Gottfried, is a thinly disguised and not unloving portrait of Amiri Baraka. The victim is Janie, "a confused, earnest, warm and admirably dignified girl, [who is] perhaps like Baraka's ex-wife." See Martin Gottfried, "A Radical Idea," *The New York Post,* (5 May 1975): 23.
40. Gottfreid, "Radical Idea."
41. Julius Novick, "The Taking of Miss Cegnation," *The Village Voice* (12 May 1975).: 87.
42. Ibid.
43. Bullins Journal, 14 May 1975, TBC.
44. Bullins Journal, 2 January 1975, TBC.
45. Charles M. Young, "Is Rape a Symbol of Race Relations?" *The New York Times* (18 May 1975): II-1.
46. Barbara Mackay, "Studies in Black and White," *The Saturday Review* (12 July 1975): 52.
47. Jervis Anderson, "Profiles: Dramatist Ed Bullins," *The New Yorker* 49 (16 June 1973): 40.
48. Novick, "Taking of Miss Cegnation."
49. Richard Cohen, "Black Play Smacks of Anti-Semitism," *The Sun-Reporter* (17 June 1975): 12. Referring to Cohen's notions that Sharon and Len's marriage had failed, Bullins said that Len's marriage had not failed—as indicated by Sharon's monologue. Bullins further believed that Cohen's notion about a Jewish poet's trying to steal the black man's pleasures shows that Cohen is not only racist but also uninformed about *Miss Janie* (marginal note to author).
50. Bullins, "An Open Statement," *The Village Voice* (13–19 August 1980): 76.
51. Quoted in Joe Kornfeld, "Playwright Ed Bullins: Soft-Spoken Giant on the Black Literary Scene," *The Boston Herald American* (24 January 1975): 32.
52. Lionel Mitchell, "Ed Bullins: Shadow and Flame," *The Village Voice* (29 October-4 November 1980): 87.
53. Ibid.
54. Ibid.
55. Munk, "Bullins: I Had My Way with Her."
56. Ibid.
57. Bullins, telephone interview with author, 16 October 1992.
58. Bullins Journal, November 1976, TBC.
59. Munk, telephone interview with author, 26 October 1992.
60. Harry Overstreet, "Images and the Negro," *Saturday Review of Literature* (26 August 1944): 5–6.
61. Bullins, letter to author, 15 October 1992. See also Bullins, "Chester Himes: Protest and Autobiographic Novels," paper presented to graduate seminar at San Francisco State University (spring 1992), 6, TBC.

62. Bullins, "Chester Himes," 4.
63. Bullins, letter to author, 15 October 1992, TBC.
64. Munk, "Bullins: I Had My Way with Her."
65. Lionel Mitchell, "Ed Bullins: Shadow and Flame."
66. Bullins quoted in Mitchell, "Shadow."
67. Munk, "Bullins: I Had My Way with Her."

Chapter 2. Black Revolutionary Class of the Black Arts School of Drama

1. The first New Lafayette Theatre at 132nd Street and 7th Avenue (site of the Lafayette Theatre of the thirties) was allegedly burned by Donald Washington on 31 January 1968. He supposedly avenged being beaten by Roy Innis at the theatre while a book party was being held for Harold Cruse's *The Crisis of the Negro Intellectual*. Washington had been in a heated argument between revolutionaries and cultural nationalists.
2. Robert Macbeth, interview with author, Miami, Florida, 26 March 1989.
3. Bullins, "Notes on Literary Biography Prospectus," TBC, 1.
4. Bullins, "The Polished Protest: Aesthetics and the Black Writer," *Contact Magazine,* (July 1963), reprint, n.p.
5. Ibid.
6. Ibid, emphasis added.
7. Ibid.
8. Amiri Baraka, *The Autobiography: LeRoi Jones/Amiri Baraka* (New York: Freundlich, 1984), 249.
9. Bullins, "Bulletins," *Other Stages* (17–30 December 1981): 1.
10. Ibid.
11. Elaine Brown, *A Taste of Power: A Black Woman's Story* (New York: Pantheon, 1992), 142.
12. Eldridge Cleaver, *Soul on Ice* (New York: McGraw-Hill, 1968), 81.
13. Ibid., 74.
14. Marginal note to the author.
15. Robert Macbeth, telephone interview with author, 22 October 1992.
16. Marvin X, "Interview with Ed Bullins," in *New Plays from the Black Theatre,* ed. Ed Bullins (New York: Bantam, 1969), vii-xv.
17. "Lafayette Theatre: Reaction to *Bombers,*" *Black Theatre* #4 (1969): 16–25.
18. Bullins wrote several other black commercials that espouse brotherhood. Most of these shorts were destroyed in a fire. *Black Commercial #2,* however, is collected in *The Theme Is Blackness.*
19. Bullins, *Black Commercial #2,* 131–34.
20. Bullins, "A Street Play," in *The Theme Is Blackness,* 141–43.
21. David Hilliard and Lewis Cole, *This Side of Glory: The Autobiography of David Hilliard and the Story of the Black Panther Party* (Boston: Little Brown, 1993), 338.
22. Bullins, "Death List," in *Four Dynamite Plays,* ed. Ed Bullins (New York: William Morrow, 1972), 19–38.
23. Marginal note to author.

24. Elaine Brown alleges that the Cleaver faction in New York killed Sam Napier, circulation manager of the *Panther* newspaper. She said that "Eldridge was building an opposition army. That message was delivered with the brutal murder . . . [of Napier, who] had been tied to a chair in our main newspaper distribution office in New York, beaten, shot in the head, and left in the building, which was then set on fire. His body was found charred nearly beyond recognition." Brown, *A Taste of Power,* 266.

25. Bullins, "Night of the Beast," in *Four Dynamite Plays,* 83, 84.

26. Hilliard and Cole, *This Side of Glory,* 193.

27. Bullins, *It Bees That Way,* in *Four Dynamite Plays,* 1–16.

28. Bullins, *A Short Play for a Small Theater,* in *The Theme Is Blackness,* 182.

29. Bullins, *Dialect Determinism (or The Rally),* in *The Theme Is Blackness,* 17.

30. Hilliard and Cole, *This Side of Glory,* 319.

31. Toni Cade, "Black Theater," in *Black Expression,* ed. Addison Gayle Jr. (New York: Weybright and Talley, 1969), 134.

32. Bullins, *The Electronic Nigger,* in *Five Plays,* ed. Ed Bullins (New York: Bobbs-Merrill, 1968), 88–90.

33. Stephen G. Tompkins, "Report Says King Target of U.S. Military," *The Washington D.C. News Dimensions* (26 March 1993): 2, *passim.*

34. Harold Clurman, "Review," *The Nation* (25 March 1968): 420–21.

35. Bullins, quoted in Peter Bailey, "*The Electronic Nigger:* Controversy over Play's Title Fails to Cloud Author's Acclaim," *Ebony* (September 1968): 97.

36. Ed Bullins, *The Gentleman Caller,* in *A Black Quartet,* ed. Ben Caldwell, Ronald Milner, Ed Bullins, and LeRoi Jones (New York: New American Library, 1970), 91–92.

37. Ed Bullins, "Two Days Shie . . . ," 59.

38. Tariq Ibn Hassiz, "On that Black Administrator Sitting in Darkness," *Liberator* (March 1971): 11.

39. Bullins, *How Do You Do,* in *Black Fire: An Anthology of Afro-American Writing,* ed. LeRoi Jones and Larry Neal (New York: Morrow, 1968), 595.

40. Other plays in the Communications Project's repertory were Marvin X's *Flowers for the Trashman,* directed by Duncan Barber and Bullins; Jimmy Garrett's *We Own the Night,* Ben Caldwell's *Militant Preacher,* and Baraka's *Madheart*—all directed by Baraka.

41. Baraka, *Autobiography,* 249.

42. Ibid., 250.

43. Ibid., 255–56.

44. Bullins, *One-Minute Commercial,* in *The Theme Is Blackness,* 138.

45. Bullins, "Next Time . . . ," TBC.

46. Bullins, *State Office Bldg. Curse* in *The Theme Is Blackness* 136–37.

47. Bullins, *The American Flag Ritual,* in *The Theme Is Blackness,* 135.

48. Marginal note to author.

49. Kingsley B. Bass Jr. (Bullins) *We Righteous Bombers,* in *New Plays from the Black Theatre,* ed. Ed Bullins (New York: Bantam, 1969), 21–22.

50. See Hilliard and Cole, *This Side of Glory,* 131.

51. "Lafayette Theatre: Reaction to *Bombers,*" *Black Theatre #4* (1969): 16.

52. Bullins, "Notes on Literary Biography Prospectus," 1, TBC.
53. Ms. marginal notes to the author.
54. Ms. marginal note to author.
55. Bullins chose the *nom de plume* Kingsley B. Bass Jr., a concoction from King-fish, one of the characters in the *Amos and Andy* television show: The first name, "Kingsley," was taken from the first syllable of "Kingfish." The surname "Bass" is the "fish." Interview with Robert Macbeth, Miami, Florida, 26 March 1989.
56. Larry Neal, "Toward a Relevant Black Theatre," *Black Theatre #4* (1969): 14–15.
57. Ibid.
58. Robert Macbeth, telephone conversation with author, 22 October 1992.
59. Bullins, letter to the editor, *New York Times* (25 May 1975): 8.
60. Bullins, "Talking of Black Art, Theatre, Revolution, and Nationhood," *Black Theatre #5* (1971): 18.

Chapter 3. Binding Relationships Class of Black Experience Drama

1. Alain Locke, "The New Negro Speaks," in *The New Negro*, ed. Alain Locke (New York: Albert & Charles Boni, 1925), reprint New York: Atheneum, 1969), 47.
2. Samuel A. Hay, *African American Theatre: A Historical and Critical Analysis* (New York: Cambridge University Press, 1994), 29.
3. James Lacy, letter to Ed Bullins, n.d., TBC.
4. For details, see Hay, *African American Theatre*, 33–35.
5. Mel Gussow, "Bullins's *In the Wine Time*," *The New York Times* (30 April 1976): 9.
6. Edith Oliver, "Off Broadway: Superior Vintage," *The New Yorker* (10 May 1976): 33.
7. James Lacy, letter to Ed Bullins, n.d., TBC.
8. Thomas Johnson, "Black Drama Gains as Way to Teach, Unite—and Amuse," *The New York Times* (1 October 1968): 49.
9. Lindsay Patterson, review of *In the Wine Time*, *The New York Times* (22 December 1968): III-1.
10. Lance Jeffers, "Bullins, Baraka, and Elder: The Dawn of Grandeur in Black Drama," *CLA Journal* 7 (September 1972): 32.
11. The Twentieth-Century Cycle is, according to Bullins, "a structure or vehicle to write twenty plays." Bullins planned to give African Americans "some fresh impressions and insights into their own lives in order to help them consider the weight of their experience of having migrated from the North and the West, from an agricultural to an industrial center." Bullins, quoted in James P. Draper, ed., *Black Literature Criticism* (Detroit: Gale, 1992), 321. Many of the characters in the seven plays are linked by blood or association. Bullins has completed only seven of the planned twenty cycle plays: *In the Wine Time* (1968), *The Duplex* (1970), *In New England Winter* (1971), *The Fabulous Miss Marie* (1971), *Home Boy* (1977), *Daddy* (1977), and *Boy x Man* (1995).

12. Sterling Brown, *Negro Poetry and Drama* (Washington, D.C.: Associates in Negro Folk Education, 1937; reprint, New York: Atheneum, 1969), 123.

13. Allan Wallach, "A Different Taste," *Newsday* (30 April 1976): 14.

14. Marginal note to author.

15. Edith Oliver, "Off Broadway: Superior Vintage," *The New Yorker* (10 May 1976): 33.

16. Lindsay Patterson, "New Home, New Troupe, New Play," *The New York Times* (22 December 1968): II-7.

17. Sandra Mayo, "Ed Bullins, New York's Resident Black Dramatist" in *Afro-Americans in New York Life and History,* (Buffalo, NY: Afro-Americans in New York, 1981), 51.

18. Allan Wallach, "Different Taste," 14.

19. Ibid.

20. Ibid.

21. Lindsay Patterson, "New Home," II-7.

22. Lance Jeffers, "Bullins, Baraka, and Elder: The Dawn of Grandeur in Black Drama," 32.

23. Douglas Watt, "Black-Ghetto Street Scenes." *The New York Daily News* (24 June 1972): 23.

24. Mel Gussow, *"The Corner Opens," The New York Times* (23 June 1972): 20.

25. Douglas Watt, "Black Ghetto Street Scenes," 23.

26. Jerry Tallmar, "Off-Broadway: Goss, Oyam O, Bullins," *The New York Post* (23 June 1972): 20.

27. Ed Bullins, *The Box Office, Black Theatre #3* (1969): 17–19.

28. Susanne K. Langer, *Feeling and Form: A Theory of Art* (New York: Charles Scribner's Sons, 1953), 26.

29. Cited in Marvin X, "Interview with Ed Bullins," in *New Plays from the Black Theatre,* ed. Ed Bullins (New York: Bantam, 1969), vii.

30. Henri Bergson, "Laughter," in *Comedy: Plays, Theory, and Criticism,* ed. Marvin Felheim (New York: Harcourt, Brace & World, 1962), 214.

31. Ed Bullins, *Dirty Pool,* TBC.

32. Ibid.

33. Bullins, *Michael,* TBC, 6.

34. Theresa McGriff, " 'Man-Wo-Man': The Battle Continues," *The New York Amsterdam News* (5 August 1978): D-6.

35. Sy Syna, "Bullins and Harris," *Wisdom's Child* (5 August 1978).

36. Theresa McGriff,"Battle Continues," D-6.

37. Ibid.

38. M. Mark, "Who, Men, Whoa!" *The Village Voice* (17 July 1978): 75.

39. Bullins, Notes on a Literary Biography, TBC.

40. Ethel Pitts Walker, letter to author 20 January 1993, TBC.

41. Ethel Pitts Walker, telephone interview with author, 25 August 1992.

42. Sharon Bell Mathis, letter to Viking Penguin, 26 July 1992, photocopy in TBC.

43. Sharon Bell Mathis's *Teacup Full of Roses* was chosen as one of the Child Study Association of America's Children's Books of the Year, one of the *New*

York Times Best Books of the Year, and one of the American Library Association's Best Young Adult Books—all in 1972. See *Something about the Author: Facts and Pictures about Authors and Illustrators of Books for Young people* vol. 58, ed. Anne Commire (New York: Gale Research, Inc., 1990), 123.

44. Ibid.

45. Sharon Bell Mathis, *Teacup Full of Roses* (New York: Viking, 1972; reprint, Boston: G.K. Hall, 1973), 109–10.

46. Janet Harris, review of *Teacup Full of Roses, The New York Times Book Review* (10 September 1972): 8.

47. Sharon Bell Mathis, *Teacup Full of Roses,* 143–44.

48. Mathis, *Something about the Author,* 123.

49. Ibid.

50. Mathis, *Teacup Full of Roses,* 154.

51. Eugene C. Van Horn, M.D., letter to author, 30 January 1993, TBC.

52. St. Clair Bourne has said that had the film been made, Bullins's screenplay would not have been used because it, unlike the novel, is more "exposing" than "nurturing." Playwright Charles Fuller wrote a second screenplay, which, "like the film *Sounder,* was more family oriented." St. Clair Bourne, telephone interview with author, 13 May 1993.

53. Ed Bullins, Marginal Notes to Author. TBC, 56.

54. Ed Bullins, Notes on the manuscript, "Ed Bullins: A Literary Biography," 98, TBC.

55. Bullins, *City Preacher,* TBC, 47.

56. Hilda Scheib, "*Preacher* Says Little about Powell," *Alameda County Gazette* (18 January 1984): 45.

57. Robert Taylor, "Actors Try to Save a Shapeless *Preacher,*" *The Oakland Tribune* (14 January 1984): 24.

58. Steve Winn, "Play You Have to Take on Faith," *The San Francisco Chronicle* (13 January 1984): 8.

59. Ibid.

60. Ibid.

61. Bernard Spunberb, "From Booze to Pews," *Bay Area Reporter* (12 February 1984).

62. Hilda Scheib, "*Preacher* Says Little."

63. Alfred Kay, "New Work by Noted Playwright Bullin Misses Mark," *The Sacramento Bee* (13 January 1984).

64. Bullins, *C'mon Back to Heavenly House,* TBC.

65. Nancy Scott, "One Cheer for New Bullins Play," *The San Francisco Examiner* (13 January 1984).

66. Quoted in Scott, "One Cheer."

67. Bullins's rehearsal notes for rewrites included the following:

    May be too simple
    Not enough climatic scenes
    Show growth of leading character
    A little bit too simple
    Dialogue too formal, too stilted
    Naturalness of language

> Made it too easy
> Have not made it terrible enough
> Sucked down into the morass (Aaron)
> Must root for him
> Have to change the conflict from an intellectual one to *guts*
> Go into GUTS of problem
>
> Involve them in background conflicts/choices
> sub-plot or two
> show/not talk
> communists
> poverty
>
> psycho-points of legitimate self-confidence
> give picture of Harlem/1930s
> human story
> black/white relationships
> personalize
> can't happen purely through supernatural devices
> struggle against environment
> story hook—character development
> social state/ment
> strange backgrounds
> human story (Bullins, "*City Preacher* Re-Write Notes," TBC).

68. Steve Winn, "Play on Faith," 8.
69. Huey P. Newton, *Revolutionary Suicide* (New York: Harcourt Brace Jovanovich, 1973), 251–52.
70. Ibid.
71. Ibid.
72. Ibid.
73. Bullins, *Snickers,* TBC.
74. Todd R. Clear, cited in Francis X. Clines, "Prisons Running Out of Cells, Money, and Choices," *The New York Times* (28 May 1993): 1, *passim.*
75. Ibid..
76. Bullins, *The Hunk,* TBC.
77. Cornel West, *Race Matters* (Boston: Beacon, 1993), 86.
78. Jon L. Clayborne, "Modern Black Drama and the Gay Image," *College English* 36 (November 1974): 381.
79. Ibid.
80. Molefi Kete Asante, cited in Henry Louis Gates Jr., "Blacklash?" *The New Yorker* (17 May 1993): 42.
81. Michael Smith, "Theatre Journal," *The Village Voice* (11 April 1968): 39.
82. Langston Hughes, *Little Ham,* in *Black Theater U.S.A: Forty-Five Plays by Black Americans 1847–1974,* ed. James V. Hatch (New York: Free Press, 1974), 775–811.
83. Eldridge Cleaver, *Soul on Ice,* 102.
84. Ibid., 110.

85. Linda Villarosa, "Readers Respond to Coming Out," *Essence* (October 1991): 89.

86. Bullins, "The Polished Protest," *Contact Magazine* (July 1963):

87. Bullins, "Travel from Home," in *The Hungered One,* 85–91.

88. Bullins, "The Drive," in *The Hungered One,* 21–25.

89. Michael Smith, "Theatre Journal," 50.

90. James V. Hatch, "Three at the Afro American Studio," *The Village Voice* (6 November 1969): 42.

91. Edith Oliver, "Three Cheers," *The New Yorker* (9 November 1981): 155.

92. Michael Smith, "Theatre Journal," 39.

93. Harold Clurman, "Review," *The Nation* (25 March 1968): 420–21.

94. Ibid.

95. Michael Smith, "Theatre Journal," 39.

96. In marginal notes, Bullins said that "The views which the public has about Bullins are often much more negative and fixed than his beliefs really are—whether they concern homosexuality, social status, growth, lying or confusion. Bullins is perceived, for example, as a gay- and woman-basher." The intended meaning was that he is believed to be quite anti-gay because of his bashing gays and women. Bullins underlined "gay," and he wrote in the margin: "By whom? Let me know so I can sue them." See "Notes on Prospectus for Ed Bullins: A Literary Biography," 102.

97. Bullins, letter to author, 12 February 1993, TBC.

98. James Lacy, letter to Ed Bullins, n.d. TBC.

Chapter 4. The Flow Class of Black Experience Drama

1. Ed Bullins, telephone interview with author, 1 August 1994.

2. Marginal note to author.

3. The playwrights, calling themselves the New York Theatre Strategy, included Ken Bernard, Julie Bovasso, Robert Heide, Paul Hoffman, Murray Mednick, Leonard Melfi, Ronald Tavel, Megan Terry, Marie Irene Fornes, along with some friends.

4. This event was recreated from eyewitness accounts of this incident by some of the participants, especially the writer Maria Irene Fornes, "Playwrights' Lib Meets Mr. Irving," *The Village Voice* (30 March 1972): 58, *passim.*

5. Quoted in Clayton Riley, "Bullins: It's Not the Play I Wrote," *The New York Times* (19 March 1972): C-1.

6. Ibid.

7. Tice L. Miller, "Jules Irving," in *Cambridge Guide to American Theatre,* ed. Don B. Wilmeth and Tice L. Miller (New York: Cambridge, 1993), 250.

8. Alain Locke, "Max Reinhardt Reads the Negro's Dramatic Horoscope," *Opportunity* (May 1924): 145.

9. Alain Locke, "The Negro and the Theater" in *Theatre,* ed. Edith J. R. Isaacs (Boston: Little, Brown, 1927), 290.

10. Bullins Press Release on *Duplex* 25 February 1972, TBC.

11. Alain Locke, "The Negro and the American Stage," in *Anthology of the Ameri-*

can Negro in the Theatre: A Critical Approach, ed. Lindsay Patterson (New York: Publishers Company, 1968), 21.

12. Alain Locke, "Negro Youth Speaks," in *The New Negro,* ed. Alain Locke (New York: Albert & Charles Boni, 1925; reprint, New York: Atheneum, 1969), 51.

13. Bullins, "The Mystery of Phillis Wheatley," in *New/Lost Plays by Ed Bullins: An Anthology,* ed. Ethel Pitts Walker (Aiea, HI: That New Publishing Company, 1993), 123.

14. Carll Tucker, "She Went to London, Not Senegal," *The Village Voice* (2 February 1976): 110.

15. Charles Garo Ashjian, photo copy of letter to Carll Tucker, 2 February 1976, TBC.

16. J. Saunders Redding, *To Make a Poet Black* (College Park, MD: McGrath, 1939; reprint, Chapel Hill, NC: University of North Carolina Press, 1968), 5.

17. Mel Gussow, "Stage: *Phillis Wheatley,*" *The New York Times* (5 February 1976): 18.

18. Phillis Wheatley, "On Being Brought from Africa to America," in *Cavalcade: Negro American Writing from 1760 to the Present,* ed. Arthur P. Davis and Saunders Redding (Boston: Houghton Mifflin, 1971), 11.

19. Carll Tucker, "She Went to London," 110.

20. Mel Gussow, "Stage: *Phillis Wheatley,*" 18.

21. Bullins, *I Am Lucy Terry,* in *New/Lost Plays* of Ed Bullins 17–69.

22. Burt Supree, "Lucy Gets Her Man," *The Village Voice* (5 April 1976): 46.

23. See Ann Allen Shockley, *Afro-American Women Writers 1746–1933* (Boston: G. K. Hall, 1988), 13–16. Although the poem says that the attack occurred on 25 August, Shockley says that it was three days later.

24. *The Red Moon* tells the story of the cooperation between Native and African Americans to rescue a woman's bi-racial daughter, who has been kidnapped by her irresponsible Native American father. Du Bois undoubtedly saw the possibilities of further highlighting the important historical links between the two oppressed peoples. See Henry T. Sampson, *Blacks in Blackface* (Metuchen, NJ: Scarecrow, 1980), 287.

25. Ibid.

26. Bullins, *High John da Conqueror,* in *New/Lost Plays by Ed Bullins,* 71.

27. Barbara Firger, "*Storyville:* Creators Tell Story behind the Scenes," *The UC San Diego Weekly* (2–8 May 1977): 1.

28. Don Shirley, "*Storyville:* Not Feeling that Jazz," *The Washington Post* (29 January 1979): B-9.

29. Bullins, *Journal,* 1 November 1976, TBC.

30. Kayden quoted in "The Story behind *Storyville,*" Sylvie Drake, *Los Angeles Times* (26 May 1977): 18.

31. Bullins, *Journal,* 18 May 1977, TBC.

32. Alain Locke, "The Negro and the American Stage," in *Anthology of the American Negro in the Theatre,* ed. Lindsay Patterson (New York: Publishers, 1968), 21.

33. Idris Ackamoor, "Director's Notes," Program for *Raining Down Stars,* 23 January 1992, TBC.
34. Steven Winn, "Kids from Street Stage Their Play," *San Francisco Chronicle* (27 October 1993): E-5.
35. Bullins, letter to author, 10 November 93, TBC.
36. Selaelo Maredi and Ed Bullins, *Sinning in Sun City: A Musical Play,* TBC.
37. Edith Oliver, "Off Broadway," *The New Yorker* (11 October 1976): 81.
38. When Bullins read an early version of this manuscript, he noted that he would prefer that the word "art" be substituted for "money," making the sentence read: "These Romantic revues, significantly, show that producer/director Bullins has no qualms about putting the knife and suture to playwright Bullins when there is some *art* to be made." Ha.
39. Stephen Holden, "Chilling Life on the Rock Curcuit," *The New York Times* (5 March 1990): 29.
40. Bullins, et al., *I Think It's Gonna Work Out Fine,* TBC.
41. Bernard Weiner, "Curtain Calls: A Story Like Ike and Tina's," *The San Francisco Chronicele* (30 September 1989): 30.
42. Beth Coleman, "American Gothic: Ed Bullins and Company Show Us What We Do Not See," review of *I Think It's Gonna Work Out Fine, The Village Voice* (20 March 1990): 106.
43. Robert Hurwitt, "*It's Gonna Work Out Fine* Works Out," *The San Francisco Examiner* (23 September 1989): 38.
44. Beth Coleman, "American Gothic".
45. Stephen Holden, "Chilling Life."
46. Beth Coleman, "American Gothic," 106.
47. Stephen Holden, "Chilling Life," 29.
48. Bullins, *The Work Gets Done,* TBC.
49. Bullins, *The Play of the Play,* in *The Theme Is Blackness,* ed. Ed Bullins, 183.
50. Michael Kirby, *Happenings* (New York: Dutton, 1965), 9.
51. Kirby, 13.
52. Mel Gussow, "Forty Informative Vignettes of *Street Sounds,*" *The New York Times* (23 October 1970): II-1.
53. Ibid.
54. Ibid.
55. Oscar C. Brockett, *History of the Theatre* (Boston: Allyn & Bacon, 1987), 30.
56. Bullins, *Salaam, Huey Newton, Salaam,* in *New/Lost Plays by Ed Bullins,* 311.
57. See Hugh Pearson, *The Shadow of the Panther: Huey Newton and the Price of Black Power in America* (New York: Addison-Wesley, 1994).
58. Helen Merrill, telephone interview with author, 29 September 1994.
59. El Muhajir (Marvin X), letter to Helen Merrill, 25 May 1992, TBC.
60. Bullins, letter to author, 25 July 1992, TBC.
61. Bullins, telephone interview with author, 29 September 1994.
62. El Muhajir (Marvin X), *The Devil and Marvin X: Autobiography of a Crack Monster,* 1994, TBC. A copy of this play was obtained by this author from Marvin X. Interestingly, a production of the play was prevented from opening on 3 August 1994. The lease was cancelled by the owner of the building

rented to the producing company, A Black Box Theatre, a new Tenderloin repertory company of African American actors, activists, and recovering addicts. Marvin X suspects that the owner was pressured into this action by government officials.

63. Bullins, telephone interview with author, 29 September 1994.

64. Marvin X, telephone interview with author, 18 September 1994.

65. Glenn Young, letter to Helen Merrill, 19 March 1991, TBC.

66. Lourdes Lopez for Helen Merrill, Ltd., letter to Ed Bullins, 3 April 1991, TBC.

67. Bullins insists that he never saw the galley of *Best Plays:* "Had I, I would have given my primary source credit, but I didn't see it. I credited Marvin in *New/Lost Plays,* but it was edited out—not by me." Marginal note to author.

68. Bullins did not make his directorial debut with *Dr. Geechee.* He directed his *Michael* for the New York Shakespeare Festival in 1978. The critic M. Mark said that Bullins had directed "rather well" (*Village Voice* [17 July 1978]: 75). When he moved to California, Bullins did quite a bit of directing, with credits including Ishmael Reed's *Savage Wilds* (1987), as well as several plays by Jonal Woodward: *Some Mo' Street Sounds, The Burial of Prejudice, A Smokey Affair,* and *The Burial of Prejudice* (1992).

69. Bullins, "Program Note," *Dr. Geechee and the Blood Junkies,* City College of San Francisco, January 1986, TBC.

70. Bullins, *Dr. Geechee and the Blood Junkies: A Modern Hoodoo Horror Yarn,* 1986, 80 TBC.

71. *Plato: Collected Dialogues,* Michael Joyce, trans., ed. Edith Hamilton and Huntington Cairns (Princeton: Princeton, 1969), 526.

72. Ed Bullins, *The Fabulous Miss Marie,* in *The New Lafayette Theatre Presents: Plays with Aesthetic Comments By Six Playwrights,* ed. Ed Bullins (Garden City, N.Y.: Anchor, 1974), 3.

73. John Lahr, "On Stage," *The Village Voice* (25 March 1971): 47.

74. Sege, "Review," *Variety* (6 April 1971): 7.

75. William B. Collins, "Eloquent Piece of Black Drama," *Philadelphia Inquirer* (19 May 1975): A-8.

76. Ibid.

77. Mel Gussow, "Bullins's *Miss Marie* Comes to New Lafayette," *The New York Times* (31 May 1979): C-16.

78. Sege, "Review."

79. Edith Oliver, "An Evening with Bullins and Company," *The New Yorker* (20 March 1971): 94–95.

80. Collins, "Eloquent Piece."

81. Martin Gottfried, "Approaching Masterwork Status," *Women's Wear Daily* (9 March 1971): 6.

82. Oliver, "An Evening with Bullins."

83. Ibid.

84. Sege, "Review." of *The Fabulous Miss Marie.*

85. Gussow, "Bullins's *Miss Marie.*"

86. Sege, "Review."

87. Ibid.
88. Bullins, *The Duplex: A Black Love Fable in Four Movements* (New York: Morrow, 1971).
89. John P. Desmond, review of "World Premiere," *The Northeastern University Artscene* (February 1978): 1.
90. I am indebted to an anonymous peer reviewer of the manuscript for this insight.
91. Clive Barnes, "Humanity in *The Duplex,*" *The New York Times* (15 March 1972): C-46.
92. George Oppenheimer, "Black Playwright Protests Play Production," *New York Newsday,* (15 March 1972): D-11.
93. John Lahr, "On Stage," *The Village Voice* (16 March 1972): 52.
94. Jack Kroll, "In Black America," *Newsweek* (20 March 1972): 98–99.
95. Oppenheimer, "Black Playwright Protests." review of *Duplex.*
96. Roscoe Orman, "The New Lafayette Theatre," *Black Theatre #5* (1971): 12–13.
97. Bullins, telephone interview with author, 10 August 1994.
98. Jules Irving, "Two Answers to Ed Bullins," *The New York Times* (26 March 1972): II-1.
99. Bullins, quoted in Clay Goss, "Review," *Black Books Bulletin* 1 (spring/summer 1972): 34–35.
100. Bullins, interview with J. C., *The San Francisco Sun Reporter* (20 March 1973): 23.
101. Agreement between Ed Bullins and The Repertory Theater of Lincoln Center, TBC.
102. Bullins, quoted in Jervis Anderson, "Profiles: Dramatist Ed Bullins," *The New Yorker* (16 June 1973): 40.
103. Bullins, telephone interview with author, 10 August 1994.
104. The St. Louis Black Repertory Company, founded in 1976 and directed by Ron Himes, is the largest African American performing arts organization in Missouri. The "Black Rep," as it is commonly known, specializes in programs for education and community, for professional internships, for touring shows, workshops, and student matinees. The touring company is composed of recent college graduates and/or experienced and committed college theatre students who have been accepted into the professional intern program. The three-year program provides paid internships. The touring company performs 150 shows each year for schools, community centers, corporations, churches, and other organizations in St. Louis, as well as throughout the midwest. Over fifty thousand children have seen the shows, which are sponsored by various corporations. Year-round children's workshops are offered, along with adult workshops that focus on communication skills through the use of music, movement, and creative drama. For its annual awards show in 1994, called "An Evening at the Woodies," the Black Rep went all out to honor Woodie King Jr. by bringing in such national stars, writers, directors, and designers as Glynn Turman, Kiki Shepard, John Cothran Jr., Judy Dearing, Antonio Fargas, Lincoln Kilpatrick, Ted Lange, Ron Milner, Ntozake Shange, and Dick Anthony Williams.
105. Bullins, telephone interview with author, 8 August 1994.

Chapter 5. Inner Life versus Inner Life Class of Black Experience Drama

1. Clayton Riley, telephone interview with author, 9 August 1994.
2. Clayton Riley, "Introduction," in *A Black Quartet: Four New Plays by Ben Caldwell, Ronald Milner, Ed Bullins, and LeRoi Jones* (New York: New American 1970), vii.
3. Clayton Riley, telephone interview with author, 5 September 1994.
4. Clayton Riley, "It's Not the Play I Wrote," *The New York Times* (19 March 1972): D-1.
5. Quoted in Riley, "Bullins: 'It's Not the Play I Wrote.' "
6. Ibid.
7. Alain Locke, "Negro Youth Speaks," in *The New Negro,* ed. Alain Locke (New York: Albert & Charles Boni, 1925; reprint, New York: Atheneum, 1969), 53.
8. Bullins, *Goin' a Buffalo* in *Black Theater, U.S.A.: Forty-Five Plays by Black Americans 1847–1974,* ed. James V. Hatch (New York: Free Press, 1974), 826.
9. Mel Gussow, "W.P.A. Stages Bullins Play on Young Adults," *The New York Times* (16 February 1972): 28.
10. The comparison of Bullins with European absurdists, rather than with other African Americans, is important here because Bullins has been greatly influenced by the former, whom he continually studies for form and style. He enjoys experimenting with form, which often means that his plays are the sole produced examples in African American theatre of a particular kind of play. Although Bullins read the early African American dramatists, he rejected their well-made-play structures. He declined to copy the forms—and themes—of his contemporaries because he prided himself on being strikingly original. This originality was best achieved in some cases by trying out European forms for African American subjects.
11. Bullins, *In New England Winter,* in *New Plays from the Black Theatre,* ed. Ed Bullins (New York: Bantam, 1969), 129.
12. John Lahr, "On Stage," *The Village Voice* (4 February 1971): 43.
13. Ed Bullins, letter to Joel Weixlmann, 6 February 1979, TBC.
14. Bullins, *The Pig Pen,* in *Four Dynamite Plays,* 39.
15. Edith Oliver, "Off Broadway," *The New Yorker* (30 May 1970): 72.
16. Harold Clurman, "Theatre," *The Nation* (1 June 1970): 668–69.
17. Martin Gottfried, "*The Pig Pen,*" *Women's Wear Daily* (21 May 1970): 14.
18. Clayton Riley, "Theatre Review," *Liberator* 10 (June 1970): 20.
19. Ibid.
20. Edith Oliver, "Off Broadway," *The New Yorker,* (20 June 1977): 89.
21. Bullins, *Daddy,* TBC, 86.
22. Edith Oliver, "Off Broadway."
23. Terry Curtis Fox, "The Con Man in the Mirror," *The Village Voice* (20 June 1977): 71.
24. William Harris, "Off and On," *The Soho Weekly News* (23 June 1977): 48.
25. Ibid.

26. Unless otherwise stated, all quotations from the symposium are from "Lafayette Theatre: Reaction to *Bombers*," *Black Theatre* #4 (1969): 16.
27. Bullins, *To raise the dead and foretell the future,* TBC.
28. Bullins, "I'm Tired," Poem, TBC.
29. Bullins, "Creation Spell," *Journal of Black Poetry* 1 (summer-fall 1969): 58.
30. Bullins, *The Devil Catchers: A Philosophic Prophecy,* TBC, 35.
31. Bullins, *The Psychic Pretenders: A Black Ritual Mystical Drama,* TBC, 45.
32. Bullins, *The Devil Catchers,* TBC, 96.
33. Bullins, *The Psychic Pretenders,* TBC, 76.
34. Eric Bentley, review of *The Psychic Pretenders, The New York Times* (23 January 1972): II-1.
35. Marginal notes to author.
36. Bullins, telephone interview with author, 8 August 1994.
37. Ed Bullins, "Two Days Shie . . . ," 60.
38. Ibid.
39. John J. O'Connor, "Getting beyond Polemics," *Wall Street Journal* (25 March 1968): 14.
40. Bullins, *A Son, Come Home,* in *Five Plays by Ed Bullins,* ed. Ed Bullins (New York: Bobbs-Merrill, 1968), 184.
41. Bullins, "Two Days Shie . . . ," 68.
42. Bullins, "He Couldn't Say Sex," in *The Hungered One,* 26.
43. Bullins, "Baseball Bill," *Ink Margins Magazine* (1992), 79.
44. Bullins, *Boy x Man,* TBC.
45. Anne Barnhill, "*Boy x Man* Is A Must-see," *Greensboro* (NC) *News and Record,* TBC, 10.
46. Bullins, *Blacklist,* TBC, 46.
47. Bullins, telephone interview with author, 8 August 1994.
48. John J. O'Connor, "Getting beyond Polemics," *The Wall Street Journal* (25 March 1968) 13.
49. Martin Gottfried, "The Master Introduces His Pupils," *New York Post* (23 July 1977): 14.
50. Harold Clurman, "Theatre," *The Nation* (25 March 1968): 420–21.
51. Ed Bullins, letter to author, 26 August 1994, TBC.

Conclusion

1. Bullins, letter to author, 14 April 1994, TBC.
2. Ed Bullins, Notes on Literary Biography," TBC.
3. Mel Gussow, "Bullins's *Miss Marie* Comes to the New Lafayette," *The New York Times* (12 March 1971): 7.
4. Ed Bullins, letter to author, 10 November 1993, TBC.

BIBLIOGRAPHY

Works by Ed Bullins

PUBLISHED PLAYS/SCREENPLAYS

The American Flag Ritual: A Short Play or Film Scenario. One act. Unproduced. 1969. In *The Theme Is Blackness: The Corner and Other Plays*, edited by Ed Bullins. New York: Morrow, 1973.

Black Commercial #2. One act. Unproduced. 1967. In *The Theme Is Blackness*, edited by Ed Bullins. New York: Morrow, 1973.

The Box Office. One act. Unproduced. *Black Theatre #3* (1969): 17–19.

City Preacher. Long one act. First produced at Magic Theatre, San Francisco, 1984. In *New/Lost Plays by Ed Bullins: An Anthology*, edited by Ethel Pitts Walker. Aiea, HI: That New Publishing Company, 1993.

Clara's Ole Man. One act. First produced at Firehouse Repertory Theatre, San Francisco, 1965. In *Five Plays*, edited by Ed Bullins. New York: Bobbs-Merrill, 1969. Also published in *The Electronic Nigger, and Other Plays*. London: Faber, 1970.

The Corner. One act. First produced by Theatre Company of Boston, 1968. In *Black Drama Anthology*, edited by Woodie King and Ron Milner. New York: Columbia University Press, 1972. Reprinted in *The Theme Is Blackness: The Corner and Other Plays*, edited by Ed Bullins. New York: Morrow, 1973.

Death List. One act. First produced by Theatre Black, University of the Streets, New York, 1970. In *Four Dynamite Plays*, edited by Ed Bullins. New York: Morrow, 1972.

Dialect Determinism. One act. First produced by Firehouse Repertory Theatre, San Francisco, 1965. In *The Theme Is Blackness: The Corner and Other Plays*, edited by Ed Bullins. New York: Morrow, 1973.

269

The Duplex: A Black Love Fable in Four Movements. Four acts. First produced at New Lafayette Theatre, New York, 1970. New York: Morrow, 1971.

The Electronic Nigger. One act. First produced at American Place Theatre, 1968. In *Five Plays,* edited by Ed Bullins. New York: Bobbs-Merrill, 1969. Also published in *The Electronic Nigger, and Other Plays.* London: Faber, 1970.

The Fabulous Miss Marie. Long one act. First produced at New Lafayette Theatre, New York, 1971. In *The New Lafayette Theatre Presents,* edited by Ed Bullins. New York: Anchor, 1974.

The Gentleman Caller. One act. First produced with other plays as *A Black Quartet* by Chelsea Theatre Center, Brooklyn Academy of Music, 1969. In *A Black Quartet: Four New Plays by Ben Caldwell, Ronald Milner, Ed Bullins, and LeRoi Jones,* edited by Ben Caldwell, Ronald Milner, Ed Bullins, and LeRoi Jones. New York: New American Library, 1970.

Goin' a Buffalo. Three acts. First produced at New Lafayette Theatre, New York, 1969. In *Five Plays,* edited by Ed Bullins. New York: Bobbs-Merrill, 1969. Also published in *The Electronic Nigger, and Other Plays.* London: Faber, 1970. Reprinted in *New Black Playwrights,* edited by William Couch Jr. New York: Bard Books, 1970. Also reprinted in *Black Theater U.S.A.: Forty-Five Plays by Black Americans, 1847–1974,* edited by James V. Hatch and Ted Shine. New York: Free Press, 1974.

The Helper. One act. First produced by New Dramatists' Workshop, New York, 1970. In *The Theme Is Blackness: The Corner and Other Plays,* edited by Ed Bullins. New York: Morrow, 1973.

High John da Conquerer: The Musical. Two acts. First produced at Black Repertory Theatre, Berkeley, Calif., 1985. In *New/Lost Plays by Ed Bullins: An Anthology,* edited by Ethel Pitts Walker. Aiea, HI: That New Publishing Company, 1993.

How Do You Do: A Nonsense Drama. One act. First produced at Firehouse Repertory Theatre, San Francisco, 1965. San Francisco: Illumination Press, 1967. Reprinted in *Black Fire,* edited by LeRoi Jones and Larry Neal. New York: Morrow, 1968.

I Am Lucy Terry: An Historical Fantasy for Young Americans. Two acts. First produced at American Place Theatre, 1976. In *New/Lost Plays by Ed Bullins: An Anthology,* edited by Ethel Pitts Walker. Aiea, HI: That New Publishing Company, 1993.

In New England Winter. Long one act. First produced at Henry Street Settlement's New Federal Theatre, New York, 1971. In *New Plays from the Black Theatre,* edited by Ed Bullins. New York: Bantam, 1969.

In the Wine Time. Two acts. First produced at New Lafayette Theatre, New York, 1968. In *Five Plays,* edited by Ed Bullins. New York: Bobbs-Merrill, 1969. Also published in *The Electronic Nigger, and Other Plays.* London: Faber, 1970. Reprinted in *Black Theatre,* edited by Lindsay Patterson. New York: New American Library, 1971. Also reprinted in *Black Drama in America: An Anthology,* 2d ed., edited by Darwin T. Turner. Washington, DC: Howard University Press, 1994.

It Bees Dat Way. One act. First produced at Ambience Lunch-Hour Theatre Club, London, 1970. In *Four Dynamite Plays,* edited by Ed Bullins. New York: Morrow, 1972.

Bibliography

It Has No Choice. One act. First produced by Black Arts/West Repertory Theater/ School, San Francisco, 1966. In *The Theme Is Blackness: The Corner and Other Plays,* edited by Ed Bullins. New York: Morrow, 1973.

Jo Anne!!! Two acts. First produced at Theatre of the Riverside Church, New York, 1976. In *New/Lost Plays by Ed Bullins: An Anthology,* edited by Ethel Pitts Walker. Aiea, HI: That New Publishing Company, 1993.

Malcolm: '71, or Publishing Blackness. One act. Unproduced. *The Black Scholar* (June 1975): 84–86.

The Man Who Dug Fish. One act. First produced by New Dramatists, New York, 1970. In *The Theme Is Blackness: The Corner and Other Plays,* edited by Ed Bullins. New York: Morrow, 1973.

A Minor Scene. One act. First produced by Black Arts/West Repertory/School, San Francisco, 1966. In *The Theme Is Blackness: The Corner and Other Plays,* edited by Ed Bullins. New York: Morrow, 1973.

The Mystery of Phillis Wheatley: An Historical Play for Young Americans. Long one act. First produced at Henry Street Settlement's New Federal Theatre, New York, 1976. In *New/Lost Plays by Ed Bullins: An Anthology,* edited by Ethel Pitts Walker. Aiea, HI: That New Publishing Company, 1993.

Night of the Beast. Screenplay. Unproduced. 1971. In *Four Dynamite Plays,* edited by Ed Bullins. New York: Morrow, 1972.

One-Minute Commercial. One act. Unproduced, 1973. In *The Theme Is Blackness: The Corner and Other Plays,* edited by Ed Bullins. New York: Morrow, 1973.

The Pig Pen. Long one act. First produced at American Place Theatre, 1970. In *Four Dynamite Plays,* edited by Ed Bullins. New York: Morrow, 1972.

The Play of the Play. One act. Unproduced. 1973. In *The Theme Is Blackness: The Corner and Other Plays,* edited by Ed Bullins. New York: Morrow, 1973.

Salaam, Huey Newton, Salaam. One act. First produced at Ensemble Studio Theatre, New York, 1991. In *Best American Short Plays of 1990,* edited by Howard Stein. New York: Applause Theatre Books, 1991. Reprinted in *New/Lost Plays by Ed Bullins: An Anthology,* edited by Ethel Pitts Walker. Aiea, HI: That New Publishing Company, 1993.

A Short Play for a Small Theater. One act. Unproduced. 1973. In *The Theme Is Blackness: The Corner and Other Plays,* edited by Ed Bullins. New York: Morrow, 1973.

A Son, Come Home. One act. First produced at American Place Theatre, 1968. In *Five Plays,* edited by Ed Bullins. New York: Bobbs-Merrill, 1969. Also published in *The Electronic Nigger, and Other Plays.* London: Faber, 1970.

State Office Bldg. Curse: A Scenario to Ultimate Action. One act. Unproduced. 1973. In *The Theme Is Blackness: The Corner and Other Plays,* edited by Ed Bullins. New York: Morrow, 1973.

A Street Play. One act. First produced at San Francisco State College, 1966. In *The Theme Is Blackness: The Corner and Other Plays,* edited by Ed Bullins. New York: Morrow, 1973.

Street Sounds. Long one act. First produced by La Mama's GPA Nucleus, 1970. In *The Theme Is Blackness: The Corner and Other Plays,* edited by Ed Bullins. New York: Morrow, 1973.

The Taking of Miss Janie. Long one act. First produced at Henry Street Settlement's New Federal Theatre, New York, 1975. In *Black Thunder: An Anthology of Contemporary African American Drama,* edited by William B. Branch. New York: Mentor, 1992.

The Theme Is Blackness. One act. First produced at San Francisco State College, 1966. In *The Theme Is Blackness: The Corner and Other Plays,* edited by Ed Bullins. New York: Morrow, 1973.

To raise the dead and foretell the future. One-act ritual. First produced by New Lafayette Theatre, New York, 1970. New York: New Lafayette Theatre Publications, 1970.

We Righteous Bombers (under the alias Kingsley B. Bass Jr.). Three acts. First produced by New Lafayette Theatre, New York, 1969. In *New Plays from the Black Theatre,* edited by Ed Bullins. New York: Bantam, 1969.

UNPUBLISHED PLAYS

With Idris Ackamoor. *American Griot.* One-act, one-man musical. First produced at La MaMa E.T.C., 1991. The Bullins Collection.

At the Bottom. Adaptation of Maxim Gorky's *The Lower Depths.* Fragment. Unproduced (written for Joseph Papp), 1979. The Bullins Collection.

A Black Time for Black Folk. One-act mime. First produced at the New Lafayette Theatre, 1970. No known copies extant.

Blacklist. Long one act. Unproduced. 1982. The Bullins Collection.

Boy x Man. Two acts. First produced at North Carolina A. & T. State University in Greensboro, North Carolina, 1995. The Bullins Collection.

C'mon Back to Heavenly House. Two acts. First produced at Amherst College, 1977. The Bullins Collection.

City Preacher. Teleplay. Unproduced. 1978. In The Bullins Collection.

Daddy. Three acts. First produced at Henry Street Settlement's New Federal Theatre, 1977. The Bullins Collection.

The Devil Catchers. Long one-act with music. First produced by the New Lafayette Theatre, 1970. The Bullins Collection.

Dirty Pool. One act. Unproduced. 1985. The Bullins Collection.

Dr. Geechee and the Blood Junkies: A Modern Hoodoo Horror Yarn. Three acts. First produced at City College of San Francisco, 1985. Revised in 1986. The Bullins Collection.

Dr. Geechee and the Blood Junkies. Screenplay. Unproduced. 1986. The Bullins Collection.

The Electronic Nigger. Screenplay. Unproduced. 1979. The Bullins Collection.

With Rhodessa Jones and Danny Duncan. *Emergency Report.* Two-act musical drama. First produced by Cultural Odyssey at the Lorraine Hansberry Theater in San Francisco, 1993. The Bullins Collection.

Ethiopian Comedy. One act. Unproduced. 1985. No known copies extant.

With Shirley Tarbell. *The Game of Adam and Eve.* One act. First produced by the Theatre Company of Boston, 1966. No known copies extant.

With Bill Lathan. *Go Go: A Story of Dancing Girls.* Screenplay. Unproduced. 1969. The Bullins Collection.

Bibliography

Goin' a Buffalo. Screenplay. Produced by the New Lafayette Theatre, 1971. The Bullins Collection.

The Home. Teleplay. Unproduced. 1974. The Bullins Collection.

Home Boy. Long one-act musical drama. First produced at the Perry Street Theater in New York City, 1976. The Bullins Collection.

House Party. Musical revue. Production concept by Robert Macbeth, music by Pat Patrick. First produced by the American Place Theatre, 1973. Produced as "Women I Have Known" in 1976. The Bullins Collection.

The Hungered One. Radio play. Unproduced. 1984. The Bullins Collection.

Hunk. One act. Unproduced. 1980. The Bullins Collection.

With Idris Ackamoor, Rhodessa Jones, and Brian Freeman. *I Think It's Gonna Work Out Fine: A Rock and Roll Fable.* Music by Rhodessa Jones, Idris Ackamoor, Peter Fuji, and Rock of Edges. Two-act musical drama. First produced by Cultural Odyssey at the South of Market Climate Theater in San Francisco, 1989. The Bullins Collection.

Judge Tom Strikes Back: A Seriously Vicious Satire. Long one act. Unproduced. 1992. The Bullins Collection

Leavings. One-act musical drama. First produced by Solid Productions at Syncopation in New York City, 1980. In The Bullins Collection.

Michael. One act. First produced at Northeastern University, 1978. The Bullins Collection.

Next Time . . . One act. First produced at Bronx Community College, 1972. The Bullins Collection.

"No Man Who Believes in Freedom Shall Ever Die." Incomplete treatment for screenplay. N.d. The Bullins Collection.

The Psychic Pretenders. Long one-act music drama. First produced by the New Lafayette Players, 1971. The Bullins Collection.

With Idris Ackamoor and Rhodessa Jones. *Raining Down Stars.* Music by Idris Ackamoor, Hakeem Muhammad, and Famoudou Don Moye. Long one-act musical drama. First produced by Cultural Odyssey at Theater Artaud in San Francisco, 1992. The Bullins Collection.

A Ritual to Bind Together and Strengthen Black People So That They Can Survive the Struggle to Come. Long one-act musical drama. First produced by the New Lafayette Theatre, 1969. The Bullins Collection.

Safety Check. Screenplay. Unproduced. 1971. In The Bullins Collection.

"The Seance." *Sanford and Son.* Outline. Unproduced. 1972. The Bullins Collection.

Satchmo: An American Musical Legend. Musical. Unproduced. 1981. The Bullins Collection.

With Mildred Kayden. *Sepia Star.* Musical. First produced by Solid Productions at Stage 73 in New York City, 1977. The Bullins Collection.

With Selaelo Maredi. *Sinning in Sun City.* Long one-act musical drama. First produced by the Julian Theatre at the Buriel Clay Memorial Theatre in San Francisco, 1987. The Bullins Collection.

Snickers. One act. Unproduced. 1985. The Bullins Collection.

A Son, Come Home. Teleplay. Unproduced. 1972. The Bullins Collection.

273

Steve and Velma An Epilogue to the Duplex. One act. First produced at Northeastern University, 1978. The Bullins Collection.

With Mildred Kayden. *Storyville.* Two-act musical. First produced at University of California-San Diego, 1977. The Bullins Collection.

With Marshall Borden. *A Sunday Afternoon.* Two acts. First produced at San Francisco City College, 1987. The Bullins Collection.

"The Taking of Miss Janie." Treatment for screenplay. Unproduced. 1976. The Bullins Collection.

A Teacup Full of Roses. Screenplay. Adapted from the novel by Sharon Bell Mathis. Unproduced. 1975. The Bullins Collection.

A Teacup Full of Roses. Three acts. Adapted from the novel by Sharon Bell Mathis. Unproduced. 1985. The Bullins Collection.

Women I Have Known. Musical revue. Production concept by Robert Macbeth, music by Pat Patrick. First produced at the American Place Theatre, 1976. First produced as *House Party* by the American Place Theatre, 1973. The Bullins Collection.

The Work Gets Done. One act. First produced by the New African Company in Boston, 1980. The Bullins Collection.

You Can't Keep a Good Man Down. One act. Unproduced. 1978. No copies extant.

You Gonna Let Me Take You Out Tonight, Baby? One-character one-act drama. First produced at the Syncopation in New York City, 1980. No copies extant.

PUBLISHED FICTION

"Baseball Bill." *Ink Margins Magazine* (1992): 79–81.

"The Harlem Mice." *Black World* (June 1975): 54–55.

The Hungered One: Early Writings of Ed Bullins. New York: Morrow, 1971.

"Miss Minnie and Her New Hairdo." *Discourse* (October 1992): 11.

The Reluctant Rapist. New York: Harper, 1973.

UNPUBLISHED FICTION

"Bunky Learns to Read." Short story. 1979. The Bullins Collection.

"Dirty Story." Short story. Ca. 1968. The Bullins Collection.

"Funky Chicken." Novella. 1995. The Bullins Collection.

"The Home: A Contemporary Parable." Novella. Ca 1968–82. The Bullins Collection.

"Night of the Beast." Novella. Ca. 1968–82. The Bullins Collection.

With Sheryl P. Whitmore. "The Drug Zombie." Short story. ca. 1968–82. The Bullins Collection.

PUBLISHED ARTICLES, ESSAYS, AND INTERVIEWS

"Black Revolutionary Commercial." *The Drama Review* 13 (summer 1969): 144–45.

"Black Theatre." *Other Stages* (10 July 1980): 2.

"Black Theatre Art—Structured Black Collaboration: A Discussion between Romare Bearden and Ed Bullins." *News of the American Place Theatre* (14 September 1973): 1–4.

"Black Theatre Roundup." *Black Theatre Newsletter* 2 (June-August 1986): 1–4.

"Bulletins." *Other Stages* (28 January-10 February 1981): 1.

"Celebrating La Mama's 20th." *The Villager* (15 October 1981): 16.

"Comments on Production of *In New England Winter.*" *The New York Times* (20 December 1970): 6.

"the electronic nigger meets the gold dust twins: Clifford Mason Talks with Robert Macbeth and Ed Bullins." *Black Theatre* #1 (1968): 24–28.

"The Eugene O'Neill Memorial Theater Foundation." *Black Theatre* #1 (1968): 4–7.

"Interview." *Black World* (April 1969): 9–11.

"Introduction: Black Theatre: The 70's—Evolutionary Changes." In *The Theme Is Blackness,* edited by Ed Bullins. New York: Morrow, 1973, 1–15.

"Like It Was: Review of Jones' *The Dutchman* and *The Toilet.*" *Black Dialogue* 1 (spring 1996): 72–75.

"No Nothin'." *The New York Times* (21 September 1977): 18.

"On Baraka." *Other Stages* (17–30 December 1981): 1, (31 December 1981): 2.

"Open Letter to Douglas Watt." *Soho Weekly* (10 June 1976): 15.

"Open Letter to Joan Little: 'Stay Off Fast Track.'" *New York Amsterdam News* (13 December 1975): D-2.

"An Open Statement on the Review of 'Leavings.'" *The Village Voice* (13–19 August 1980): 76.

"Playwrights Workshop at the Public Theatre." *Other Stages* (14–27 January 1982): 1.

"The Polished Protest: Aesthetics and the Black Writer." *Contact Magazine* (July 1963): reprint, n.p.

"Lafayette Theatre: Reaction to *Bombers.*" Edited by Ed Bullins. *Black Theatre* #4 (1969): 16–25.

"Review of *A Hero Ain't Nothin' But a Sandwich* by Alice Childress." *The New York Times Book Review* (4 November 1973): 36.

"Short Statement on Street Theater." *The Drama Review* 12 (summer 1968): 93.

"Should Black Actors Play Chekhov?" *The New York Times* (4 February 1973): 16.

"The So-called Western Avant-Garde Drama." *Liberator* (December 1967): 16. Reprinted in *Black Expression,* edited by Addison Gayle Jr. New York: Weybright and Talley. 1969.

"Talking of Black Art, Theatre, Revolution and Nationhood: Interviews at the First Pan African Cultural Festival and in Manhattan and Harlem." *Black Theatre* #5 (1971): 18–37.

"Theatre of Reality." *Negro Digest* 15 (April 1966): 60–66.

"Two Days Shie . . . " In *Contemporary Authors Autobiography Series,* vol. 16, edited by Joyce Nakamura (Detroit: Gale Research, 1992), 59–70.

"What Lies Ahead for the Blackamericans?" *Black World* (November 1969): 8.

UNPUBLISHED ARTICLES AND ESSAYS

"Adrienne Kennedy and the 'Magic Realism' Question." 1992. The Bullins Collection.

"Bay Area Black Theatre, Or 'The Renaissance Will Not Be Televised.'" 1983. The Bullins Collection.

"The Black Male and Cultural Studies." 1992. The Bullins Collection.

"The Blackening of Oakland." 1984. The Bullins Collection.

"Ce Chien Est A Moi." 1992. The Bullins Collection.

"Chester Himes: Protest and Autobiographic Novels: A Personalized Reader Response." 1992. In The Bullins Collection.

"The Color Line." 1991. The Bullins Collection.

"Conformity/Nonconformity." 1991. The Bullins Collection.

"Deconstruction: The Nihilism of Postmodern Western Literary Theory." 1992. The Bullins Collection.

"The End of *The Member of the Wedding*." 1992. The Bullins Collection.

"Friedman Does Angela Carter." 1992. The Bullins Collection.

"Housekeeping?" 1991. The Bullins Collection.

"Journal Notes: 'Tit for Tat,' 'Journals,' 'Bluest Eyes,' 'Various Approached,' 'The Not-So-Invisible Man Listening . . .,' 'Random,' 'You Take the High Road, and . . .,' and 'Unsexy Sex.'" 1991. The Bullins Collection.

"Levi's Men." 1992. The Bullins Collection.

"A Moor in the Taco Bowel." 1991. The Bullins Collection.

"The Slave in the Cave: A Zora Neale Hurston Heroine and the Parables of the Cave." 1991. The Bullins Collection.

"TDC = PC + LT." 1992. The Bullins Collection.

"The Transcendent Stereotype; or the Confessions of an Epiphanic Black Rogue." 1991. The Bullins Collection.

Works by Other Authors

BIBLIOGRAPHIES

Arata, Esther Spring, and Nicholas John Rotoli. *Black American Playwrights, 1800 to the Present*. Metuchen, NJ: Scarecrow Press, 1976.

———. *More Black American Playwrights*. Metuchen, NJ: Scarecrow Press, 1978.

Turner, Darwin T., editor. *Black Drama in America*, 2d ed. Washington, DC: Howard University, 1994.

BOOKS AND ARTICLES

Anderson, Jervis. "Profiles: Dramatist Ed Bullins." *The New Yorker* 49 (16 June 1973): 40–78.

Baraka, Amiri. *The Autobiography: LeRoi Jones/Amiri Baraka*. New York: Freundlich, 1984.

Bourne, Kay. "Wesley and Bullins." *Bay State Banner* (12 April 1979): 15.

Brown, Elaine. *A Taste of Power: A Black Woman's Story*. New York: Pantheon, 1992.

Brown, Sterling. *Negro Poetry and Drama*. Washington, DC: Associates in Negro Folk Education, 1937. Reprint. New York: Atheneum, 1969.

"Bullins' Appointment to American Place Theatre." *Critical Digest* 14 (12 February 1973).

Bibliography

"Bullins in Algiers." *Bay State Banner* (4 September 1969): 5.

Cade, Toni. "Black Theater." In *Black Expression,* edited by Addison Gayle Jr. New York: Weybright and Talley, 1969.

Clarke, Constance. "About Ed Bullins." *Applause* (22 December 1971): 17.

Clayborne, Jon L. "Modern Black Drama and the Gay Image." *College English* 36 (November 1974): 381–84.

Cleaver, Eldridge. *Soul on Ice.* New York: McGraw-Hill, 1968.

Draper, James P., editor *Black Literature Criticism,* vol. 1. Detroit: Gale Research, 1992, 321–42.

"Ed Bullins on the Go: Becomes Own Producer." *Show Business* (15 February 1973): 1.

Goncalves, Joe. "The Mysterious Disappearance of Black Arts West." *Black Theatre* #2 (1969): 21–25.

Gottfried, Martin. "The Master Introduces His Pupils." *New York Post* (23 July 1977).

———. "Playwrights: The Inner Four." *Vogue* (July 1973): 72–73.

Hawkins, Van. "Ed Bullins Is Baddest Brother in Black Theater." *The Newport News Times-Herald* (25 May 1974): S 1.

Hay, Samuel A. "African American Drama, 1950–1970." *Negro History Bulletin* 36 (1973): 5–8.

———. *African American Theatre: A Historical and Critical Analysis.* New York: Cambridge University Press, 1994.

Hilliard, David, and Lewis Cole. *This Side of Glory: The Autobiography of David Hilliard and the Story of the Black Panther Party.* Boston: Little Brown, 1993.

Jeffers, Lance. "Bullins, Baraka, and Elder: The Dawn of Grandeur in Black Drama." *CLA Journal* 7 (September 1972): 32–48.

Johnson, Thomas. "Black Drama Gains as Way to Teach, Unite—and Amuse," *The New York Times* (1 October 1968): 49.

Jones, LeRoi, and Larry Neal, editors. *Black Fire: An Anthology of Afro-American Writing.* New York: Morrow, 1968.

Kirby, Michael. "Introduction." *Happenings.* New York: E. P. Dutton, 1965.

Knickerbocker, Paine. "Quiet Revolution under Way by Black Playwrights." *Datebook* (29 April 1973): 9.

Kornfeld, Joe. "Playwright Ed Bullins: Soft-Spoken Giant on the Black Literary Scene." *The Boston Herald American* (24 January 1975): 32.

Locke, Alain. "Max Reinhardt Reads the Negro's Dramatic Horoscope." *Opportunity* (May 1924): 145.

———. "The Negro and the Theater." In *Theatre,* edited by Edith J. R. Isaacs. Boston: Little, Brown, 1927, 290–303. Rpt. in *Anthology of the American Negro in the Theatre: A Critical Approach,* edited by Lindsay Patterson. New York: Publishers Company, 1968, 21–24.

———, ed. *The New Negro.* New York: Albert & Charles Boni, 1925. Rpt. New York: Atheneum, 1969.

McManus, Otile. "Playwright Ed Bullins and the Black Ethos." *Boston Evening Globe* (28 January 1975).

Marowitz, Charles. "America's Great Hopes, White and Black?" *New York Times* (13 April 1969): D3.

277

Mayo, Sandra. "Ed Bullins, New York's Resident Black Dramatists." In *Afro-Americans in New York Life and History*. Buffalo: Afro-Americans in New York, 1981, 51–57.

Miller, Jeanne-Marie A. "Images of Black Women in Plays by Black Playwrights." *CLA Journal* 20 (June 1977): 494–507.

Mitchell, Lionel. "Ed Bullins: Shadow and Flame." *The Village Voice* (29 October–4 November 1980): 87–88.

Nelsen, Don. "Basing Plays on Tragic Fact." *Daily News* (16 January 1980): 23.

"New Lafayette Theatre Recognized in Europe." *New York Amsterdam News* (10 October 1970).

Newton, Huey P. *Revolutionary Suicide*. New York: Harcourt Brace Jovanovich, 1973.

O'Haire, Patricia. "Bullins: A Philadelphia Story." *The New York Daily News* (7 June 1975): 25.

Pearson, Hugh. *The Shadow of the Panther: Huey Newton and the Price of Black Power in America*. New York: Addison-Wesley, 1994.

"Philly Court Awards $201,792 to Bullins for Son's Crash Death." *Variety* (4 March 1981).

"Playwright Ed Bullins' Son Crushed to Death; Compensation: $5,822." *Variety* (26 December 1979).

Raidy, William A. "In Art There Is Nothing You Cannot Do." *The Staten Island Sunday Advance* (13 July 1975): E-5.

Riley, Clayton. "Introduction." In *A Black Quartet: Four New Plays by Ben Caldwell, Ronald Milner, Ed Bullins, and LeRoi Jones*. New York: New American, 1970, vii–xxiii.

Sampson, Henry T. *Blacks in Blackface*. Metuchen, NJ: Scarecrow, 1980.

Sanders, Leslie Catherine. *The Development of Black Theater in America: From Shadows to Selves*. Baton Rouge: Louisiana State University Press, 1988.

Simms, Donna A. "Looking at Ed Bullins from Different Places in the Room." *Aquarian* (12–19 October 1977).

Tener, Robert L. "Pandora's Box: A Study of Ed Bullins' Dramas." *CLA Journal* 19 (June 1976): 533–44.

Wallach, Allan. "His Universe in Black." *New York Newsday* (July 1975): II-3.

Wesley, Richard. "Black Theater in New York." *Third World* (31 March 1972): 4.

Williams, Mance. *Black Theater in the 1960s and 1970s: A Historical-Critical Analysis of the Movement*. Westport, CT: Greenwood Press, 1985.

X, Marvin. "Autobiography of a North American African." Unpublished manuscript, 1994.

———. "Interview with Ed Bullins." *In New Plays from the* Black Theatre, edited by Ed Bullins. New York: Bantam, 1969, vi-xv.

Dissertations

Cipriani, Barbara. "Ed Bullins." University of Florence, Italy, 1995.

Hennessy, Mary-Frances C. "Soul on Stage, The New Black Dramatists: A Definition." Trinity College, 1973.

Bibliography

Mayo, Sandra M. "The Cultural Roots of the Drama of Ed Bullins." Syracuse University, 1987.

Ogunbiyi, Yemi. "New Black Playwrights in America (1960–75): Essays in Theatrical Criticism." New York University, 1976.

REVIEWS OF INDIVIDUAL PLAYS

American Griot

Oumano, Elena. "Idris Ackamoor Honors His Musical Heritage." *The Oakland Sun* (6–12 March 1991): 25.

Seymour, Gene. "Autobiography of a Jazz Great." *New York Newsday* (5 February 1991): II-1.

Boy x Man

Barnhill, Anne. "*Boy x Man* Is A Must-See." *The Greensboro (NC) News and Record* (28 October 1995): G-2.

City Preacher

Berson, Misha. "Bullins Falls from Grace." *The San Francisco Bay Guardian* (18 January 1984).

————. "Magic Preacher: Playwright Ed Bullins Comes Home to San Francisco." *The San Francisco Bay Guardian* (11 January 1984).

Kay, Alfred. "New Work by Noted Playwright Bullins Misses Mark." *The Sacramento Bee* (13 January 1984).

Morgan, Maggie. "An Unnecessary Harangue in Tired Plotting." *The California Aggie* (24 January 1984).

Mote, Sue. "A View of Black Harlem." *The Vacaville Reporter* (19 January 1984).

Scheib, Hilda. " 'Preacher' Says Little about Powell." *Alameda County Gazette* (18 January 1984): 45.

Scott, Nancy. "One Cheer for New Bullins Play." *The San Francisco Examiner* (13 January 1984).

Spunberb, Bernard. "From Booze to Pews." *The Bay Area Reporter* (12 February, 1984).

Taylor, Robert. "Actors Try to Save a Shapeless 'Preacher.' " *The Oakland Tribune* (14 January 1984): 24.

Winn, Steve. "Play You Have to Take on Faith." *The San Francisco Chronicle* (13 January 1984): 8.

Clara's Ole Man

Brukenfeld, Dick. "Off-Off." *The Village Voice* (28 May 1970): 51.

Clayborne, Jon L. "Modern Black Drama and the Gay Image." *College English* 36 (November 1974): 381–84.

Clurman, Harold. "Review." *The Nation* (25 March 1968): 420–21.

Gussow, Mel. "The New Playwrights." *Newsweek* (20 March 1968): 114–15.

Hatch, James V. "Three at the Afro-American Studio." *The Village Voice* (6 November 1969): 42.

Lowrie, Barbara Woller. "A Homecoming for the Family." *The Westchester Weekend* (15 April 1977): D17.

Oliver, Edith. "The Theatre: Off Broadway." *The New Yorker* (9 November 1981): 155.

———. "Three Cheers." *The New Yorker* (13 April 1968): 133–34.

Smith, Michael. "Theatre Journal." *The Village Voice* (11 April 1968): 39.

Watts, Richard. "A Trio of Short Plays by a Negro Dramatist." *The New York Post* (7 March 1968): 24.

The Corner

Gussow, Mel. " 'The Corner' Opens." *The New York Times* (23 June 1972): 18.

Novick, Julius. "No Place Like Rome." *The Village Voice* (29 June 1972): 58.

Raidy, William A. "Three One-Acters Paint Portrait." *The Long Island Press* (23 June 1972): 11.

Tallmer, Jerry. "Off-Broadway: Goss, Oyam, Bullins." *The New York Post* (23 June 1972): 20.

Wallach, Allan. "Theatre." *Newsday* (23 June 1972): 11.

Watt, Douglas. "Black-Ghetto Street Scenes." *The New York Daily News* (24 June 1972): 23.

Daddy

Baker, Rob. "Bullins Bares a Hit." *The New York Daily News* (14 June 1977): 17.

Fox, Terry Curtis, "The Con Man in the Mirror." *The Village Voice* (20 June 1977): 71.

Harris, William. "Off and On." *The Soho Weekly News* (23 June 1977): 48.

Lask, Thomas. "Stage: Black to White." *The New York Times* (17 June 1977): C10.

Oliver, Edith. "The Theatre: Off-Broadway." *The New Yorker* (20 June 1977): 89.

The Devil Catchers

Munk, Erika. "Bullins: 'I Had My Way with Her.' " *The Village Voice* (8 November 1976): 87.

Oliver, Edith. "The Theatre: Off Broadway." *The New Yorker* (30 November 1970): 132.

Dialect Determinism

Barnes, Clive. "Four Black Plays: Bullins' 'Short Bullins's Done by La Mama." *The New York Times* (5 March 1972).

Sainer, Arthur. "Up For Adoption." *The Village Voice* (2 March 1972): 51.

Sanders, Leslie. " 'Dialect Determinism': Ed Bullins' Critique of the Rhetoric of the Black Power Movement." In *Beliefs vs. Theory in Black American Literary Criticism,* edited by Joe Weixlmann and Chester J. Fontenot. Greenwood, Fla.: Penkeville, 1986, 161–75.

The Duplex

Barnes, Clive. "Humanity in 'The Duplex.' " *The New York Times* (15 March 1972): 46.

Berman, Audrey. "Off-Stage." *The Village Voice* (23 March 1972): 60.

"Bullins Criticizes Staging of 'Duplex.' " *New York Times* (24 February 1972).

Clarke, Sebastian. "Ed Bullins: Possessed by a Demon." *The Metropolitan Review* (15–21 June 1972): 37–38.

Bibliography

"Ed Bullins Demands Lincoln Center Scrap 'Duplex' Production." *The New York Amsterdam News* (11 March 1972).

Evans, Don. "The Theater of Confrontation: Ed Bullins, Up against the Wall." *Black World* 23 (April 1974): 14–18.

Fornes, Maria Irene. "Playwrights' Lib Meets Mr. Irving." *The Village Voice* (30 March 1972); 58, *passim*.

Goss, Clay. "Review." *Black Books Bulletin* 1 (spring/summer 1972): 34–35.

Hay, Samuel A. "What Shape Shapes Shapelessness? Structural Elements in Ed Bullins's Plays." *Black World* 23 (April 1974): 20–26.

Irving, Jules. "Two Answers to Ed Bullins." *The New York Times* (26 March 1972): sec. 2, p. 11.

Kerr, Walter. "Mr. Bullins Is Himself at Fault." *The New York Times* (19 March 1972): II-1.

Knickerbocker, Paine. " 'Duplex': Past and Present." *The San Francisco Chronicle* (26 March 1972).

———. " 'Duplex' to Re-open." *The San Francisco Chronicle* (28 February 1973).

Kornfeld, Joe. "Playwright Ed Bullins: Soft-Spoken Giant on the Black Literary Scene." *The Boston Herald American* (24 January 1975): 32.

Kroll, Jack. "In Black America." *Newsweek* (20 March 1972): 98–99.

Lahr, John. "On-Stage." *The Village Voice* (16 March 1972): 52.

"Lights for 'Duplex.' " *San Francisco Chronicle* (14 March 1973).

Lloyd, J. Steven. " 'Duplex': Controversy at Lincoln Center." *Uhuru Dun Dun* (April 1972): 1.

Lomax, Michele. "Real People Inhabit 'The Duplex.' " *The San Francisco Examiner* (20 March 1973): 27.

"Love and Laughter from the Tenements." *San Francisco Progress* (14 March 1973).

Moses, Gilbert. "Two Answers to Ed Bullins." *The New York Times* (26 March 1972): sec. 2, p. 1.

Oliver, Edith. "The Theatre: Off Broadway." *The New Yorker* (18 March 1972): 85.

Oppenheim, Irene. "Black Actors, Short Actors, and Excellent Drama." *The San Francisco Bay Guardian* (20 March 1973): 23.

Oppenheimer, George. "Black Playwright Protests Play Production." *New York Newsday* (15 March 1972): D-11.

Riley, Clayton. "Bullins: 'It's Not the Play I Wrote.' " *The New York Times* (19 March 1972): C-1, *passim*.

Smitherman, Geneva. "Ed Bullins/Stage One: Everybody Wants to Know Why I Sing the Blues." *Black World* 23 (April 1974): 4–13.

Wesley, Richard. " 'Duplex' and the Lincoln Theater." *The Washington, D.C., Third World* (January 1972): 3.

The Electronic Nigger

Bailey, Peter. "Controversy over Play's Title Fails to Cloud Author's Acclaim." *Ebony* (September 1968): 97–101.

Clurman, Harold. "Review." *The Nation* (25 March 1968): 420–21.

Eckstein, George. "Review." *Dissent* (winter 1973): 113.

Goldman, Jane Ellen. "The Electronic Nigger." *Washington Square Journal* (14 March 1968).

Lewis, Emory. "Ascent for Bullins and Foster, Descent for Williams." *Cue* (6 April 1968): 9.

Oliver, Edith. "Three Cheers." *The New Yorker* (13 April 1968): 133.

Playboy 18 (April 1971): 37.

Watts, Richard. "A Trio of Short Plays by a Negro Dramatist." *The New York Post* (7 March 1968): 24.

Emergency Report

Winn, Steven. "Kids from Street Stage Their Play." *San Francisco Chronicle* (27 October 1993): E-5.

The Fabulous Miss Marie

Alexander, Donald W. "Ed Bullins, the Leading Black Playwright." *Unicorn Times* (January 1978): 43.

Berger, Chip. "And His 'Miss Marie.' " *Unicorn Times* (January 1978): 43.

Collins, William B. "Eloquent Piece of Black Drama." *Philadelphia Inquirer* (19 May 1975): A-8.

Gottfried, Martin. "Approaching Masterwork Status." *Women's Wear Daily* (9 March 1971): 6.

Gussow, Mel. "Black Festival in Bullins's 'Miss Marie.' " *The New York Times* (31 May 1979): C-16.

———. "Bullins's 'Miss Marie' Comes to New Lafayette." *The New York Times* (12 March 1971): 7.

Lahr, John. "On-Stage." *The Village Voice* (25 March 1971): 47.

Oliver, Edith. "An Evening with Bullins & Company." *The New Yorker* (20 March 1971): 94–95.

Sainer, Arthur. "A New Look at the New Lafayette." *The Village Voice* (1 April 1971).

Sege. "Review." *Variety* (6 April 1971): 7.

The Gentleman Caller

Bolton, Whitney. " 'A Black Quartet' Is Recommended." *The New York Morning Telegraph* (1 August 1969).

Hurd, Myles Raymond. "Bullins' The Gentleman Caller: Source and Satire." *Notes on Contemporary Literature* 14 (1984): 11–12.

Kerr, Walter. "The Loneliness on Both Sides." *The New York Times* (4 May 1969): C-1.

Kraft, Daphne. "A Black Quartet." *The Newark Evening News* (31 July 1969).

Marowitz, Charles. "America's Great Hopes, White and Black?" *The New York Times* (13 April 1969): D-3.

Raidy, William A. " 'Black Quartet' Says It." *Long Island Press* (31 July 1969).

Riley, Clayton. "Adjust Your Binoculars, Uncle Sam." *The New York Times* (3 August 1969): C-1.

Shepard, Richard F. "Theater: Black Quartet." *The New York Times* (31 July 1969): C-1.

Bibliography

Goin' a Buffalo

Gussow, Mel. "W.P.A. Stages Bullins Play on Young Adults." *The New York Times* (16 February 1972): 28.

Oliver, Edith. "Off-Broadway." *The New Yorker* (4 March 1972): 83.

Richie, Mark L. "Another 'Inspired' Don Evans Hit." *Utimme Umana La Voz Oculta* (20 November 1973): 11.

Washburn, Martin. "On the Way to the Big Time." *The Village Voice* (24 February 1972): 49.

Home Boy

Oliver, Edith. "Off-Broadway." *The New Yorker* (11 October 1976): 81.

Jenner, Cynthia Lee. "Taking Bullins by the Horns." *Villager* (30 September 1976): 8.

House Party

Barnes, Clive. "The Theater: Lower-Vintage Bullins." *The New York Times* (30 October 1973).

Brukenfeld, Dick. "More Gray than Black & White." *The Village Voice* (1 November 1973): 60.

Evans, Don. "The Theater of Confrontation: Ed Bullins, Up against the Wall." *Black World* 23 (April 1974): 14–18.

Watt, Douglas. " 'House Party' a Dull Black Inferno." *Daily News* (30 October 1973): 56.

Watts, Richard. "About a 'Soulful Happening.' " *New York Post* (30 October 1973): 52.

How Do You Do

Barnes, Clive. "Four Black Plays: Bullins's 'Short Bullins' Done by LaMama." *The New York Times* (5 March 1972).

Brewster, Townsend. "A Word on Plays." *Big Red* (17 August 1980): 19.

Davis, Thulani. "Stick Figures in Black and White." *The Village Voice* (6 August 1980): 69.

Gussow, Mel. "Three Bullins One-Acters at Bill Cosby's Hangout." *The New York Times* (31 December 1980): C-9.

Hart, Steven. "Solid Bullins Experiment." *The Villager* (4 September 1980).

Marowitz, Charles. "America's Great Hopes, White and Black?" *The New York Times* (13 April 1969): D-3.

Mintz, Ed. "The Lively Arts." *Brooklyn Daily Bulletin* (18 September 1980): 12.

Nelsen, Don. " 'Oedipus,' Euripides, et al Lurking in the Wings." *Daily News* (10 September 1980): 21.

Williams, Julinda Lewis. "Theatre: 'Leavings.' *The Black American* 19 (August 1980): 4.

I Am Lucy Terry

Davis, Curt. "Will the Real Lucy Terry Please Stand Up?" *Encore* (5 April 1976): 41.

Gussow, Mel. "Bullins Turns 'Lucy Terry' into History Lesson." *The New York Times* (12 February 1976).

Oliver, Edith. "Off Broadway." *The New Yorker* (23 February 1976): 82.

Supree, Burt. "Lucy Gets Her Man." *The Village Voice* (5 April 1976): 46.

I Think It's Gonna Work Out Fine

Berson, Misha. "Critic's Choice." *The San Francisco Bay Guardian* (4 October 1989).

Coleman, Beth. "American Gothic: Ed Bullins and Company Show Us What We Do Not See." *The Village Voice* (20 March 1990): 106.

Helbig, Jack. "Review." *Chicago Reader* (22 June 1990).

Holden, Stephen. "Chilling Life on the Rock Circuit." *The New York Times* (16 March 1990).

Hurwitt, Robert. "*It's Gonna Work Out Fine* Works Out." *The San Francisco Examiner* (23 September 1989): 38.

Smith, Sid. "A Sizzling Duo Lifts Musical at Black Ensemble." *Chicago Tribune* (19 June 1990).

Weiner, Bernard. "Curtain Calls: A Story Like Ike and Tina's." *The San Francisco Chronicle* (30 September 1989): 30.

Worsham, Doris G. " 'I Think It's Gonna Work Out Fine' Does a Lively Ike and Tina Turn." *The Oakland Tribune* (4 January 1990).

In New England Winter

Bourne, Kay. "Bullins's Play Staged by BU Collective." *Bay State Banner* (9 May 1974): 14.

Lahr, John. "On-Stage." *The Village Voice* (4 February 1971): 43.

Oliver, Edith. "Off Broadway: Heart of Blackness." *The New Yorker* (6 February 1971): 72.

Phillips, Julian. "Playwright Offers 'Black Perspective.' " *The Purdue Exponent* (17 April 1972): 6.

Weiner, Bernard. "Brothers' Struggle at Edge of Despair." *San Francisco Chronicle* (4 October 1992).

In the Wine Time

Bourne, Kay. " 'In the Wine Time' Is Positively Black." *Bay State Banner* (19 November 1970): 12.

"Brief Note." *The Village Voice* (24 May 1976).

Gussow, Mel. "Bullins's 'In the Wine Time.' " *The New York Times* (30 April 1976): 9.

Harris, Jessica B. " 'In Wine Time' . . . Fine, Fine!" *New York Amsterdam News* (22 May 1976).

Lewis, Barbara. "Models of Maturity." *Soho Weekly News* (13 May 1976).

Mayo, Sandra. "Ed Bullins, New York's Resident Black Dramatist." In *Afro-Americans in New York Life and History* (July 1981): 51–57.

Nelsen, Don. "High Spirits in 'Wine.' " *Daily News* (11 May 1976).

Oliver, Edith. "Off Broadway: Superior Vintage." *The New Yorker* (10 May 1976): 33.

Patterson, Lindsay. "New Home, New Troupe, New Play." *The New York Times* (22 December 1968): II-7.

Riley, Clayton. "Theatre Reviews." *Liberator* 9 (January 1969): 20–21.

Bibliography

Rosenberg, Scott. "Black Theater Gaining Ground." *San Francisco Examiner* (6 June 1990): F-3.

Wallach, Allan. "A Different Taste." *New York Newsday* (30 April 1976): 14.

It Has No Choice

Barnes, Clive. "Four Black Plays: Bullins's 'Short Bullins' Done by LaMama." *The New York Times* (5 March 1972).

Brukenfeld, Dick. "The Worst Thing about It Is the Title." *The Village Voice* (21 June 1973): 79.

Sainer, Arthur. "Up for Adoption." *The Village Voice* (2 March 1972): 51.

Jo Anne!!!

De Lappe, Pele. "Pluses & Minuses in Joan Little Play." *People's World* (18 July 1981): 10.

Gussow, Mel. "Reviews." *The New York Times* (19 October 1976).

Hamer, Gail. "Theatre Politico: Leading Playwright Focuses on JoAnn Little Subject." *Washington, D.C., Afro-American News* (24 July 1976).

Lewis, Barbara. "A Woman Scorned." *The Villager* (25 October 1976).

Munk, Erika. "Bullins: 'I Had My Way with Her.'" *The Village Voice* (8 November 1976). 87.

Nelsen, Don. "Review of Jo Anne." *The New York Daily News* (5 February 1976): 76.

Oliver, Edith. "Off Broadway." *The New Yorker* (25 October 1976): 62.

Rabkin, Gerald. "Saint Jo Anne." *The Soho Weekly News* (21 October 1976): 30.

Syna, Sy. "Review: Jo Anne BeLittled." *Wisdom's Child.* (25 October 1976).

Steele, Mike. "Playwright Tries to Expand Work beyond Black Theatre Audiences." *The Minneapolis Star* (28 October 1977): 19.

Thompson, Kenneth. "Joanna: New Black Theatre." *The University of Washington Daily* (8 November 1983).

Weiner, Bernard. "A Dramatic, Surrealistic Interpretation of a Trial." *San Francisco Chronicle* (26 May 1981): 42.

Wilkins, Roger. "Review of *The* Innonence of Joan Little." *The New York Times* (17 December 1977).

Leavings

Davis, Thulani. "Response to Ed Bullins's 'An Open Statement.'" *The Village Voice* (13 August 1980): 76.

———. "Stick Figures in Black and White." *The Village Voice* (6 August 1980): 69.

Williams, Julinda Lewis. "Leavings." *The Black American* 19 (August 1980): 4.

Michael

Johnson-Moyler, Wista. "'Man-Wo-Man' at New Heritage Repertory Theatre." *Big Red* (14 May 1978): 25.

Lewis, Barbara. "'Man-Wo-Man' Looks at Relationships." *New York Amsterdam News* (13 May 1978).

McGriff, Theresa. "'Man-Wo-Man': The Battle Continues." *The New York Amsterdam News* (5 August 1978): D-6.

Mark, M. "Whoa, Men, Whoa!" *The Village Voice* (17 July 1978): 75.

Oliver, Edith. "The Birds and the Bees." *The New Yorker* (22 November 1978): 91–92.

Syna, Sy. "Bullins and Harris." *Wisdom's Child* (5 August 1978): 6.

A Minor Scene

Barnes, Clive. "Four Black Plays: Bullins's 'Short Bullins' Done by LaMama." *The New York Times* (5 March 1972).

The Mystery of Phillis Wheatley

Gussow, Mel. "Stage: 'Phyllis Wheatley.' " *The New York Times* (4 February 1976).

Norton, Elliot. "Opening Here of Play on Slave-Girl Poet." *Boston Herald* (23 September 1972).

Tucker, Carll. "She Went to London, Not Senegal." *The Village Voice* (2 February 1976): 110.

The Pig Pen

Barnes, Clive. "Bullins Views 'The Pig Pen.' " *The New York Times* (21 May 1970).

Brukenfeld, Dick. "Off-off." *The Village Voice* (28 May 1970): 51.

Clurman, Harold. "Theatre." *The Nation* (1 June 1970): 668–69.

Gottfried, Martin. "The Pig Pen." *Women's Wear Daily* (21 May 1970): 14.

Kraft, Daphne. "New Bullins Drama." *The Newark Evening News* (21 May 1970): 30.

Kroll, Jack. "The Pig Pen." *Newsweek* (1 June 1970).

Oliver, Edith. "Off Broadway." *The New Yorker* (30 May 1970): 72–73.

Riley, Clayton. "Theatre Review." *Liberator* 10 (June 1970): 20, 22.

Stasio, Marilyn. "The Pig Pen." *Cue* (30 May 1970).

Tallmer, Jerry. "Not So Simple." *New York Post* (21 May 1970): 52.

Psychic Pretenders

Bentley, Eric. "I'll Take Diahann Carroll, Sidney Poitier and Genet." *The New York Times* (30 April 1972).

———. "Must I Side with Blacks or Whites?" *The New York Times* (23 January 1972): II-1.

Raining Down Stars

E., Jonathan. "One World Beat." *Bay Area Music Magazine* (7 February 1992).

Elwood, Philip. " 'Raining Down Stars' Celebrates a Heritage." *San Francisco Examiner* (24 January 1992): D-10.

Gere, David. "Captains Courageous." *Dance Magazine* (April 1992): 86.

———. " 'Raining Down Stars' a Fresh, Brave Look at Issue of Race." *Oakland Tribune,* 25 January 1992.

Kelp, Larry. " 'Stars' Illuminate Diversity." *Oakland Tribune* (22 January 1992).

Ritual to Bind Together and Strengthen Black People So They Can Survive the Long Struggle that Is to Come

Elder, Arlene A. "Ed Bullins: Black Theatre as Ritual." In *Connections: Essays on Black Literatures.* edited by Emmanuel S. Nelson. Canberra, Australia: Aboriginal Studies Press, 101–9.

"Ritual." *Bay State Banner* (4 September 1969): 5.

Bibliography

Salaam, Huey Newton, Salaam

Gussow, Mel. "Four New Plays, One Act Each." *The New York Times* (19 June 1991).

Harvey, Dennis. "Razor-Sharp Writing." *The San Francisco Bay Guardian* (20 July 1994).

Michel, Sia. "Raging Angst." *San Francisco Weekly* (20 July 1994).

Wasserman, John L. "Playwright's Plans on Huey Story." *San Francisco Chronicle* (19 July 1968).

Sepia Star

Fraser, C. Gerald. "Bullins Joins His Words to Music." *The New York Times* (19 August 1977): C-2.

A Son, Come Home

Clurman, Harold. "Theatre." *The Nation* (25 March 1968): 420–21.

Dace, Tish. "Review." *The Soho Weekly News* (28 July 1977): 36.

Gottfried, Martin G. "The Master Introduces His Pupils." *New York Post* (23 July 1977): 14.

Gussow, Mel. "Three Bullins One-Acters at Bill Cosby's Hangout." *The New York Times* (31 December 1980): C-9.

O'Connor, John J. "Getting beyond Polemics." *Wall Street Journal* (25 March 1968): 13–14.

Oliver, Edith. "Three Cheers." *The New Yorker* (13 April 1968): 133.

Watts, Richard. "A Trio of Short Plays by a Negro Dramatist." *The New York Post* (7 March 1968): 24.

Steve and Velma

Desmond, John P. "World Premiere." *The Northeastern University Arts/Scene* (February 1978): 1.

Wilson, Dave. "Ed Bullins to Open Plays Here." *Bay State Banner* (2 February 1978): 16.

———. "Obie Award Winner's New Play Opens Here." *Northeastern News* (1 February 1978): 11.

Storyville

Drake, Sylvie. "The Story behind 'Storyville.'" *Los Angeles Times* (26 May 1977): 18.

Fall, Gay. "But, Where Is the Story?" *LaJolla Light* (26 May 1977).

Firger, Barbara. "'Storyville' Creators Tell Story behind the Scenes." *The UC San Diego Weekly* (2–8 May 1977): 1.

Fraser, C. Gerald. "Bullins Joins His Words to Music." *The New York Times* (19 August 1977): C-2.

Jones, Welton. "'Storyville' Needs a Little Editing." *The San Diego Union* (20 May 1977).

Lowen, Sara J. "'Storyville': Old Style Musical." *The San Diego Triton Times* (20 May 1977): 1.

Russell, Kathlyn. "'Storyville' Has Seen-It-All-Before Air." *Escondido (Calif.) Times Advocate* (19 May 1977): A-8.

Shirley, Don. 'Storyville': Not Feeling that Jazz." *The Washington Post* (29 January 1979): B-9.

Simons, Ed. " 'Storyville' Is a Good Musical." *Clairemont (Calif.) Sentinel* (22 May 1977).

Street Sounds

Donovan, Patricia. "Spirited Sounds of the 'Street' Are Sweet." *The Buffalo News* (30 July 1992).

Gussow, Mel. "Forty Informative Vignettes of 'Street Sounds.' " *The New York Times* (23 October 1970): 32.

Stanley, John. "Playwright Captures Ghetto's Street People." *San Francisco Chronicle* (21 August 1988): 43.

" 'Street Sounds': Familiar, Painful, Funny." *The Challenger* (5 August 1992): 4.

The Taking of Miss Janie

Barnes, Clive. "Miss Janie." *The New York Times* (5 May 1975).

Blackman, Brandon R. IV. "Black Hope of Broadway," *Sepia* (December 1975): 61–68.

"Bullins' 'Janie' Moves to Lincoln Center." *Pittsburgh Courier* (3 May 1975).

Christon, Lawrence. " '60s Hindsight in 'Miss Janie.' " *Los Angeles Times* (4 March 1977): IV-19.

Cohen, Richard. "Black Play Smacks of Anti-Semitism." *The Sun-Reporter* (17 June 1975): 10.

Glover, William. "Ed Bullins's Crusade Mellows." *Camden Courier Post* (18 July 1975). Rpt. as "Ed Bullins' Vision: To Be 'Drama's Ali.' " *Jackson Miss. Daily News* (20 July 1975).

Gottfried, Martin. "A Radical Idea." *The New York Post* (5 May 1975): 23.

Grandchamp, Kathy. "Tensions Deftly Handled in Play." *The Minneapolis Star* (28 December 1977): B-18.

Gussow, Mel. "Bullins's 'Taking of Miss Janie.' " *The New York Times* (18 March 1975).

Hema. "Ein Bitterböses Stück von Ed Bullins." *Aufbrau* (16 May 1975): 7.

Kalem, T. E. "Requiem for the '60s." *Time* (19 May 1975): 80.

Kauffmann, Stanley. "Now and Also Then." *The New Republic* (7 June 1975): 20.

Levine, Faiga. "Absorbing, Confusing 'Janie' at Back Alley." *The Jewish Week* (29 July-4 August 1976): 22.

Lewis, Emory. " 'Miss Janie': Haunting Blues for the Lost '60s." *The Record* (5 May 1975): A-17.

McGinnis, Juliette. "Reliving the '60s with Ed Bullins in New Play, 'Taking of Miss Janie.' " *New York Voice* (16 May 1975): 17.

Mackay, Barbara. "Studies in Black and White." *The Saturday Review* (12 July 1975): 52.

Mancini, Joseph. "Bullins' 'Miss Janie' Brings Cliches to Life." *New York Post* (14 March 1975): 28.

Novick, Julius. "The Taking of Miss Cegenation." *The Village Voice* (12 May 1975): 87–89.

O'Haire, Patricia. "Bullins: A Philadelphia Story." *Daily News* (7 June 1975): 25.

Bibliography

Oliver, Edith. "Fugue for Three Roommates." *The New Yorker* (24 March 1975): 61.

Pennington, Ron. "Comments on 'The Taking of Miss Janie.' " *Hollywood Reporter* (8 July 1975): 6.

Popkin, Henry. "Bungled Portrayal of the Black Experience." *Westchester Rockland* (5 May 1975): B-5.

Raidy, William A. "Taken by 'Miss Janie.' " *Long Island Press* (5 May 1975).

Richards, David. "Ed Bullins, Angry Playwright Who Has Cooled Out." *The Washington Star* (1 August 1976).

Riley, Clayton. "Review." *Critique* (1975): 3.

Rowe, Billy. "Notebook." *San Francisco Post* (23 May 1975).

Ryweck, Charles. "Stage Review." *Hollywood Reporter* (13 May 1975): 12.

Simon, John. "Theater." *New York* (19 May 1975): 93.

Stasio, Marilyn. "After the Party's Over." *Cue* (12 May 1975): 28.

Taylor, Clarke. "New Theater." *The New York Press* (July 1975): 13.

Trescott, Jacqueline. "Betrayals of the '60s." *The Washington Post* (30 July 1976): B-9.

———. "Playwright Ed Bullins: A Mellowed Scenario." *The Washington Post* (21 August 1976): C-1.

Watt, Douglas. " 'Miss Janie' Is a Stunner." *Daily News* (5 May 1975): 50.

Watts, Richard. "Ed Bullins' Best Play." *New York Post* (10 May 1975).

Young, Charles M. "Is Rape a Symbol of Race Relations?" *The New York Times* (18 May 1975): II-1.

The Work Gets Done

Mitchell, Lionel. "Monologues: One Man's Meat, Another's Poison." *New York Amsterdam News* (6 December 1980): 36.

Don Nelsen. "It's Tough Setting Sights on a Name in Lights." *Daily News* (9 April 1980).

———. "In the Buff for Art's Sake." *Daily News* (17 February 1992).

You Gonna Let Me Take You Out Tonight, Baby?

Gussow, Mel. "Three Bullins One-Acters at Bill Cosby's Hangout." *The New York Times* (31 December 1980): C-9.

Hart, Steven. "Solid Bullins Experiment." *The Villager* (4 September 1980).

Mintz, Ed. "The Lively Arts." *Brooklyn Daily Bulletin* (18 September 1980): 12.

Nelsen, Don. " 'Oedipus,' Euripides, et al Lurking in the Wings." *Daily News* (10 September 1980): 21.